OTHER BOOKS BY GEORGE GARRETT

Novels

The Finished Man
Which Ones Are the Enemy?
Do, Lord, Remember Me
Death of the Fox
The Succession

Short Fiction

King of the Mountain
In the Briar Patch
Cold Ground Was My Bed Last Night
A Wreath for Garibaldi
The Magic Striptease
To Recollect a Cloud of Ghosts
An Evening Performance

Poetry

The Reverend Ghost: Poems
The Sleeping Gypsy and Other Poems
Abraham's Knife: Poems
For a Bitter Season: New & Selected Poems
Welcome to the Medicine Show
Luck's Shining Child
The Collected Poems of George Garrett

Plays

Sir Slob and the Princess
Enchanted Ground

Biography

James Jones

Poison Pen

Poison Pen;

o r,

Live Now and Pay Later

George Garrett

Drawings by Jonathan Bumas

If the serpent bites before it is charmed,
        there is no advantage in a charmer.
                ECCLESIASTES 10:11

    From a good face gone mad,
    From False and hissing tongue,
    What comforts to be had,
    What sweetness can be wrung?

                RICHARD WILBUR
                  "Another Voice"

"Where everything goes, the creative
   imagination, of course, leaps."

                GEORGE STEINER
          New York Times, 26 May 1985

"In our society speech may be controversial and conten-
tious; words may be intended to arouse, disturb, provoke,
and upset. For a primary function of free speech under our
system of government is to invite dispute. It may indeed
best serve its high purpose when it induces a condition of
unrest, creates dissatisfaction with conditions as they are,
or even stirs people to anger."

            JUDGE J. SKELLY WRIGHT
        The United States Court of Appeals
             for the District of Columbia
     [from *The Washington Post*, 14 April 1985, p. 3 (A)]

STUART WRIGHT, PUBLISHER

FIRST EDITION

Library of Congress Catalog Number: 833-062169

ISBN 0-913773-06-9   *Trade Issue*
ISBN 0-913773-07-7   *Signed and Limited Issue*

This book is dedicated to the memory of

JOAN RIVERS*

*The publisher offers a prize of $25.00 for the best one-liner based on the memory of Joan Rivers. Something beginning: "Joan Rivers? Her memory is so bad that . . ."

Psst . . . . *a little preface*

Hey, listen! Please . . . Before you even get cranked up and going on this thing pay attention for just a big minute. All right? Okay? Seriously . . .

Please don't skip this note. There are plenty of places and spaces in the pages that follow where you can skip and skim as much as you please. I won't claim that it's brilliantly designed that way—it just kind of happened. Just growed like Topsy, like the incredible Christie Brinkley . . .

God, she is wonderful, isn't she? Fan-fucking-tastic, tip to toe, aft to stern! Besides which I would like to think she has character and intelligence commensurate with her outward and visible physical splendor. And the beauty of it is that since I'll never actually meet her, in the *flesh*, if you'll pardon the expression, I can cheerfully attribute to her whatever I.Q. and character I wish to. But I won't take advantage of that privilege and allow myself to imagine that she may have a brain the size of a peanut and the limited social values of, say, Lucretia Borgia on a bad day. No siree. None of that stuff. You are the Top, Christie Brinkley. And the ultimate Bottom, too, I reckon.

I would buy the hardcover edition of your beauty and exercise book (the title of which I forget at the moment), brazen it out with the snot-nosed, mustachioed kid at the counter of the Little Professor Book Store, who knows me and would laugh at me and even would tell on me if I bought your exercise and beauty book, either with cash or my Visa card. I am willing to brazen it out with him and anybody else who may be hanging out at or hanging around the cash register if only to possess that one marvelous full page photo of you in a scanty bathing suit and all covered with sand. I would do that, but I sure don't have enough nerve to bring it home and let my wife see that I spent good money for it. Not that she would get upset. I could probably handle that or, if worse came to worst, put on my earphones and turn on my Walkman II and listen to *Halftime Classics* by the 258-member Michigan Marching Band, which tends to drown out even the angriest of wives. No, she wouldn't make a big scene or anything. She would just laugh. She has a good, rich, mellow laugh, a confident and somewhat sexy laugh if the truth be known, a laugh I like to hear . . . *except when I am being laughed at.* You know? Being laughed at by women, especially the woman you are married to, is no fun at all.

You don't laugh at people, do you, Christie?

Let me see.

Where was I?

Oh, yes. Excuse me, Reader, for the digression.

Anyway . . .

I want to be (as poor old Nixon always used to say) very, very *clear* about this. How can I put it, directly and simply? Here's how: I DID NOT WRITE THIS STUFF! IT WAS NOT ME! I mean . . . uh . . . IT WAS NOT I.

Let me explain.

All that follows was written by John Towne. Who is really a *character*. I mean that literally. He is really and only a character in a novel that I *am* writing and have been working on, off and on, since the early 1960's. The novel was/ is called *Life With Kim Novak Is Hell*. Which is not a fact or even a reasonable supposition, but a headline from *The National Enquirer*. Which is just the sort of tacky and trashy publication that John Towne tends (almost always) to read instead of important and intelligent and uplifting stuff like the fiction of John Updike or, say, the serious poetry of Mark Strand. I mean, he could be improving himself, couldn't he?; but he won't. He just won't. It is not Towne's goal to leave the world a little bit better place than he found it.

Towne wrote most of what follows—all of the letters and, I guess, a lot of the rest, too. Poison pen letters to various public figures and celebrities were something he produced (and actually *mailed!*) here and there in the novel. I mention this, indeed I stress it; because in no way whatsoever does this Towne person reflect my views or opinions. His idea of a joke, then or now, is not my idea of a joke. His screwball notions and cockamayme philosophy have nothing to do with me or mine. I reject him and them utterly, here and now.

Unfortunately his half-assed *style* seems to have had some pernicious influence on me, as well as on other characters in *Life With Kim Novak Is Hell*. At least my friends say so. They say that at times, *stylistically*, you can't tell us apart. Content-wise, however, we are worlds apart. Believe me.

I am allowing these letters to go public in exactly the way, shape, and form that Towne wrote them (and as many of them were published in obscure little magazines). Some of the prominent people he addresses or mentions are dead and gone now. And I am sorry about that. At the time he wrote to them, they were all just fine, thank you. And that is how you should try to think of them, too, as alive and well and worthy of attention. Towne's intentions were limited—to insult living, prominent and powerful public figures and to outrage his audience (if any) with juvenilian blackface, buck-and-wing. Neither he nor I would trouble the dead. Who, if St. Augustine is right (and I think he always is/was) are at least entirely untroubled by, careless of this world, world without end.

I leave the letters from the 1960's as Towne wrote them. In the final section there are a few letters from the 1980's. Which seem to indicate that Towne— who dropped out of sight if not out of mind in the early 70's—is back again and probably no wiser than before.

Judge for yourself.

In a way I hope he is not back among us. For if he is, then I may yet have to finish *Life With Kim Novak Is Hell*, if only to be rid of him for good and all.

Of course, chances are that no self-respecting American publisher, large or small, would ever publish that novel. I certainly hope not. As values and standards all around us crumble like Hostess Twinkies in the little grubby fists of children raised on Wonder Bread and Captain Kangaroo, it is reassuring to know that the American publishing business remains what it has always been—a serious, if not especially profitable industry devoted to long boozy lunch hours and to the ceaseless search for . . . well, for lack of a better word, *quality*.

(Try not to get any of that quality on your shoes. It is hard to get off. And it stinks.)

G.G.

P.S. Oh, yes, I nearly forgot. Because I have let the earlier letters go out as they were originally written and (sometimes) published, I must confess that there are certain repetitions and even inconsistencies in the text. So what? That's the way he is (Towne, I mean)—repetitious and inconsistent. It can't be helped. And if any of you smartasses plan to give me (or Towne) a bad time based on the argument of the fallacy of imitative form, forget it. You look after your fallacy and I'll look after mine. Okay?

G.G.

Poison Pen

Part One

Front Matter

NOVELIST IRVING STONE SAYS
WRITING TAKES STRUGGLE

(Headline from *The Washington Post*)

1.

"Many readers may be completely unaware that, following his disastrous sojourn in Hollywood, John Towne somehow managed to resume his long-interrupted academic career during the tag end, the doggy days of the 1960s. It may come as a surprise to some, even among the best informed. . . ."

2.

The paragraph (above) is one of a series of aborted first paragraphs written by an Assistant Professor of English by the name of Lee Holmes. For some time now and for various reasons Holmes has been trying to put together, to hoke up and whomp out, something in the nature of a scholarly-critical article about John Towne, an utterly unimportant writer and a generally worthless bum. Who was Holmes' colleague and peer at the bottom of a very modest academic totem pole a few years ago. One of the reasons behind Holmes' apparently irrational enterprise is that if he doesn't publish something (anything) somewhere, and pretty quick too, he is flat finished as far as his career is concerned as the oldest Assistant Professor at the small women's college in southwest Virginia. Which might be Sweet Briar or Hollins or Southern Seminary or even Randolph Macon, but which Holmes, out of fear as much as any innate sense of decency and decorum, insists on calling Nameless College. Another reason, of course, is that the raw materials are at hand, indeed *in hand* among the miscellaneous papers that Towne left in Holmes's safe-keeping when he simply vanished from Nameless just before Graduation Day. It is only meet and right that Holmes should be the one to find some use for the papers and letters and unfinished manuscripts Towne left behind, not only because Towne urged him to feel free to do so, but also because Towne left them (he said so in a brief note, alas, destroyed by Holmes in a moment of thoughtless anger) in at least partial security and payment for the credit cards, gold pocket watch, U.S. Passport, Lamy 2000 fountain pen, the Brooks Brothers necktie, Ronson lighter, and roughly forty dollars in miscellaneous

5

cash and small change, all belonging to Holmes, which Towne took with him when he left Nameless.

Holmes can still remember (more or less) the brisk and cheery tone of Towne's argument. "Old buddy-buddy," he may have written, "you know that I would never borrow anything without asking first if I didn't have to, especially from a friend. But that's it, the definition. Friendship is when you can always feel free to take what you need without all the unseemly charades of begging and pleading. You are too big of a person, too humane a spirit to quibble and make a fuss about . . . *material things*! Besides I am leaving you all of my papers and letters and bills and manuscripts—including the first draft of my KIM NOVAK novel. Which, even if they won't make you rich and famous, may help you get tenure and keep your job if you play your cards right."

After he had torn the note into confetti, Holmes's second strong impulse was to burn all of Towne's papers. And he probably should have done that. Except that Towne was right. Smugly and perversely right. His miscellaneous manuscripts and papers are Holmes' last best chance not to have to join the growing ranks of the unemployed. Somehow, in spite of all protestation to the contrary, Towne knew that Holmes' adventure into scholarship—a Tom McCann shoebox full of index cards, the only outward and visible sign of his long-planned and much-deferred dissertation on "Milton's Use of Dreams and Dream Visions," would never manage the transformation to typescript. Somehow Towne knew, too, that his own papers—and with them his reputation, if you can use that word—were and are as safe in the possession of Lee Holmes as they would be, for instance, in The Rare Book Room of Princeton's Firestone Library or in a safe deposit box at the Peoples' National Bank.

The irony of it all can give Holmes a terrible headache, so he tries not to think about it too much.

If you play your cards right. . . .

One thing that Towne played right, used freely and adventurously for some months, until it expired, was Holmes' American Express Card. For a time Holmes was able to follow the direction of Towne's travels and adventures, mostly in western Europe, by means of the monthly statements of charges in his own name which he received from American Express. And, as much with envy as outrage, Holmes could reconstruct even more details of Towne's itinerary by means of the random, irregular, mildly cryptic postcards mailed to him from colorful interesting places. Even now, though the credit cards have long since expired, Holmes may, from time to time, still find a bright postcard, depicting some famous beach or mountain, an ancient cathedral, temple ruins, or a grand hotel, sneering at him from the window of his mailbox. Lately most of these have been coming from the South Pacific, and, allowing for the fact (as ever and always) that Towne may be trying to trick him, Holmes infers that Towne has tired of Europe's pleasures and is now exploring and enjoying, in a leisurely fashion, these more exotic places. The other day Holmes read something in *The Washington Post* which seemed

6

to him to bear the unmistakable signature (not the story, but the occasion of it) of John Towne. In an article about the persistence of Cargo Cults in Papua-New Guinea, he learned of the rise of a new cult there. The article stated that "as far as can be determined, an unknown American, apparently in jest, told native villagers that the key to wealth and prosperity was to vote for Lyndon Baines Johnson. A national election was to be held at that time. When a government election team arrived to collect the votes for local candidates, they were informed that all the people wanted to vote for LBJ and no one else. The cult spread to neighboring islands and organizers began to collect an 'American Tax' in order to buy LBJ. It was widely believed that the Australian administration had kidnapped LBJ and was deliberately keeping him away from them as well as the cargo which LBJ wanted them to have."

Meantime Holmes has not had much luck in the rough and tumble literary marketplace with the things Towne left behind. For example, the draft copy of the novel, *Life With Kim Novak Is Hell*, has been rejected, not so much flatly as furiously, by most of the major publishers. Undaunted, however, Holmes is now trying to put together a documentary, scholarly-critical article dealing with Towne's brief career at Nameless and arguing that the man and his actions are symptomatic, indeed exemplary of the worst excesses of the Sixties. Hard to do in any case, but the problem is compounded by the invincible ambiguity of Holmes' feelings. On the one hand it behooves him to strain himself to the limits of sophistry in order to inflate and heighten Towne's apparent significance as a proper subject for scholarly and critical inquiry. Any small signs of some critical interest in this deplorable man's literary works would certainly enhance Holmes' chances of selling off some of the trash Towne left behind him. Yet against these practical considerations must be balanced matters of principle, the rude injustice of it all. Why should Holmes have to spend his precious time and energy writing to serve a man who had (and continues to) fooled, foxed, and fiddled him? Pulling his own teeth with an old pair of rusty pliers would be a more pleasant pastime to Holmes than trying to write the article.

So it remains a very serious question whether or not Holmes will ever be able to get beyond the first paragraph.

But that, after all, is his problem, not ours.

3.

Of course, both Lee Holmes and John Towne are imaginary characters. There shouldn't be any real problem about that. Not nowadays. The trouble is that like a great many other fictional characters they are both (separate and equal) engaged in what could be called a subversive conspiracy to prove that they are something more than the dimensionless figments of some lazy writer's fancy. Like all kinds of uppity people, both in and out of books, they insist on having some kind of identity. They profess to believe that they can cast real shadows.

7

Ordinarily the appropriate response to this kind of refractory behavior on the part of one or more fictional characters is at once simple and effective, aiming more toward rehabilitation than punishment. Characters can be confined in the cold print, cheap paper, binding, and jacket of a manufactured book. Once they're locked within the limits of a contemporary novel, the odds are highly favorable that very, very few other people (leaving aside the variable network of the author's friends and relatives, who are doubly variables anyway since they may or may not actually open the book and read any pages of it, though they are certain to demand free copies of same and to feel free to use and abuse it in any way they see fit) will ever hear of these characters again. True, a very few people may accidentally make their acquaintance, see them briefly as they writhe and groan in the chains and shackles of printed pages, as, for example, and once upon a time, our more civilized ancestors viewed the miseries and masquerades of Bedlamites, feeling at the time, perhaps, a slightly pleasurable inner shudder which was, then, soon shaken off, easily and mercifully forgotten.

Sentenced to a term of imprisonment in a book, Holmes and Towne would soon come to learn the simple virtues of necessity and would soon enough be willing to accept and settle for oblivion and its constant climate of sweet and dusty silence.

Unfortunately neither one of these guys is in a book at this time and they are not likely to be in the near future. They are both free and (separate and equal) taking advantage of their freedom, pushing liberty to the sheer edge of license, as they run amok in two old footlockers full of the chaotic and disorganized typescript pages of an unfinished novel. Towne actually began as the (pardon the expression) protagonist of that story. Not satisfied with that perfectly honorable station, he has been working and scheming ever since with ceaseless mischief and occasional cunning, to try to make himself the *hero* of the tale. All right-thinking readers will be pleased to know that his rebellious insolence has been sternly and strictly checked. Barring some unforeseen development of a catastrophic nature, John Towne will never be a hero in any book of mine. Or anybody else's either, if I can help it.

There remains an additional topic to mention here—the whole question of Towne's style and influence. It can be safely said, and without fear of serious challenge, that Towne's style, in his own writing as well as in Real Life, is at once slovenly and unscrupulous, wholly without any redeeming social value. He is (as he was and always will be) a writer entirely indifferent to such common concerns as objectivity, coherence, consistency, decency, dignity, decorum and *le mot just*. He probably never heard of *le mot just*; and if he did, it went in one ear and out the other. His chief literary strength is to be found in a certain passionate vulgarity. The problem is that his style appears to be (like certain unmentionable social diseases) quite contagious. Holmes appears to have succumbed to the infection. And some of my so-called friends have implied that Towne has lately even managed to sneak into my own prose, from time to time, coming on in surprising places like a club-footed thief in the night, not only to rip off the silverware, the Polaroid and my RCA Color TV, but also to leave behind his muddy footprints and his graffiti on the walls. I deny that. I vehemently deny even the possibility of it. I say it is a crock of shit! But, in fairness, assuming that such a thing were not only possible, but also true, I can here assure everyone, including John Towne, that all of his halfass efforts will come to no avail. He is doomed to be a rather unpleasant character in a minor novel. Sooner or later, no matter how much he tries to distract me, I shall manage to complete the manuscript. Sooner or later some publisher dumb and foolish enough to publish it will be found. Then none of us will ever again be troubled by Towne. Until that happy day, however, it is up to Lee Holmes to do his duty, to do the best he can with the raw materials under difficult and admittedly unenviable circumstances.

IMPORTANT
(DO NOT IGNORE)
A Note from the Publisher to the Reading Public at Large

As the oldest senior editor of this firm, I have insisted upon my rights and, in especial, the privilege of addressing you, members of the Reading Public.

If I may be permitted to say so, in all humility, it took some doing. The young, bearded, shaggy-haired scroyle (a good Elizabethan word implying an homogenized character, part rogue, part rascal, part base and upstart knave) who calls himself Jonathan Folger (God knows what his *real* name is), a fellow of less than infinite jest foisted upon the Trade Department of this house as a result of a recent and unfortunate merger for the express purpose of (and here I quote Folger's first memo to our distinguished staff) "jazzing up the crummy line of literary tea party books we like to lose money on," young Folger resisted my demand to the last. "Rights?" he cried. "When I get through with you, you'll lose your key to the unisex washroom."

Poor boy. I may well be, as he describes me, "a tweedy fart," but a man can't be in this business for forty years without making a few friends in power, friends who can come in handy on a "rainy day," as it were. In short, dear unknown friends, though I was unable to prevent the publication of this book, I won a clearcut victory over Folger by being permitted to address you briefly at the outset. And, you'll be pleased to know, I retain my key to the washroom.

Publishing in the U.S. was once a gentlemanly business, friendly and fun. Editors were gentlemen and even authors strove to emulate them. Everybody knew his place in the scheme of things. In paneled offices we puffed our pipes and weighed and sifted the wheat from the chaff, taking the greatest care in deciding what was good for you to read. Printers wore bib overalls and said yes, sir, to Senior Editors. Tea was served daily at 4:00 P.M.

I am sorry to report that the winds of change have blown that whole scene into untidy oblivion. The publishing business these days is conducted by greedy, unmannerly young whippersnappers who gulp down martinis at lunch, pinch secretaries, abuse expense accounts, and spend most of their working hours looking for a better job. Printers drive Cadillacs and sports cars while Editors with seniority and long, honorable records of achievement must jostle hostile Spades for space on the subway.

I am not so senile as to claim that all was, in Arnold's phrase, "sweetness and light," in the good old days. It is true that we at one time "pirated" editions of popular works by foreign authors, even Englishmen. Pray remember that most of them would never have been heard of on these shores had we not done so. Copyright agreements have changed all that. Now we are content to acquire the works of foreigners for "peanuts," as they say, and bring culture to the masses while making a few dollars at the same time. It is true that we weren't very nice to our own native writers in those days. So? Show me a nice writer. They better they write the worse they are. Besides which, as all have agreed, struggle is good for an artist. How can you have art without struggle? We never considered publishing as a part of any poverty program.

Enough fond reminiscence. I merely wish to say that in my day we would never have seriously considered such a manuscript as this one, let alone permitted it to appear under our imprint. It is trash, pure and simple. It is subversive and negative. It is poorly written and badly edited. An illiterate Darkey could have done a better job. Let Jonathan Folger take upon himself the onus. If, after perusing these horrid pages, you are outraged, you can never get your money back. But at least you can still express yourself. Write Folger c/o this publishing house and let him know what you think. Bombard the little bastard with letters, telegrams and phone calls. Make him rue the day. Then, ladies and gentlemen, we may get back to our proper business of publishing a few good books and true, quiet stories about good decent people and their amusing pets. There are times when it seems as if *The New Yorker* is our last bastion against massive and unseemly vulgarity. Let us here resolve to rally around and drive the vulgarians and barbarians back across the Hudson to the provinces. Caviar is wasted upon those who prefer a Whopper-burger at the nearest Tasteefreeze.

Let us stand together. If we must fall before the Folgers of this world, let us fall like the Spartans.

God bless you one and all.

Written this day at the Men's Bar of the Yale Club,

    with sincerity,

    H. Worthington Snood

Rebuttal

(1) Snood is a nice old guy, but a drunk.

(2) We carry him on the payroll to keep him off the Welfare Rolls. It's like a public service.

(3) As per *Poison Pen*: don't blame me. I only work here. The MS came down from High Above with PRINT IT stamped boldly on the cover. I can read. Even between the lines.

(4) But I have not read this MS. We've got copyeditors for that. I have very little time for reading these days. Snood hasn't read a book in twenty years. And he has all the time in the world. The phone never rings in Snood's office. I am thinking of disconnecting it as an economy measure. Snood's idea of the *avant garde* is the work of Floyd Dell or maybe that wild swinger Joseph Hergesheimer.

(5) This is a business. Art is for kids.

(6) If you want to write somebody, write Snood. Tell him to do himself a favor and go have a stroke.

(7) Snood still wears separate collars. When he pretends he's reading, he puts on a green eyeshade. He plays tennis with red tennis balls. Snood is a fink. No, he's more like a *feep*, which is a combination of a fink and a creep.

(8) He never ever went to Yale.

(9) If you don't like the book, tough about you. Nobody twisted your arm.

(10) High praise for the Production Dept. Great jacket! At least it will look good on your coffee table. Leave it there. Go watch T.V. You'll live longer and worry less. Take it from me, ulcers are no joke.

> J. Folger, Esq.
> Director of Trade Books

CONFIDENTIAL
Memo From Copy Editor to Whom It May Concern . . .

I am only a humble, overworked, underpaid, much-abused and little-honored sort of a proofreader around this so-called publishing house. Therefore probably nobody, living or dead, cares two hoops about what I think. I just work here, as I have done ever since I graduated from Vassar many years ago with honors in English and a promise that if I were patient I might even move up the ladder to become a manuscript reader-rejector. I'm still waiting. I am very patient.

Be that as it may, I must call someone's attention to certain facts concerning this MS. It is my duty to check the facts. And while we do not make a (pardon the expression) *fetish* out of accuracy around here, especially in our non-fiction (I'm assuming that's what this is; it surely isn't a novel, at least the definition of a novel we learned at Vassar, Class of '49, doesn't apply; and my roommate who attended Smith says her definition won't work either), it is important that someone check into certain basic things. I can find no record anywhere in the world, public or private, of any such person as JOHN TOWNE. I can find no record, starting right in the fouled up files of this publisher, of anyone named LEE HOLMES. Which (if you look closely) is supposed to be the name of the ignorant boor who "edited" Towne's papers. Though our staff is large here and, like that of every other publishing business, constantly changing from day to day (except for one faithful Copy Editor), we have never had on our payroll any editors named either WORTHINGTON SNOOD or JON-ATHAN FOLGER. Furthermore, we haven't merged with anyone. The plain naked truth is that we tried to merge several times over the past few years—with General Foods, Tiger Airlines, Bernard Geis Assoc. etc. And every time, as soon as they took a look at our books, they gave us the whinnying horse laugh. We are going it alone. Toughing it out.

In short, I should like to call to the attention of somebody (if only the Printer's devil), that there is something phoney about this MS.

To our distinguished editorial staff (in the hope that you read this while you are still sober, i.e. before lunch) let me say this. I know full well that proof-readers aren't supposed to muck around with complex and subtle things like style. Nevertheless there are a few things which, to an ordinary Vassar grad-uate, seem rather obvious. Stylistically there is something in common in the prose of all these people. My roommate, Smithy to the core, puts it succinctly: "None of them can write worth a shit." However, it is not exactly that simple. Please note that *even the characters, so-called, created in synopses etc. by this, so-called, John Towne have exactly the same stylistic faults.* If Towne is the master of anything, it is the sudden and overwhelmingly vulgar descent into bathos and the crudely vernacular. Decorum is definitely not his bag.

Stylistically, this MS. is so much of a piece (never mind of what) that I can only conclude that the same disturbed personality is responsible for every bit of it, from guggle to zatch. And I'm sure that any sane person would agree with me.

Ergo: the gimmick doesn't work. Verisimilitude-wise, it's a definite big loser.

If you really want to publish this trash, why not do it right? My roommate and I have many free evenings. If the price were right, I'm sure we could fix it up properly in no time. Given a little more freedom, we might add the value of the intelligent feminist touch. To break even a book has to sell to the ladies. All men are beasts, of course, but why wave it in their faces? Why let this "JOHN TOWNE" come on like Malvolio, unzipped and unashamed? If anybody wants a rewrite, we're available.

Molly Sassey
Copy Editor

Dedication

I fully and firmly intended to dedicate this work, as is my custom, to my good wife Minerva. She has put up with a lot, through thick and thin. But I cannot. And if you are reading this, Minerva, I certainly hope you will try to understand.

I owe the dedication, a solemn promise, to my graduate research assistant, a talented and attractive young lady who was truly a Trojan when it came to working on this MS. All work and no play, especially when you're editing somebody else's confused papers, is bad news. From time to time my assistant and I would take a coffee break at the Student Union Building. It was there that she taught me how to play Strip Ping Pong. She probably figured to put me down in front of the students who crowded around to witness our match. It was a mismatch. It is true that I am clumsy and inept at many things and especially games and sports. But the one thing I can really do (Minerva will testify to this) is play Ping Pong. I am a demon when it comes to Ping Pong. Well, the long and the short of it, is that in about ten minutes after my assistant dared me to play her a game of Strip Ping Pong, she was down to her Scanty Panties, the kids were hooting and jeering, she was crying, and I was trying to let her win enough points to spare her the final shame of revealing what crude students at our institution refer to as "beaver" or "squirrel shot." I fed her many easy shots, but she was too distraught to take advantage. The result? One bareass research assistant.

In order to console her I made a rash impulsive promise (after we had returned to the relative privacy of my office and I had managed to cheer her up a little) to dedicate this book to her. A man is only as good as his word, even his rash and impulsive word. That's why this book is dedicated, with fond appreciation to

Miss Betty Lou Savage

Rough Draft of a Speech by the Rev. "Radio" P. King, Possibly to be Delivered in Hyde Park, London, at Some Future Date. . . .

—Ladies and Gentlemen, please permit me, your friendly American blackface cousin and righteous comedian, to say a few words about why I love England so much and what I am doing over here at this time. You may think me some kind of a kook to have left the shores of the affluent and booming U.S.A. behind me, to be here in jolly old, grimy old England telling you why you should love your own little country.

—Now, I could tell you that you might as well love it, you better love it, because if you don't surely nobody else will. I could say that, but wait!, I won't. Because it ain't true. The plain truth is that your attitude, one way of the other, doesn't much matter any more. We, your fun-loving, loud-talking, power-wielding, double-dealing American cousins, we love it just the way it is and you just the way you are or, anyway, the way we think you are. Therefore, the facts of life being what they are whether you like it or not, because that's the way we want them. . . .

—You, sir, you with that brick in your hand! Don't do something you'll regret. Hear me out first. Show me a little of that celebrated British patience and fortitude, and then when I'm done, if you still want to throw rocks, I'll have to take my chances and my lumps, won't I?

—Not to worry. Oh, never and not to worry. The insulting and negative part of my peroration is nearing its (pardon the expression) climax and will soon be over and done with. After that, rhetoric and good manners demand an encomium. Which I am sure enough fixing to give you, too.

—Now then, I can judge by your tired and pale and somewhat angry faces that you don't much like the present state of affairs. You helped win the War and you have suffered ever since. You have, within a lifetime not actually lost, but in fact *given away* the greatest single Empire in the history of the world. You see yourselves now as rather like the Japanese, though of course not half so industrious or energetic these days, cramped on your little island set in a shrinking sea, surrounded as once before by hostile Celts of all kinds, condemned to your ghastly weather, your fading traditions, your notorious mutton, boiled veggies and brussels sprouts.

—Others, perhaps more optimistic, see some kind of a future role for your nation and your people. Having dropped the torch of actual and practical leadership in the Western World, you are now free, cleanhanded and pure-hearted, to take up that more perfect torch whose symbolic and invisible flame is supposed to be *moral* leadership of freedom, custodian of right reason and disinterested integrity.

—A fine idea, but forget it. Just fucking forget it, you hear?

—So far as I can tell no nation in the history of the world has ever been able to assume such a role, and not bloody likely now. Greece exerted its great power and influence, but only as an idea, an abstraction after the place itself was in ruins, the sites of the temples and theatres mere gazing land for a lot of scruffy goats and sheep, herded by illiterate shepherds as far from Orpheus as I from Hercules. In short, moral power can be exercised only by dead nations in an honest state of *rigor mortis*, not dying Empires with the *delirium tremens*. The irony is that you are not dead enough.

—Anyway, since most of your powers of moral persuasion would have to be squandered upon us, your wheeling-dealing American cousins, since we do speak more or less the same language, what would you tell us, if you could? What to do in Viet Nam? Ridiculous! Truly ridiculous. The only reasons you aren't there too are: (a) you can't afford it, (b) you've already got a disproportionate and quite necessary percentage of your manpower and wealth committed elsewhere.

—Would you try to tell us how to manage our unruly Niggers? Really!! Stand on the podium of Smethwick and tell us. Wasted breath!

—I'm not really trying to be insulting when I say that you have nothing at all to tell us; for this is not true. You have the Beatles to tell us. You have fashions and plays and pansy poets to tell us. You have Mandy and Christine and Jean Shrimpton and Diane Celinto and James Bond and Sir John Gielgud reading "The Seven Ages of Man" on T.V. You have Herman's Hermits and C.P. Snow. What else do you want or need? Oh yes, not to forget all those lady novelists you have to tell us: your Iris Murdoch, Muriel Spark, Doris Lessing, your Margaret Drabble and Brigid Brophy and so forth and so on. To reply with Mary McCarthy or Rona Jaffe would be like trying to

put up the wife of Bath against the patient Greselda in a contest for Best Housewife of the Middle Ages. We know when we're licked!

—No, I do not wish to say you don't have something to say. You do. I wish merely to point out that this idea of becoming the forged and moral conscience of any known world beyond Land's End, the borders of Scotland and Wales, and the territorial limits of your cold and windy waters, is pure, pardon my yiddish, *dreck*. History, past and present, tells us that morals have nothing whatsoever to do with politics—local, national or international. Morals are the nosegay of winners. To win is to be moral. To lose is to have your history written by less than sympathetic, probably immoral strangers. Conscience is a luxurious quality, like guilt, reserved for those who have retired from the fray. Live with yours.. . .

—Wait! Don't go away yet. I still have a few more pertinent remarks to make. I have come as a sort of ambassador to you, bearing good news. Listen and learn. In the first place, things are not quite as bad as they may seem where you're standing in your shabby, ill-fitting and uncomfortable clothes. All is not lost by any means. Sinking you may be, but the island didn't go down when I stepped on board.

—Let me get down to facts and figures. In *World Statistics* (for 1966) there is an interesting section on "Riches and Resources" of nations. Under *minerals and metals* sixteen key ones are listed. You have four of these. You are 6th in cement, 5th in lead, 6th in pig iron and 10th in zinc. Of the eighteen categories of agricultural riches you are mentioned in seven of them: 5th in barley, 6th in meat, 6th in milk cows, 7th in oats, 7th in potatoes, 10th in sheep and 9th in wool. Under "Industry, Trade and Communications" you're holding up pretty well. You are 2nd in airlines, 8th in aluminum, 3rd in electricity, 2nd in merchant fleets, 3rd in motor vehicles, 5th in steel production, and 10th in telephones. I am sorry that you do not appear in the top ten in such categories as "Employment-Index," "Retail Trade Index" etc., but no matter. Cheer up. You've still got cement, barley and oats and plenty of telephones.

—But wait. These figures do not tell the whole story and are likely to fool the unwary. In point of fact, viewed from any long-range perspective, all the English-speaking world is one and will be judged so. Boundaries are irrelevant. We share a common basis of language and many traditions—though we don't understand them all, of course. Moreover, as an irony of history, that greenhouse and hotbed or ironies, you have now become a sort of colony in the vast process and program of the *Pax Americana*. We need you, just as we need our own St. Augustine, Williamsburg, Concord, and Lexington. We need you as you are, to prove our legitimacy. Otherwise literally and not just metaphorically we are nothing but a bunch of bastards.

—We need you. Didn't our President Johnson, then Vice-President I believe, enter one of your Saville Row tailor shops and say, speaking on behalf of us all: "Make me look like a fucking British diplomat!"

—Didn't Roger Miller come to England and sit in his hotel room and write "England Swings Like A Pendulum Do"?

—Swing on Brittania! Be forever quaint and colorful for us. Pose for our cameras and take our money. And stop worrying about the Bomb. Nobody is going to waste one on you. It isn't worth it according to the computer-tested criteria of kill ratio. And for heaven's sake stop trying to update everything. For example, take this Royalty business. You may be tired of it. You may agree with angry old John Osborne, that cliché image of his about royalty being the gold filling in a decaying mouth. Or some such rude remark. Never mind, we like your Royalty. We need it! Our own worthies are assholes. Our ceremonies are pretty silly. Therefore we need yours. So you are stuck with them whether you like it or not.

—The point is that you have now become a kind of International Fun Park. Don't try to change. Don't fret and fume, it's hopeless. While everybody else is sweating the whole business of *becoming*, you've already been there. All you have to do is—be! And not without pride. After all, you are not and never have been cowards. I was in Los Angeles during the so-called Cuban Missile Crisis and I just thank the Lord they didn't drop a bomb anywhere around there. Even an automobile backfire could have started an apocalyptic ethnic panic among the natives. With nothing to lose you can afford to be brave and to tell the truth. The rest of the world will certainly marvel at that, though none will practice it either. You can even afford, as you've recently discovered, the rare luxury of the very poor—you can be as silly as you please. There is far too little silliness in this solemn, sick world of ours.

—And that, ladies and gents, is why I'm here. I have come back to Playland, the Land of Cockaynge, the old ship of fools my n'er-do-well ancestors fled—like rats—some centuries ago. Well, you didn't sink and won't for a while yet. So you lost India and Africa. Who needs them? You've found Twiggy, that sweet and skinny young lady, and as the poet says "long may ye live and toughly I hope ye may thole."

—Thank you very much for your kind attentions.

—Contributions in coin of the realm will be gratefully accepted etc. etc. etc.

Part Two
Life of John Towne, Esq.

I am not he such eloquence to boast
    To make the crow in singing as the swan,
     Nor call the lion of coward beasts the most
That cannot take a mouse as the cat can . . . .
        (Sir Thomas Wyatt—*Satires*)

Notes Toward an Outline of the
Life & Character of John Towne

1.

What manner of man is this so-called John Towne?

To begin the search for preliminary answers one must bear in mind that, beginning with the use of a pseudonym, he is forever furtive and in disguise. Therefore we can take very little for granted and almost nothing at face value.

Even allowing for all difficulties, however, we can deduce, discover, and infer some relevant things, implicit and explicit from the confused MS of *Life With Kim Novak Is Hell* and his other papers. For Towne, though often sly, is seldom genuinely shrewd or clever, try as he will. A neatly balanced arrangement of ignorance and arrogance betrays him again and again.

I have managed to put together a sketchy *vita* by an exhaustive and exhausting examination of "KIM NOVAK" and the other papers. Incomplete as this is, it will have to do until the time (*when and if*) the entire MS is to be perpetrated upon the public.

2.

CURRICULUM VITAE—John Towne

At the time of the ostensible composition of this so-called confessional novel, John Towne must have been close to the age of forty. Close enough to be called so.

It would seem that in the Academic Year 1967–1968 he was employed on a one year contract on a trial basis as Instructor of English at a private college for women, quite likely located in southwestern Virginia. He refuses to give the correct name, preferring to call it Nameless College. In general, however, it sounds very much like Randolph Macon or Hollins or even Sweet Briar.

In my opinion it may have been Hollins College. For in several places he refers to "the millstones in the central quadrangle." That institution is known to be decorated with a number of huge millstones. Secondly, there are a number of bad jokes and unspeakable puns which would seem to be based upon the fact that the Administration Offices of that beautiful and picturesque school, nestled beneath the Blue Ridge Mountains, are located in a building with a name which amused him—Cocke Hall.

More cryptic are references made from time to time to one Levy the Occulist. And in one place a reference to The Chapel of Levy the Occulist. After investigation I have discovered that the Chapel at Hollins College bears the inscription "Levavi Occulus," from the *Psalms*, across the front facade.

Since Towne's Latin is execrable, it is entirely possible that he assumed the Chapel to be the gift of one Levy, the Occulist. In any case, even allowing for some sort of private (and perhaps anti-semitic) "joke," the whole thing is altogether apt to the revealed character of Towne.

There is no evidence either of professional competence or seriousness on Towne's part. A series of events involving both the college and the local authorities seems to have formed a background to the termination of his affiliation with that institution.

There were a great many minor difficulties, controversies, and problems. But the most serious occurred when Towne, attempting to outrun a police vehicle while driving a Volkswagen, ran off the road and wrecked and demolished that little car. He emerged from the heap, "laughing and scratching," and he puts it, and unscathed. Since it was a stolen automobile ("borrowed" from the Dean of Women without her permission) and since Towne was drunk at the time, he found himself in fairly serious difficulties with the Law. He was charged with grand larceny, reckless driving, driving while intoxicated, disorderly conduct, resisting arrest, assault upon a Police Officer and, finally, driving without a valid driver's license. For, as it was soon painfully evident, his own license had been permanently revoked earlier in the year when he was apprehended and convicted for driving while intoxicated.

It appears that Towne never stood trial for his series of serious charges. On the original date scheduled for a hearing he was in the hospital. By the time of the second date he had vanished.

In a section of the MS, apparently written prior to that date and prior to his disappearance, he states that he will soon fly off to London, cleverly disguised as a Negro Clergyman, under the assumed name of the "Reverend Radio P. King."

Any British Readers are hereby warned that Towne appears to don and to doff all kinds of disguises with blithe abandon and without the least twitch of conscience or remorse. He is not without skill in the assumption of new identities. However, true to form, pattern or a flaw of his nature, whenever Towne plays a role there is always something outlandish, ridiculous, and indeed offensive about his style. He tends to throw himself into the part of some imaginary character (or sometimes, by the same token, into an hypothetical "intellectual" position) with such childish enthusiasm as to inflate or exaggerate the role beyond all the bounds of credibility, pushing it, therefore himself, stumbling and staggering, into the precincts of farce and self-parody.

Thus, no matter how well he disguises himself in the electric atmosphere, rich and various and strange, of "the new swinging London," it seems likely that he will sooner or later reveal himself by the habit of outraging common sense and decency. Experts have long noted that there exists a strong impulsive pattern of self-destruction in the criminal phycology. In short, should there be a literal or metaphorical banana peel anywhere in the vicinity of John Towne, he will, as it were, seek it out, step down upon it firmly, and take a mighty pratfall.

It would be pointless here to enumerate his many difficulties at Nameless College. Imagine the worst and you will still be giving him the benefit of the doubt. The range of his folly extends all the way from matters of deportment, social behavior, and general incompetence in the classroom, through every conceivable form of cheerful irresponsibility towards his students and the College. It includes some serious troubles involving faculty wives, unmarried female faculty, and, I am very sorry to report, certain of his young students. He was a source of constant friction and irritation to both the Faculty and the Administration. He continually annoyed all of his superiors, especially the patient Chairman of the Department of English, not only by his inexcusable actions and his elaborate excuses for them, but also by his unceasing complaints and "constructive criticism" on all subjects from curriculum to trash disposal.

It should surprise no thoughtful person that Towne's contract to teach at Nameless was not renewed. Of course, Towne was surprised, "deeply shocked by this blatant demonstration of injustice," as he puts it. In his view he justly deserved not only the renewal of his contract but a promotion and a raise in salary. Or so he professes, with all the sincerity he can muster, in a final "letter of resignation" submitted to the President of the College.

In appearance Towne would seem to be of medium height, just under six feet tall, of average weight and proportion for his size and age, possessed of thinning sandy hair, blue eyes, a complexion by turns sallow or ruddy. Apparently he has bad teeth or false teeth. He has no noticeable scars or deformities. However he refers in several places to the tattoo upon his chest. The tattoo being the words "Death Before Dishonor," together with the insignia of the U.S. Marine Corps. He also possesses a rather remarkable "washboard" stomach. Although he gives every indication of loathing all forms of physical exercise and exertion, he admits to the most careful preservation of the definition and muscle tone of his abdomen. He owned, and used with an obsessive Spartan regularity, several items of equipment designed to keep his stomach muscles in good shape. These included: a Relax-a-Cisor, an inclined exercise board, a mechanical massage belt, and an electrically powered wooden roller of the type found in many professional health studios.

23

Whatever justification there may be for his inordinate concern for the muscles of his stomach, we have his own words and observations on the matter.

"Women don't give a shit one way or the other about muscles in general. The truth is there's only one muscle of the male anatomy that is relevant. Weightlifters, body-builders, jocks of all description are really wasting their time if their purpose is to impress women and score.

"However, despite the truth of the above, it has been my experience that women are powerfully curious if not downright fascinated by the prospect of a flat, ridged, well-defined, muscular gut. How else can you explain the popularity of Paul Newman, for example? He can't act for sour apples, his whole *shtick* being a rather inferior impersonation of the early Marlon Brando.

"Anyway, all you have to do is get your shirt off under some pretext or other. Right away they will want to touch it. The stomach, I mean. Once a woman is engaged in touching your stomach, you are well on your way. The rest is up to you, but if you know anything at all about women, a score should follow.

"In my own particular case, the tattoo serves at once to distract and repel them. It also amuses them mildly. I have found that, faced with its gaudy and emphatic glory, they tend to avert their eyes. It has been my observation that women, who seldom waste even an impulsive gesture, do not, as a rule, while averting their eyes from anything, look upwards towards a distant and dubious heaven. Nine times out of ten they look down. Whereupon the muscles of my upper abdomen serve to catch their attention. At even the most indirect and oblique invitation they will admit to a curiosity concerning the entire abdominal area. From there on it's just a matter of giving curiosity free reign and letting nature take its course."

Shortly before he fled to London (or wherever he went), as stated earlier, Towne entered the hospital for an operation. He had his appendix removed. This may have spoiled the muscular symmetry of at least one side of his lower abdomen.

It should be added that Towne never served in the U.S. Marine Corps.

His military service consisted, among other things, of combat duty as an enlisted man in the Infantry, U.S. Army, during the Police Action in Korea. After service overseas he finished up his tour of duty with the rank of Sergeant.

Although he is clearly not patriotic in any conventional sense, Towne has expressed interest in the Vietnamese conflict in several places in the MS. In one place he states that he would seriously consider re-enlisting if he could be certain to get his old rank back and be assured of duty in Saigon.

"I don't enjoy being shot at by slope-heads and gooks and I don't figure that killing a few more of them will make much difference in the general demographic picture one way or the other. But from what I hear and can find out the Black Market in Saigon is one of the best deals in recent times. A man with my experience might be able to come back home a legitimate Capitalist instead of a candidate for the Poverty Program. In fact, that strikes

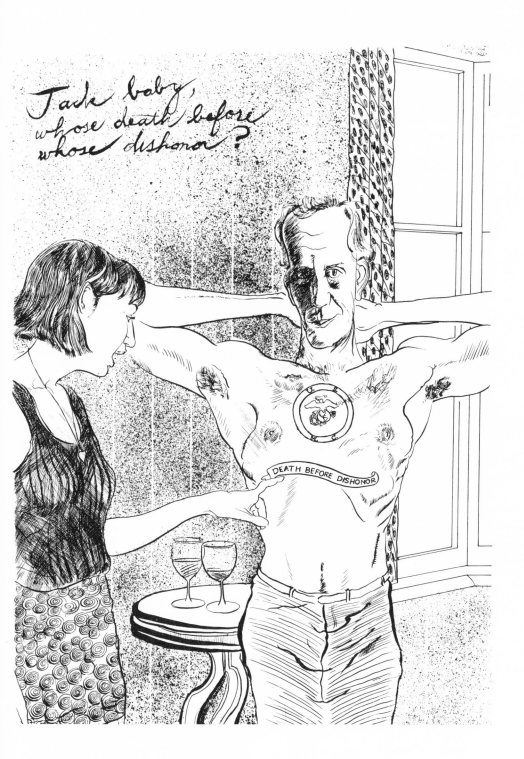

me as a sound reason to keep the war going as long as possible. It could save the American taxpayer a lot of loot in the long run."

These sentiments, openly expressed at a solemn Vietnam Teach-In held at Nameless College, appear to have been a contributing factor in the outburst of the only riot ever to take place at that institution.

Shortly after receiving his honorable discharge from the U.S. Army, Towne took advantage of the educational opportunities afforded by the G.I. Bill by enrolling in a training school for professional masseurs. Which may seem an odd choice for a graduate of Princeton University. But he argues that he was without means or ambition at the time and had no desire to tax his brain with serious studies. He graduated from the course and apparently became a masseur at a winter ski resort in New England.

It was there, as she lay upon his massage table, that he met his bride-to-be, whom he refers to as "Annie" and "Fanny" and, in someplaces, as "Franny," in the MS. She was apparently a wealthy girl of good family, though somewhat prematurely "liberated" it would appear, at least by the standards of The Silent Generation of the Fifties.

By agreeing to return to graduate school to study towards a Ph.D. in English, he managed to win over her suspicious parents. And he married the girl. He attended graduate school, and though he seems to have survived and to have progressed far enough to settle upon a dissertation topic—"Milton's Use of Dreams and Dream Visions"—it is extremely doubtful, despite his claims otherwise, that he ever received his degree.

One major piece of evidence. As late as the time of the composition of "KIM NOVAK" he seems to have been working on the dissertation topic in a desultory manner. It is a fact that he assigned his entire Seminar on Contemporary Fiction to the task of doing research on that subject.

Circa 1956 he found himself teaching at "John Wesley College," in New England, bored to distraction by his work, but living in a rather grand style, by dint of his wife's income, of course, in a beautifully restored 18th century house in the country. He was the father of two young children—a son, whom he calls "Monster" in the MS and for whom his implaccable hostility is unconcealed, and a daughter referred to only as "The Princess."

Apparently his marriage was not going well at the time. According to Towne, his most attractive and desirable young wife could be sexually aroused only by reading pornography. The Reader is here reminded that due to the persistence of the Puritan Ethos and the composition of the Supreme Court of the United States at that time, dirty books were not so easily accessible in those days as now, when any friendly neighborhood drugstore offers a full range of vicarious erotic pleasure at a decent and democratic price. Towne swears that he never had any interest whatsoever in creative writing—and it is easy enough to see why—until that fateful day when he discovered that he had exhausted the entire Locked Books Section of the John Wesley Library. "At that point I realized painfully that there was a simple choice before me—

26

either start being creative and creating like a madman or doing without nooky. Needless to say, reason prevailed. I became a writer overnight."

His artistic problem was intensified by the awkward fact that any given composition, addressed to and written for his audience of one, would work its magic *one time only* . . . ! But he wrote steadily and indefatigably during that time, building up an impressive canon of pornographic MSS.

At the same time he was actively engaged in several "affairs," including a rather prolonged relationship with one Geraldine Wadley, identified as "the wife of my best friend." He justifies all this hanky panky as "research," denying any self-indulgence whatsoever. "It was all a sacrifice to my art," he writes.

Finally, reaching a state of mental and physical exhaustion as a result of his intensive literary production and other related activities, he convinced his wife to see a psychiatrist. (With characteristic hostility and ignorance he calls this doctor "Dr. Smartheim" and "Dr. Smartass" in the MS.) The immediate results of her visits and treatment were less than gratifying to the troubled and weary Towne. In order to study and know his patient properly, Dr. Smartass soon had Towne cranking out more pornography than ever before.

"I do not know how long this might have lasted," Towne writes, "had not a lucky break spared me from my fate."

The "lucky break" he refers to was the occasion when his "best friend" returned home unexpectedly and found Towne enjoying the intimacy of Geraldine. Much confusion and trouble followed upon this moment, all dutifully recorded in the MS "KIM NOVAK." (Which is, in fact, addressed and dedicated to his former friend, Ray Wadley.) However, to make a long complex story short, Towne went off to New York with Geraldine. Ray Wadley was fired from the college for "moral turpitude," for he attacked Towne with his fisticuffs on college property and in the presence of students. Dr. Smartass moved into the Towne residence to keep a close watch on his patient during this difficult transitional period, a gesture of concern which *Mrs.* Smartass persisted in misinterpreting.

It must be added that, after divorces all around, the doctor did the honorable thing and married his former patient.

Recently, according to Towne, his former wife lapsed back into her old condition. A seriously concerned Dr. Smartass wrote him, offering him an attractive sum of money as a retainer if he would begin to write pornography again. Towne states that he flatly refused to come to the aid of the doctor, "not out of malice or, pardon the expression, hard feelings, but out of professional and artistic pride."

It was in New York that Towne, now being supported by Geraldine who had taken a job as a secretary, managed to complete his first novel, *Live Now & Pay Later*. He now admits that it was "freely adapted from" an unpublished manuscript entitled "A Home for Reckless Spenders," by Ray Wadley.

"Sure it looks bad, Ray," he writes. "But in reality I did you a favor. You are much more the scholarly-critical type. Why waste your valuable time and energy on these trivial things? I saved you from a terrible mistake. The literary life is for the birds. Take it from me. I might add, in all fairness, that I also saved you from a lifetime with Geraldine. Who is a stupid bitch even if she is a good piece of ass. There are more important things than sex, believe me. If you can think it through, logically and rationally, you cannot help agreeing with me that in one (pardon) stroke I gave you a new lease on life. What more could a friend do? I can understand why you were upset, but even the best of us are overwhelmed by our emotions sometimes. I am willing to forgive you and let bygones be bygones."

When an unfortunate movie producer purchased *Live Now & Pay Later* for the movies (it was never to my knowledge filmed and released), Towne left for Hollywood to write the screenplay, travelling in the company of an aspiring young actress.

"As for Geraldine," he writes, "I left her to find her own identity and to seek a happy and productive life. I had done all that I could for her. In the last analysis any identity crisis is a very personal thing. Each individual must face it boldly on his/her own. She seemed extremely angry and embittered when I left her and said any number of rude things to me. But she was overwrought and not in control of herself. I choose not to remember her that way, cursing and throwing things and, indeed, threatening me with physical harm, and exaggerating her importance in my success. It is true that she typed the novel for me and made a few suggestions and minor corrections, but anyone would have done that. No, I shall always remember her with affection and gratitude. And I shall always wish her well."

In the circus of Hollywood John Towne prospered for a time. Working on the adaptation of *Live Now & Pay Later* for the silver screen and receiving an excellent payment for his efforts, he managed to keep the project alive over a considerable period of time and through innumerable drafts and revisions. Part of the Producer's patience can be attributed to the fact that the Producer's wife developed a great faith and enthusiasm for Towne's talents.

All this came to an end when Towne was "discovered" in a Santa Monica motel room with that same lady. He was promptly fired. Shortly thereafter, emerging from a nightclub on Sunset Strip he was badly beaten up by some professional hoodlums. He sustained permanent damage to his teeth, and repairing that damage has been one of his chief concerns ever since.

Of that beating Towne writes: "I am not sure who to blame for setting those guys on me. I should be less than candid (and a confession without candor is like rice without gravy) if I did not admit that there were any number of misguided people in and around L.A. who may have felt some hostility towards me. The pressures of that world inevitably breed intense paranoia. However, it is my guess that Bitch Baby [*Editor's Note:* his name for the Producer's wife] is responsible. It would be typical of that slut. I made a terrible mistake in her case. I paid her the compliment of honesty. After I got fired and she got her ass booted out of her house, she started grasping for straws. She wanted to get married. To me! I simply explained to her that it would never work. She was too old for me. I stated honestly and succinctly that for the happiness and well-being of both of us I could see no need to prolong our awkward and tedious relationship. And a couple of days later I woke up in the hospital.

"Of course, I knew better. It never pays to be honest with a woman. But I genuinely respected her intelligence, so much so that I did not think of her as a woman, really. I remember I told her that, too, but she did not seem pleased by the compliment."

When Towne left the hospital, he moved in with a kindly and concerned nurse he had met there, a fellow southerner evidently named Billie-Sue. She supported him during his long period of convalescence and readjustment to society, and she continued to do so while he sought unsuccessfully to find some suitable employment.

Eventually, with Billie-Sue's financial backing, he took up the art of photography. He opened a small studio, "Figure Photos of Live Models," where, for educational purposes only, he rented out cameras, with or without film, and provided models "for interested amateur shutterbugs who might otherwise have missed the great artistic challenge of trying to capture the beauty of the undraped female form." It is not at all clear that Towne possessed either much knowledge or experience in this difficult type of photography or, indeed, in any kind of photography. In no place in the MS does he even so much as allude to such basic and interesting matters as lenses, focal lengths, light settings and arrangements, or specific cameras and films. However, there are a few references to the published works of Bunny Yeager. And at one time or another he mentions the names of such photographers as Peter Basch, Andre de Dienes, and Peter Gowland, indicating that Towne may not be entirely unfamiliar with the art form which he persists crudely in calling "skin pics and horn shots."

Towne later landed a job, scripting a low budget "nudie" film entitled MONDO TEENY BOPPO. Which he claims also to have "novelized" and asserts was published as an original paperback by Totem Pole Press. As a part of the "package," Billie-Sue reluctantly agreed to star in this picture in return for a highly speculative percentage of the net profits, if any, and upon the firm understanding that Towne would marry her upon the completion and release of the aforesaid picture.

Towne did not marry Billie-Sue, though he insists that he intended to, just as soon as he was earning enough money to support her in a proper style. In any case, this picture seems to have been "released" and to have played the shabby circuit of theatres devoted to that sort of thing. Ironically, a number of Billie-Sue's old friends and relatives happened, purely by accident no doubt, to see the picture when it appeared in a Drive-In not far from her home town of Charlotte, North Carolina. Among these was a certain evangelical Preacher whom she greatly respected and admired. Some people wrote to her that she ought to be ashamed of herself. The Preacher was not so uncharitable. He wrote a most kindly and forgiving letter, allowing as how he was in fact glad that she had done this thing, for the sake of her soul. "The Lord has given you beauty and talent, and no man in his right mind can deny that," he wrote. "But your beauty and talent were not given you to be squandered upon lowgrade movies made in America's Sodom and Gommorah. And the Lord did not give you beauty and acting talent so that you could use it to tease and tantalize poor frustrated men all across the wide world. No, Billie-Sue, it would be blasphemy to think that the Lord intended to use you as a temptation and a test of international male self-discipline. We are not given temptations that are so powerful that we cannot possibly withstand them. According to the experts in these matters, the sin of self-abuse is sharply on the rise in this sick society, along with smoking, drinking, playing cards, and mixed dancing. Self-abuse in a man breeds guilt, as well it should. For out of guilt can come repentence and contrition, among other things. Some might say that jacking off is a good thing, then, which feels good at the time and has after-effects which can help to fill up churches and revival tents with nervous men looking for some way to break the habit. Those who say this disregard the side effects. It will put hair on the palms of your hands and pimples on your face for all the world to see. And it is medically proven to dry up the vital juices and humors of the human brain.

"Wouldn't you hate to be personally responsible for thousands of hairy-palmed, acned men of low, not to say moronic I.Q. level, wandering all across the face of our land?

"A couple more pictures like that one there and you alone could achieve what all the atheists and Communists and perverts and Earl Warren combined have failed to do with all their sneaky and concerted efforts. Now, Billie-Sue, you wouldn't want that on your conscience would you?

"Your Aunt Ella, who happened to be sitting with me at the time, cried like a baby all during the picture show. But I just smiled. I took it for a sign. The Lord wants you to put your talent and beauty to work for Him. Think what you could accomplish in the name of good!

"You think about it, honey. And if you ever feel like shaking the dust of that wicked place off of your pretty little feet, you just let me know. There is a place for you always waiting in my Choir of Angels. Just remember that. . . ."

When Billie-Sue, deeply touched by this response, insisted that Towne should marry her at once and return with her to live a more wholesome life in Charlotte, he evidently (in a blind panic at the prospect) refused outright, adding that in all fairness she could not expect him to marry someone who had "exposed herself to the public like that."

Thereupon she left him. Rather he left first while she shot at him repeatedly with a .22 caliber Colt Woodsman Automatic Pistol.

There is another version of this "sad parting" which, while it sounds quite probable and in perfect character for John Towne, I, myself, would rather not believe. I prefer to believe there is some poetic justice in this world, even if that flies in the face of all the evidence.

However, in the interest of objectivity, I must mention it, wishing and hoping that it is not so.

In this second version, Towne, anticipating just such a possibility, had secretly loaded Billie-Sue's Colt Woodsman with *blank cartridges!* When she began to shoot at him, he fell groaning to the floor, feigning a mortal wound. Her nursing instincts and training aroused, she rushed to his side to aid him. And she was tearfully, gratefully relieved to discover his little joke. Promptly he effected a loving reconciliation and promised to marry her in Nevada the next day.

Unspeakable, if undaunted, Towne adds: "For fun and for real fervor there is no kind of a Score that is quite the equal of a good old Reconciliation Lay!"

Sometime much later that night or in the early dawn hours, he told Billie-Sue that he had one small, trivial confession to make before they took off to Nevada.

Towne told her that, even though he was certain that it would make absolutely no difference to her, he must in conscience tell her that he had a very modest amount of Negro blood in his veins. "I look white," he said. "It's my brother Roy who got the heredity shaft. Poor old Roy, he is as black as a coal shovel!"

The effect of this sudden revelation upon a young lady of Southern upbringing need not be detailed or elaborated. Let us avert our eyes from the sad and sordid scene, allowing only the closing information that within less than 15 minutes, Billie-Sue had packed her suitcase and was long gone and gone for good. Stunned, she departed in such haste that she left behind most of her worldly possessions, including an FM radio, a good stereo set, kitchen utensils, *objets d'art* and even an expensive hair drier. For all of these items Towne managed to fetch a fair price a bit later when he found himself in need.

Shortly thereafter John Towne was hired by Totem Pole Press in the capacity of "Doctor Wisdom." Doctor Wisdom being an imaginary savant or sage who answers personal queries, chiefly of an erotic nature, of poor deluded individuals writing to him in response to a wide advertising and promotion campaign in some of the more tawdry magazines on the market. Magazines which no Reader will ever have glanced at since they are largely unknown to members of polite society. As "Doctor Wisdom" Towne seems to have functioned with some competence and success, a fact which should not surprise us considering the rapport he would have with sex-crazed weirdos of the lower orders of society and not ignoring that Towne demonstrates some facility, crude though it be, in the epistolary vein.

He might have gone on indefinitely, I suppose, handing out misinformation and crackpot, half-baked theories to desperately needy and confused individuals, having found his true vocation, his proper cranny in the wall, so to speak, had not his usual arrogance and ambition blinded him. He demanded a large increase in salary and more favorable working conditions. And, of course, in less time than it takes me to type these words, he found himself once again a statistical member of the unemployed.

Never one to accept an inevitable defeat gracefully, Towne's self-indulgent self-righteousness led him to one parting shot. He fired off a final series of "Doctor Wisdom" letters intended to outrage the recipients and likely, at the least, to add to their tribulations and perplexities. Heavily in debt then and without any possibility of remedy, Towne tried a number of tricks to save his skin, if not his soul. One of these was to prepare a *Vita*, which if not downright fraudulent, must be called deliberately misleading, which he mailed off to every college and university listed in the back of the *Webster's Collegiate Dictionary*. To his pleased surprise (and to my dismay!) he received at least two replies offering him a one-year job. One was from Austin Peay State College in Tennessee, which, upon the simple strength of having another offer, he declared to be "completely out of the question!" The other came from "Nameless College." Formerly a finishing school, now known as an adventurous liberal arts college for *nouveau riche* young ladies, it seemed to him, of course, like a summons to Eden. He wired (collect) his acceptance of the offer and left L.A. without delay or regret, hitch-hiking across the country, and arriving just in time for the beginning of the fall term in 1967–68.

At some time during his Hollywood period, the novel, *Goldwyn Boy*, was brought out by Totem Pole. There is no evidence that it did not receive the fate it most certainly deserved, i.e., shortly after publication it vanished forever without murmur, protest, or a trace.

During that academic year at Nameless College, Towne is supposed to have written *Life With Kim Novak Is Hell*, as an act of confession and expiation for his sins (the actual word he uses is *pecadillos*) and signal proof that he had "changed his ways."

The Reader will note that he remained busy, too, trying to sell ridiculous plots to publishers during the same period.

He appears to have been "engaged" for a time to a young Dental Technician, at least long enough to arrange for some preliminary repair work on his teeth.

Outside of the college he seems to have engaged in various contradictory activities. For example, he held simultaneous membership in The Patriots' Gun Club (whose targets were larger than life photographs of Che Guevara, Ho Chi Minh, Abdul Nasser, Charles De Gaulle, Earl Warren etc., need I say more?) and The Southwest Virginia Association of Benevolent Mau Mau. Which had formerly been affiliated with the Black Panthers but was expelled from that organization for their "extremist and violently simplistic views." Which, if either, represented a genuine political allegiance on Towne's part is impossible to determine. It would seem possible that he acted as a spy and informer for one or the other or for both at the same time.

In any event, except for the duffel bag and the wardrobe trunk containing his papers and the confused MS of "Kim Novak," it is safe to say that for all practical purposes and for the time being the man who calls himself John Towne has vanished off the face of the earth.

Which might be a cause for rejoicing, an occasion for bell ringing celebration by all right-thinking men were it not for a final warning, call it a threat, he has left us.

"My hero is a mythical Greek whose name escapes me. Every time they knocked him on his ass he came back again. And so will I. Don't count me out just because I am down and out. I'll be back one of these days—you better believe it!—louder and funnier than ever.

"I am a hustler. So what? So is everyone these days. I don't care who you are, from a Bowery Bum to the Pope in Rome, you either hustle or you get hustled. It's all the same. Difference of degree, not kind.

"Sure, I have been known to equivocate once in a while, times of dire peril and emergency. Well, if you have even bothered to flip through the pages of the *Patrilogia Latina*, you will have noticed that again and again the old Church Fathers, just like the great Jewish patriarchs before them, allowed as how a lie told in self-defense, to preserve life and limb, isn't all that serious. Of course, if you are bucking for sainthood, it would be your slickest move to tell the truth under all circumstances. But I have always been inhibited by my essential humility from considering myself as a possible candidate for beatification. So I have merely carried the logic of the Fathers to its logical conclusion.

"Satchel Paige gave me my practical philosophy of life when he said: 'Never look behind you. Something might be gaining on you.'

"Sure, I have made mistakes and done some things wrong. But am I not the first to admit it?

"Moreover, don't forget, in your pious superiority, that I, too, may have my place and purpose in the great boloxed up scheme of things that people sometimes call Providence. Let us assume that I have wronged someone. Just for the sake of argument. When someone is wronged, gets reamed and shafted without so much as a kiss, why the experience educates them to recognize that the values of this world have nothing whatever to do with justice. They can then conclude and console themselves that the values of this world are transitory and ephemeral. Besides which injustice is wonderful for the character. It gives people something palpable, tangible to try to rise above. There is nothing like a fist in the face (metaphorically speaking) to bring out the best in a man. It is a golden opportunity to turn the other cheek. If he does not, if he chooses to stand and fight or haul ass, he has only himself to blame. And there is justice. If he fails to turn the other cheek, he feels guilty as all get out. And rightly so.

"And, hypocrites, bear this in mind. Do not ignore the undeniable fact that I go along cheerfully, somehow surviving, more or less enduring, proves something. It proves that God was not kidding around about Love and Forgiveness. If God was playing fair, dishing out what people deserve, I and many others of my ilk would have been wasted, aced, wiped out, totally zapped long ago. That really ought to be a great source of comfort and joy to the rest of you. Because if each and every one of us got exactly what was coming to him, there wouldn't be any people around to enjoy the scenery of Creation.

"I would like to add that in a purely social way I am not nearly so negative as I may seem to the unthinking and the retarded. I am all for life, love, liberty, and the pursuit of . . . well, *happiness*. The latter, of course, as I imagine, conceive of, and understand it. Let no man misunderstand. I am committed to the Good Life and The American Way.

"Let it be others who scoff and scorn, criticize and satirize. Jack Towne has no (pardon the expression) truck with Nay-sayers. I laugh at winter and say yes to life.

"In short, undefeated and undaunted, I am out to get mine and to get it here and now while I can still enjoy it. Heaven is far away, and, not being musical, I doubt I could ever learn to play the harp even with an eternity to practice. I expect Hell is at once a lot worse and different than people imagine. But I'll worry about that when the time comes.

"I repeat. I'm out to get the most out of life. And what I can't get, I can imagine. As my favorite theologian, Brother Dave Gardner has said: 'Beloved, I believe the mind is beautiful, and I know you can always think about a whole lot more than you can get.' "

"The idea is to stay as loose as you can until *rigor mortis* sets in, then hope your friendly Undertaker puts a permanent smile on your face. Even if he doesn't, you don't have to give up hope. Have you ever seen a skull that wasn't grinning?"

Part Three
The Final Tape of Doctor Wisdom

Who judgeth well, well God him send.
Who judgeth evil, God them amend;
To judge the best therefore intend,
For I am as I am and so will I end.
> (Sir Thomas Wyatt—"I am as I am
> and so will I be")

1. A Blatant Intrusion by the Author

Note: Ever since that Professor Wayne C. Booth sat down and actually read all those novels that everyone had been talking about and teaching for years . . . and then had the courage to write an entire book about his experiences and *aperçus*, despite the fact that such action on his part exposed a couple of generations of teacher-scholars as speed-readers at best and con men at worst, not to mention that he also ended up proving conclusively that many famous authors spoke with the forked tongues of the worst sort of Paleface when they claimed that they never actually entered into their works, preferring to stand aside and clean their fingernails, ever since this particular Booth hurled his message into the fan, serious literature has been entirely different; and it is safe to say that even if teams of graduate students can assemble massive evidence to prove that Booth did a little skimming of pages too, nothing will ever be quite the same again. And it is also safe to say that it is perfectly all right and not even considered bad manners any more for an author to *intrude*. True, some people still cling to the old, shopworn ethics and frown every time they catch an author in the act of intruding. And some, citing old wives' tales and folk wisdom, will shake their heads and point out that intrusion is "bad" for you and will stunt your growth. But, like it or not, intrusion is a fact of life and here to stay. The main thing, in my opinion, is not to flaunt it at the expense of the feelings of others. It is my belief that if an author has to intrude, if he just can't help himself, why, he can still do so in a polite manner, acknowledging his debt to Professor Booth and begging the indulgence of all gentle readers, if any.

Listen, I sympathize. I honestly do. There is more intrusion going on nowdays than you can shake a stick at. Everywhere you look authors are intruding. Let them get a foot in the door and they not only sign you up for lifetime subscriptions to *Boys' Life, Guns and Ammo* and *The Journal of English and Germanic Philology*, but they are just liable to run off with your wife and car (leaving the squalling kids behind) together with your complete collection of Beatles' albums and the *Harvard Classics* to boot! Intrusion is rampant everywhere, and you don't know the half of it. Do you realize—I hate to bring this up and spoil things for many readers but we must face facts bravely and see Truth bare as Euclid did if we can stand it—that authors are intruding on *other authors?* Living or dead, it doesn't matter. Some of the dead are the biggest intruders. Of course some authors are more . . . well, susceptible than others.

There are some among you—there are always a few wise-acres in any crowd—who will detect the intrusion of Calder Willingham in my prose. I won't argue with you. Have it your way. I'll just say this. If Willingham got in, he came in through the back window. I didn't *let* him in. But once somebody's crashed a party, you might as well be an affable host. Live now and pay later, I always say.

What follows here is an edited transcription of a tape recording. Although it is clear enough, in and of itself, a word or two of explanation may help. The tape recording happens to be part of the papers and effects (two footlockers and one duffel bag) belonging to one "John Towne" which are still in the process of being sorted out and edited by a scholar-teacher by the name of "Lee Holmes." Holmes did not ask for this unenviable task. It was forced upon him by a Publisher as a means of repaying the publisher for an advance on a novel to be freely adapted from the romantic, truelife adventures of Gabrielle D'Annunzio and Eleanora Duse. When Holmes couldn't or wouldn't write that book he had contracted to do, the publisher "allowed" him to pay off the advance by editing the papers of the aforesaid Towne. Which has turned out to be a full-time job, the papers of John Towne being in large part a confused jumble of fragments, notes, prefaces to unwritten books, synopses of unpublished and unpublishable novels, letters, postcards, laundry lists, bridge scores, etc.

However that is another story. Both Lee Holmes and John Towne are *supposed to be* characters in a novel I am writing, a novel entitled *Life With Kim Novak Is Hell.* Not wishing (see above) to intrude any more than necessary, let me simply say that if I ever finish it, it will be a wonderful book to read. And if you don't want to read it you can put it somewhere and let the title alone serve as a "conversation piece." It will be a big book, sturdy enough to prop up a window or to be used as a doorstop or to serve as a bookend. It will be heavy enough to cause injury if you throw it at someone in jest or in self-defense. Still, at the moment, it doesn't seem likely to be finished within the foreseeable future, if ever. There are many mundane reasons for that, but the real reason is the character of my protagonist, John Towne. He has a terrible character. He is the most rebellious character (in the sense of refusing to stay in his place) I have so far encountered. Not only does he refuse to follow authorial plans and schemes (perhaps because he claims, in a half-hearted way, to be a writer himself, citing as his contributions to American Letters such forgettable works as *A Home for Reckless Spenders, Mondo Teeny Boppo,* and *Goldwyn Boy: A Hollywood Novel*), but also his bad manners, lack of logic, and incorrigible style seem to be contagious. Holmes, for example, writes exactly like him. On the basis of internal evidence one might easily conclude that "Holmes" and "Towne" are one and the same individual, trying to pull the wool over our eyes. Indeed, that may be the case. I leave it for the experts to decide. Frankly I couldn't care less. I've had more than enough of both of them.

There are some of you who go around saying (not to my face, mind you, but behind your cupped palms and my back; and never mind how I know; I've got my private sources of information . . .) that Towne has done the same thing to me. That is ridiculous, and anybody who even thinks that a character could influence the style and imagination of an actual author, is so dumb he thinks a phallic symbol is an ancient Greek musical instrument. I pity the poor wretch. But since forgiveness is divine, I am willing to forgive him.

I could never be influenced by Lee Holmes. I understand him. He's a brother rat. But it brings bad luck to hang around the losers, especially in academe where it is possible to lose big. As for Towne, let me say this: there are plenty of characters throughout Literature I would gladly listen to. But I would as lief listen to the advice of Iago. The only thing Iago was good for was investment counseling ("Put money in thy purse!"), and that was probably Shakespeare speaking anyway. Scholarship has established beyond fear of refutation by anyone but malcontents and crackpots that Shakespeare wrote so fast, even without benefit of such aids as typewriter and dictaphone and apparently, according to his friend Ben Jonson, without a way to blot or to erase either, that even he occasionally let things slip by and sneak into this text. Pope noticed this in that cryptic line "And a table for Greenfields." And there are many other similar instances throughout the plays, most notably in the famous speech of Polonius. More to the point, however, Shakespeare welcomed the intrusion of other authors, and so long as English is spoken, just so long shall Shakespeare continue to intrude upon us all.

Besides all that John Towne and I are in fundamental opposition about the nature and purpose of *satire*. I believe, together with the vast majority of scribblers, that the times we live in are much too serious to make light of. The many problems we face cannot be solved by such outdated means as satire and rational persuasion. Furthermore, together with most liberal, right-thinking and concerned individuals, I think there are many beliefs and assumptions, cherished by the intellectual leaders of our land, as well as institutions (Harvard, for example) which simply ought *not* to be subjected to satire. Wantonly indiscriminate, John Towne does not confine his satire to the chastisement of the foolish and pig-headed forces of reactionary conservatism. In this time of change he makes fun of everything including the very winds of change. In the more orderly and leisurely and loving world which is bound to come (just as soon as we can eliminate all irrational opposition by education and whatever other means are necessary) there will be no place for the likes of Towne. Anybody who will, as Towne has, make fun of Arthur Schlesinger, Jr., for jumping into swimming pools with his clothes on and writing pompous movie reviews while he was supposed to be one of those who were running the country, is not only ill-advised, but also clearly pathological. Schlesinger is not a figure of fun. And just in case he or any of his buddies are reading this I hasten to disassociate myself from John Towne.

His opinions are his very own. Let him take the rap for them.

Towne is a terrible human being. No doubt about that. I could tell you things that would not only curl your hair, but indeed so work upon tip and texture that the results might be most aptly designated as "Instant Afro." I could tell you things about him that would assault your basic working assumptions about the Nature of Man and The Human Condition. But, since time and space are short and patience (yours) even shorter, I won't. I will merely explain that this tape seems to have been made sometime in the late 1950's or early 60s when Towne, living in Hollywood following a brief and disastrous career as a screen-writer, was working for a fly-by-night publishing outfit called Totem Pole Press. Shortly after this tape was made (for reasons which will be clear in context) he vanished from Hollywood, surfacing somewhat later as an Instructor of English at a woman's college in his native south. Following an unfortunate year in academe, he appears to have fled the country, armed with stolen or forged passport and credit cards, and disguised as a Negro clergyman by the name of R.P. King. There are some clues that he was in London for a time (long enough to be soundly thrashed for some highly provocative remarks concerning the private life of the Queen which he chose to make from a public soapbox in Hyde Park) before changing his "image" radically and joining a group of bearded mercenaries serving in one of the Developing Nations of what was once called "The Dark Continent." Since then (1966) he has not been heard from or of again. Some may imagine him dead and gone. I hate to be cynical, but I doubt it. I fear he will be back, unchanged, beyond redemption and utterly indifferent to the contempt reserved for him by all decent people.

The tape has been carefully edited by Lee Holmes. Holmes is a scrupulous editor and calls *Principles of Bibliographical Description* his "Bible." Unfortunately that distinguised volume doesn't have word one about how to edit a tape recording transcript, but that did not prevent Lee Holmes from doing his level best. Which, after all, is all that can be asked of any of us, editor-wise, when *Principles of Bibliographical Description* leaves us dangling.

And now, without much further ado, "The Final Tape of Doctor Wisdom."

The Author

2. Editor's Note

Among other items found in the duffel bag said to belong to the said John Towne was a battered reel of tape, obviously much used and erased. It is an old "Scotch Brand" magnetic tape reel recorded at 3¾ on a tape recording machine of indeterminate type, save that it is 2-track, monophonic and of rather poor quality. Moreover, there appears to have been something slightly wrong with the speed of the original machine; for this tape is just off, a little slow on all the conventional machines, large and small, on which we tested it. That is too bad, really, for one may presume the principal voice on the tape to be that of John Towne.

Distorted as it is, it is impossible to speak with certainty about his voice. Nevertheless some things can be said. It is a rather pleasingly soft voice, slightly hoarse, in what may be called the tenor range. The accent is vaguely southern, though there would seem to be some effort to disguise that regional quality.

Since this tape is apparently intended to be sent to a particular individual—possibly Mr. Irving Plotz of Totem Pole Press, as indicated, it is difficult to explain how it ended up among the effect of John Towne in the duffel bag.

Perhaps it is only a copy of another tape.

Maybe, after all this, in his haste to leave Los Angeles, Towne forgot to mail it.

Maybe this tape is a pure fabrication, a sort of wishfulfillment on Towne's part, a tape he made later and wished that he had made at the time.

Who knows?

In any case, the Editor here presents it as an Exhibit in Evidence.

A further word or two about the method of transcript.

This tape was transcribed, patiently and carefully, by a young student of mine, Miss Louise Piersall. Miss Piersall deserves a vote of thanks, not only from me, but from all of us, for her care and close attention. She spent many hours on the job, her labor intensified by the fact that Miss Piersall is a clumsy two-finger typist and has no shorthand. It was done as a labor of love, a favor freely volunteered to be of aid and comfort to her English teacher, your Editor at this time.

The Editor is most grateful to Miss Piersall for this and other labors "above and beyond the call of duty."

I should add this note. A young woman of Miss Piersall's tender years and decent upbringing could not force herself to type certain words. Miss Piersall is a poet, not without some talent, and nothing human is alien to her. But she is also rather shy and inexperienced. Therefore variations on the word "blank" are used from time to time.

The Reader is missing nothing and remains free to substitute any word of his or her choosing, imaginatively, to replace these "blanks." Otherwise I here attest that Miss Piersall has done a fine and accurate job under difficult circumstances.

The Editor

3. Doctor Wisdom Tape

Hello, Irving, old buddy, this is Doctor Wisdom speaking.

Don't turn off the machine yet. I think this will interest you. I really do.

Before I cut out for greener pastures where my greasy sheep may safely graze, I thought I'd share a little wisdom with you.

Nobody is single-minded any more about anything.

Please understand that. Nobody is single-minded these days. Whether or not they ever were or even wanted to be, from the earliest half-Ape who scrawled graffiti on the walls of some cave, to the latest pronouncements of Smartass Politicians and World Leaders in Life and Art, is an excellent subject for debate and a good exercise for the Imagination, but, frankly, beyond knowing.

If you want my opinion, you are welcome to it. Even before Adam let Eve talk him into chomping down on the original apple, he had mixed feelings (if you'll pardon that expression) about the whole idea.

And so it is, Irving, that I herewith and hereby dissolve our so-called relationship, sunder all so-called relations from now until forever. In short, Irv, baby, it is with mixed feelings that I resign from my duties as Dr. Wisdom effective this date.

Oh, I can see you smirking your classic smirk as you hear these words. Can imagine you parked in lard-*blank* splendor, behind your desk, puffing away on your *schimmelpenick*, and thinking to yourself. . . .

(I can even hear your thoughts in their own inimitable style and sequence.)

You are thinking: "That *blanking* Towne! That rotten ungrateful *mother-blanker*! That untalented worthless *blank*! The *blanker* thinks he can just up and quit on me, huh? Let him! Let him *blanking* well try! Before you can say go *blank* yourself, Jackie Robinson, that double *blank* so-called Jack *blanking* Towne, who is a nobody and you *blanking* well better believe it, will be back here with his hat in his hand, if he even owns a *blanking* hat, begging. Begging to be taken on again. Begging for one more *blanking* chance to be Dr. Wisdom. . . ."

Puff-puff-puff!

"He will come in here and plead and beg. He will get on his bony knees. He will offer to kiss my *blank*. I will let him have that privilege before I have him thrown out of here on his *blank*. And I will personally see to it that he never works again in the American Porno Industry! He will end up where he belongs, standing all day in the line down at unemployment. And I will feel sorry for him, of course. Because I am that way—weak and big-hearted. But enough is enough, you know? That *blanking* Towne is a menace to Society and a pain in the *blank*. So *blank* him!"

And then you will send for Trusty Lillian and tell her to get you another boy, some half-*blank*, freeloading, deadbeat, crummy, no-talent, pardon the expression, *writer*, who can handle the Wisdom File.

She will nod with tears in her lovely olive-colored eyes, because Lillian is my good friend (didn't know that, did you, Irving?), and she will turn and sashay out of your office, wagging her lovely (it's the color of Devonshire cream, Irv, you can take it from old Towne) *blank* behind her.

And I say more power to you. Lots of luck. I hope you can find somebody else to do the job. May you prosper and wax fatter than ever. May you have tax troubles and yet manage to stay out of jail. May you live long, long enough to live on milk-toast and bad memories.

See what I mean about mixed feelings?

Don't turn off this tape yet, Irving. If you do, you will miss something.

I am quitting all right, effective this date. But I am a man of honor and I owe you one more day's work. So I am finishing up here with one last creative act, doing my final bit as Dr. Wisdom. I am typing up the letters and sealing them and putting stamps on them. They are all going out by Special Delivery at my own expense.

So that even now, even as you are listening to this tape, the letters will have reached their destinations.

Weigh that, Irving.

Okay, time to get to work, fire off today's bunch of shinola. . . .

Dear Baffled,

You say that you sometimes get a great big *blank* on just imagining yourself all dressed up in women's clothes. So? So the answer is that you are an unmanly sissy. You are a fairy and you won't admit it. But if it gives you the jollies, I urge you simply to throw away your Jockey shorts and start wearing women's panties all the time. They are cheap. No use wasting money on a whole outfit. . . .

Dear Mrs. Longsuffering,

I can explain the meaning of your "Nazi Fantasies" very easily. Some people would say that you are a masochist. I would, too, except that your letter reveals that you are a terrible human being and are hypocritical to boot. You imagine yourself being stripped and beaten and "lewdly treated" by Nazi Stormtroopers, because in your heart you think that's what you deserve. And you are so right!

Since there are no Stormtroopers around these days, I suggest that you seek out the company of the nearest available motorcycle gang. Tell them your troubles. . . .

Dear Broomstick,

So you've got fat women on the brain? You could do a lot worse. Try hard to imagine making it with Twiggy, say or Verushka and you will see what I mean.

Actually fat women have many things in their favor. Even pleasingly plump ones. Take, for instance, Mrs. Irving Plotz, wife of a notorius degenerate and filth peddler, whom, by the way, you have been supporting. . . .

Dear Eagle Scout,

You say you like to imagine being President of the U.S.A. some day. That is a sick and unrealistic fantasy in every way. Sure, anybody can be President of this country. But who would want to be? No sane man, that's for sure. The whole country is a complete mess from top to bottom. Even the *Boy Scouts* are now corrupt if you are typical of the "new breed."

First you've got to admit you have a dirty mind like everyone else. Second, as Norman Vincent Peale might say, put it to work for you. Think dirty in a positive way.

Let me tell you a typical American success story of our times. Mr. Irving Plotz was not always rich. He was a poor boy and a high school drop-out. All he had going for him was a really dirty mind. . . .

Dear Miss Swimming Pool Lifeguard,

You say you are a "well-tanned and athletic young lady with an excellent figure." Except for the adjective, "excellent", the rest is redundant. If you are a lifeguard you had better be athletic, and if you don't tan, then you will probably be burned to a crisp and die of skin cancer.

I notice you don't even mention your face. I don't assume that it is un-mentionable. Just that you are probably a dog. Well, no sweat. You can take a brown paper bag and punch two holes for your eyes and start wearing that over your head. Start a new trend. Go bare-*blank*, but hide your face. Or, if you have a nice *blank*, you can always shave that and walk backwards, as they say.

So you want to pose in the nude, eh?

Can't you imagine anything more exciting than that? You must be one of the few girls in the country who hasn't already done it. About the only sensation connected with this experience (unless you go out in the woods and get redbugs and poison ivy or something) is goosepimples.

The best way to get rid of your fantasy is to try it. Find a creep with a camera. Buy him a roll of film and let him click away to his heart's content. Then don't even bother to develop it. Just mail the roll to Mr. Irving Plotz/ 1049 N. Formosa Ave./Los Angeles 46/Calif.

After a while you will see yourself, naked, cheaply reproduced in some sleazy magazine. Presented for all the world to behold, under some made-up name.

You will get a big laugh out of it. And then you can sue Mr. Plotz and get enough out of him to have your own swimming pool. Or, anyway, a blue plastic wading pool in the back yard. . . .

Dear Rastus 3-X,

You say you are "an intelligent and sensitive Afro-American Citizen," and then you proceed to outline for me your tedious fantasy life, the banality of which is equalled only by the poverty of your inventive powers.

Haven't you even read *The Invisible Man*?

Let me be candid with you, Rastus. You have got a problem, see? Because the way things are, you are only the fantasy of assorted honkeys. You have no identity whatsoever except what Whitey will permit you.

If you weren't outnumbered 10 to 1, my advice would be to fight back.

45

Or, anyway, follow your leaders and their fantasies about fighting back.

However, your best bet is to save up your money and buy a one-way ticket back to Africa. There you can take off your clothes and live in the trees and be happy.

If you cannot afford it, present Welfare payments being too miserly to permit anyone to build up a sizable Estate, there is an organization which may help you. The Santa Foundation. SANTA stands for Send a Nigger to Africa, and its president, Mr. Irving Plotz. . . .

Dear Chief Justice,

Ordinarily I take them as they come and treat everybody equal and the same regardless of race, creed, color, ethnic origin, sex, or educational background. Ordinarily I would treat your problem just as I treat the thousands of others which pass across my desk. But I must depart from my general rule in your case which is, frankly, special. Not that you or your fantasies are special by any means, but we must acknowledge that in recent years you and your eight buddies have been swinging a lot of weight around, laying down the law and socking it to all those who disagree with you. Gone are the days when the office you hold was a commonplace political appointment, a place for people who might get into trouble in the more active branches of government. Therefore your fantasies are of more importance, in a relative sense, than most people's.

First, let us be sure we have got the facts straight. (I won't be specific because, as you indicate, one never knows who's reading the mail these days.) You say this all started when you and your colleagues spent many days and nights reading dirty books in attempting to define the legal limits of obscenity. You indicate that at first you were shocked, not realizing before how widespread and largescale the American Porno Industry is. You haven't seen anything yet, your honor! Now that you guys have agreed to let it all hang out, it is going to be big business in no time. Off the record I would advise you to pick up some stock and get a (pardon the expression) piece of the action now. Your best bet, in my opinion, would be an outfit like Grove Press which bids fair to being the General Motors of Porno.

It is a very profitable business, your honor. Take my situation. As Doctor Wisdom, I work for peanuts (unshelled, unboiled and unroasted) for a guy named Irving Plotz who is ostensibly the Managing Editor of an outfit called Totem Pole Press, but actually, under a variety of companies and bogus corporations has his fingers in all aspects of the West Coast Porno (pardon) pie. He makes a good deal more money than you do. Which seems unfair. And he probably *keeps* a good deal more, proportionately, too. For he has found many wonderful ways to outwit the Internal Revenue Service. He lives like a Renaissance Prince. His house has every gadget and luxury you ever heard of, not in the best of taste of course, but bad taste is just as expensive as any other kind. He deducts his house because he uses the basement as a storeroom for old books and magazines. It is probably the only "warehouse" in Beverly Hills, California. You many wonder why the I.R.S. auditors and investigators haven't noticed this. Well, they have. And every year, along towards tax time, Irving Plotz invites them all to come out and "investigate the Warehouse, with comely 'secretaries' to guide you and answer your questions." The local I.R.S. boys seem satisfied.

He has many interesting things, one of them being an 85-foot power yacht moored at a marina in San Diego. That yacht is a legitimate business expense, though I would prefer not to discuss the business that takes place there.

Plotz dreams of being the Alfred Knopf of Porno. He might be, too, unless he is stopped or at least discouraged. I see (in the Ginzburg case) where you guys have left yourselves an out if you really want to get somebody. Of course, Ginzburg had it coming for political reasons and so far Plotz has managed to steer clear of politics. Still, you could nail his *blank* to the wall on the basis of the Ginzburg decision, and then your investment in Grove Press would be safely launched. You might (with discretion of course) pass the word on to Barney Rossett in advance. I imagine he'd be grateful and would find a way to express his gratitude. With Plotz out of the way, the whole balance of Porno Power would shift. Personally, I would advise you to lay a little bread in the lap of Bernard Geis Associates, too. That's a more speculative investment, however, so go careful.

Far be it from me to advise you in business matters, your honor. You fellows seem to know all the angles already.

Let us return to your vulgar fantasy life. Don't fight it, judge. As a rule, it eases off with time. Soon you will be able to concentrate on legal documents and briefs and the rambling arguments of lawyers as well as you ever have. Meantime keep a straight face and you can think about whatever you please.

Late in life you find yourself "hooked" by something new. That may prove to be a blessing in disguise. Recent studies in geriatrics prove that old folks can avoid senility if they develop new interests. You are in an excellent position. Let your flunky law clerks do the leg work and research for you. Relax a little, live and enjoy, that's my advice. You've done your thing. *Entre nous*, your honor, the Constitution is pretty dull reading, and there are only so many ways you can bend or twist it around. Your reputation for highly imaginative interpretation is already established for all time. Let the younger guys have a chance to show their stuff. They will find it is a lot harder than it looks.

Best wishes from one of your faithful fans. And don't let crank letters and hate mail bug you. I imagine other important men—Alexander the Great, Julius Caesar, Napoleon, Henry VIII—got their share too. Love and popularity are for lesser men. I'd rather have power and privilege any day of the week . . .

Are you still listening, Irving? I hope so because there are a couple more items in today's mail that ought to interest you. I've saved the best for the last. I realize that your attention span is short, and there isn't much tape left on this reel anyway. So, I'll skip the personal farewell I had planned. I am too sentimental anyway. It was fun while it lasted. I hope you will remember me from time to time, in idle or in pensive mood. That's about it.

Don't feel you have to answer any of this or offer explanations or apologies to me. That would embarrass me. I'm leaving no forwarding address.

So much for that. Back to Doctor Wisdom. . . .

Here's a letter that ought to grab you. My answer to it may interest you too.

Dear Doctor Wisdom,

I know this sounds silly, but I have no one else I can talk to about this.

I am a college student specializing in the study of Microbiology. Which is neither here nor there, I realize. According to this advertisement—and just never mind how a nice typical American college girl saw your ad in the first place!—you specialize in helping people adjust to their Fantasy Life. I must say, in passing, that your statement is persuasive, where you say: "Everywhere, through guidance, counseling, therapy, etc. people are being assisted in the process of adjustment to reality. Yet all the authorities agree that at least half of your waking hours and all of our sleeping time, therefore roughly three-fourths of each lifetime, are devoted to dreams, daydreams, fantasy, and imagination. We spend three-fourths of our lives in Fantasy Land! Yet nobody takes that fact seriously. Nobody that is, except Dr. Wisdom, who has devoted his entire life to the scientific study of the Imagination and is able to offer assistance to all who are seeking to live fully, not ostrichwise pretending that Fantasy Land does not exist, but who with courage and integrity are seeking the serenity which comes from the cultivation of a full, rich Fantasy life. . . ."

I couldn't agree with you more. That is why, even though I am probably better educated and of a superior social status than you or your average client, I am writing to you at this time.

Here is my problem, Dr. Wisdom. For some time now I have had this erotic fantasy. It (pardon the expression) excites me very much to imagine walking down the sidewalk and suddenly being seized by someone who drags me into a nearby alley and rapes me. It is always a perfect stranger, of course, but in my fantasy this person, this someone, even though he rapes me, always respects me for my intelligence.

What do you think of that? Is it "good" or "bad" to imagine such a thing?

I enclose a money order, as directed in your advertisement, and look forward eagerly to your reply.

Yours truly,
Miss I.Q.

Here is the reply I am sending this gooney bird, Irving:

48

Dear Miss I.Q.,

If you were half as smart as you think you are, you would never have been looking through the back pages of a filthy magazine, produced by Irving Plotz, a notorious smut-peddler, who, without qualm or conscience, makes his money at the expense of poor, deluded, frustrated, ignorant, moronic fools who are mentally disturbed or unbalanced, else they would not even dream of looking into the pages of such trash.

Irving Plotz makes lots of money and lives high off the hog, building his estate upon human misery and the enormous and complex confusion in American sexual mores.

However, I happen to work for the said Irving Plotz. Although I am merely a modest part of his whole package, I am not entirely blameless.

Nor are you blameless, Miss so-called I.Q., as I shall demonstrate to you once and for all.

Your fantasy life is in a complete mess.

How the *blank* do you expect a rapist, even an imaginary one to ascertain your level of intelligence, let alone respect it? The average rapist has very little time. He is in a great big hurry to get it over with and be long gone before anyone catches him and slaps his *blank* in jail where he can either become a faggot or else play with his *blank* after they turn the lights out.

Now, maybe you picture or imagine him asking you some questions ("Name the capital of Florida." "Define osmosis." "Discuss the, pardon the expression, position of Aristophanes in Plato's *Symposium*," etc.). And you imagine yourself giving brilliant answers. There is very little opportunity for conversation during the average rape. Fantasy is fine in its place. But even fantasy must have some truth in it.

You cannot have it both ways. You cannot expect to have your cake and (pardon) eat it too.

Ordinarily I would advise someone like you to get off your lazy *blank* and go see a headshrinker quick before you end up in the booby hatch. But your problem is so typical, so common, that I can handle it all by myself.

You are a superb example of everything that is wrong with American women. You are a classic in your own stupid way.

American women are almost beyond salvation and redemption. Instead of recognizing the simple fact that the only thing they have going for them is their sweet *blank*, they fuss around with things like Microbiology. And then they want to have what they call Careers. In college they do not even learn to cook or sew or clean house. They do not even learn how to *blank* except by pure accident. Which is a *blank* of a way to learn any lively art.

You will think I am talking through my hat, Miss I.Q. Forget it. I have been married twice and I have long since lost count of the number of scores I have made before, during, and since the time I was (unfortunately) married. And I have a valid method of comparison, having served my country overseas in both Japan and Korea. There isn't a gook or a slopehead alive, young or old, who can't outmove, outmatch, and outswing the finest American chicks when it comes to *blanking*.

Yes, when it comes to the one and only thing you women are made for, American women are for all practical purposes worthless. Read *Human Sexual Response* and you will see the proof of it.

On top of which, Miss I.Q., American women make terrible wives. What I mean is, they are even lousy roommates. You can quote your Helen Gurley Brown at me all day, and it won't cut the mustard. She is only an American woman herself. And have you ever taken a close look at a photograph of Helen Gurley Brown? Do so sometime and then try to figure out where she gets the audacity, why she doesn't go off somewhere and hide.

Be that as it may, we still need women unless we are faggots or full-time onanists. Unless we are very rich, we cannot cut out for the joys of Japan every time we get the urge. So American men are stuck with American women and have to make the best of it. It is up to the individual whether that is better than nothing.

One of the things working for us men is that even though American wives are lousy *blanks*, they do keep trying. They will try it with anyone.

Only yesterday (see date of this letter) I got restless and upset and needed some consolation. I had just been down to the office of my boss, the afore-mentioned Irving Plotz, to ask him either for a raise or a small advance. It was urgent; for with the football season in the offing, they are trying to repossess my color T.V. set among other things. Irving Plotz is rich and happy. He has a big house and two cars. Nevertheless, he kept me waiting in his office two hours and then turned me down cold. He said I make more than I deserve already and that anybody could be Doctor Wisdom and do as good a job as I have or better. And why didn't I go have a *blanking* relationship with a duck.

I told him that he could not tell Kiwi from Shinola and departed in a huff.

I took a cab to his house, arriving at approximately 3:45 P.M. I felt safe and secure, in full knowledge that the Milkman and the Postman and the Laundryman had come and gone hours before, that Irving himself would not be home before 6:00 P.M. at the earliest, and that Mrs. Irving Plotz would be bored and restless, wondering how to kill the time until Irving got home and they could get smashed together.

Like many American wives, she is a drunk, but she does not enjoy drinking alone.

When I got there I had to wait ahile because she was, as she explained, out in the sun patio working on her "all over" tan.

"Don't let me interrupt," I said. "I just came by to get drunk."

"Why, Jack," she said, "what's wrong?"

Now I could have told her that nothing was wrong, that I just felt like getting drunk and giving her a quick toss in the hay. But honesty will get you nowhere. When an American woman asks you what's wrong, you better think of something. That is because they insist on mothering you. It is a quirk of their feminine conscience or something.

Anyway, it was a snap. I told her that the pressure of this whole Doctor

50

Wisdom caper was too much for me. That the human suffering, misery, and woe that I had to deal with was breaking my heart.

"Someone has to do it," she said wisely.

"I know, I know," I said. "They need me."

"You are young and strong, Jack," she said. "Yet you are wise beyond your years. Wise and, well . . . *sympatico.*"

"I am glad you think so," I said. "I am glad even if it is not true. Because I respect you so much. What you think matters, you know."

"I didn't know you felt that way."

"Oh, I've always felt that way, but it didn't seem right, you know. I mean, you are Irving's wife and all."

"*Ho-ho-ho!*" she laughed. "Big deal!"

"I am glad I overcame my shyness," I added. "Because somehow it seems less lonely when you can talk about things."

"I know what you mean about being lonely.. . ."

I sneaked a peek at the clock, 4:15, and we had already belted a couple of stiff drinks.

"You're losing the last rays of the sun. I'm sorry."

"It doesn't matter."

"Tell you what," I said. "We can talk and you can still work on your tan. I'll turn a chair around backwards and will promise not to peek."

"How do I know I can trust you?"

"You don't. That's the beauty of it."

So we poured a refill and repaired to the sun patio.

Sometime roughly between 4:25 and 4:30 I was working on my suntan too, and shortly thereafter was working my *blank* off on top of the old *blank* leading her to that peak of experience which evoked from her some extraordinarily vivid language, capped by the immemorial American woman's cliche—"I never knew it could be like this."

Before Irving pulled into the drive (and I was forced to beat a hasty retreat around the swimming pool and over the back yard hedge) we also investigated the pleasures of his ample double bed and, yes, the shower in his bathroom, gold handles and all.

Irving Plotz may doubt this story, Miss I.Q. If so, you just ask him to check in the upper lefthand drawer of his phonus-balonus maple bureau and see if one of his "theatrical mask" cufflinks isn't missing.

I happen to have in my possession the mask of comedy. He can keep the other one.

Where was I? Oh yes, you and your little problem. Look, Miss I.Q., I've got a suggestion for you. Either shape up and forget about sex or else get with it. If you prefer the latter, I suggest you don't fool around. Do something genuinely humiliating and degrading. Like go down to the bus station and pick up two or three sailors (in a pinch soldiers, marines, or even redcaps will do) and they will take it from there.

You will feel a lot better when it's all over and can go back to Microbiology with renewed zest and enthusiasm.

Either make your fantasies come true or forget them.

Stand up and be counted, Miss I.Q.! You can't continue to be a slob all your life.

But I am wrong. Clearly you are a slob and clearly you will remain one till the day you die. Take heart, somewhere there's a guy who is a slob himself and so hard up he will even put up with you. All you have to do is find him. Lots of luck.

I hope this answers your question.

If not, please feel free to write directly to Mr. Irving Plotz/1049 N. Formosa Ave./Los Angeles 46/Calif.

> Hang in there
> (by your thumbs)
> Doctor Wisdom

I bet you don't think I can top that, Irving. Well, maybe I can't. But there is a little more tape left, just enough for a couple of fragments. See if these don't add to the total *gestalt*.

Dear Mrs. Plotz,

I am afraid I must leave town rather abruptly for pressing personal reasons.

But I do not wish to leave the City of Angels without thanking you sincerely for a most pleasant afternoon.

Irving baffles me. How he can go around complaining all the time that you are "frigid" and "a lousy lay" beats me. You are a good lay. But how would he know? He is so busy playing around with the so-called secretary of his, Lillian, that he doesn't know what time it is.

I mention this because if he doesn't die from a coronary first, *she* may end up with your house and the two cars in her name, sunning her *blank* on the sun patio. Maybe she will in any event.

If I were you, I'd check on Irving's life insurance and be sure he hasn't switched beneficiaries on you. . . .

Dear Director of Internal Revenue,

In a quiet marina near San Diego, there stands proudly, paint fresh and brightwork gleaming, the 85-foot power yacht "Fanny Hill." She is a beauty in every way, and I think this is one "sea story" that will be of interest to you. . . .

[End of tape]

Part Four

Letter to His
(pardon the expression) *Agent*

Stink and close air away my life wears;
Innocence is all the hope I have.
(Sir Thomas Wyatt—"Sighs are my food")

Letter to Agent

Friend Sam,

I realize full well that you may not think I am ready for *popular writing* yet. Maybe I need more study of the market. Maybe I could use some more seasoning. If you do feel that way, I'm not going to argue with you here, even though I'm convinced a very good case could be made for me along the lines that (a) I lack the equipment to be a really firstrate, bigshot Prestige writer. I can't see those Swedes lining up to give me The Big One. And I can't see me, somehow, ever getting all wound up and coming along with A Major Novel, one that will dent the heavy fender of the American consciousness. No, and furthermore I'm afraid I am a Lowbrow, born & bred. Which means I ought to be able at least to communicate with the other Lowbrows, huh?

Or maybe you feel that the time is not ripe for me to make the big change, to come on strong with a brand new pitch and a brand new label. For the time being maybe I should get back to the old drawing board and crank out some standard prestige work. And just wait for you to give the signal that the time is right.

In either case and on both counts I want you to know, Sam, old buddy, that I am not now nor have I been neglecting "serious" writing. And just to prove it, I'd like to include some notes for a *bona fide* literary-type novel.

Idea for a Serious Novel, by John Towne

1. Title (tentative): *The Realms of Gold*, by John Towne, author of *Last of the Bigtime Spenders* etc., etc.

This title is a quotation from the works of John Keats, a celebrated British author, whose works and words are now in the public domain. Which means, Sam, we don't have to pay even a penny for the epigraph or anything else of his we may use. The phrase comes from a very famous line of a very famous poem: "Much have I travelled in the realms of gold." It is interesting to note in passing, Sam, that other people besides Jewish comedians like to

55

turn the natural word order of the English sentence all backwards, even Romantic poets. You would probably take umbrage if I arrived at your office and in reply to your cheery "Where the hell have you been hiding?", I answered, "Sam, much have I travelled in the realms of gold." But it is perfectly legitimate poetic language. There is a literary term for this reversal of order, but I will not mention it because the word has other popular connotations which might be misleading to you. Not that I'm trying to be an egghead or to wave my Princeton diploma at you, Sam. There is nothing wrong with Rutgers. A man can get an excellent education there and go on to be a success. You are the living proof of that. You make a lot more money that I ever will, including 10% of my money, and you can afford to send your boys to Princeton if you want to, a real possibility, especially since I hear they don't have a quota system and now the old place (if you'll pardon a direct quotation from the letter of a friend who is a reactionary and because of the frustrations of his life actually gets worked up & worries about these things): "The old place is literally crawling with them!"

The poem itself deals with the moment when Cortez, described as rather fat and scant of breath (which sure changes my image of him), comes staggering out of the foliage of the Central American jungle and practically falls into the Pacific Ocean which he did not know was there and thus had to discover the hard way. Not that he was ignorant or stupid. Just that the teaching of geography at the time left a great deal to be desired. Most people had never even heard of the Pacific Ocean. Which goes to show how backward they were and how far we have come since then, for it can now be safely assumed that many people in the world today have heard of the Pacific Ocean and that many of them, though no doubt a lesser number, could actually point it out on a map, not confusing it with other large bodies of water. It remains to be seen, however, excluding, of course, those who populate its shores and islands and those hardy fisherfolk and mariners for whom it must be like a home away from home, how much the knowledge that the Pacific Ocean is there really means to your average, run-of-the-mill inhabitant of this terrestrial ball. As they walk dully along, self-absorbed, selfishly involved in their own personal day-to-day battles against poverty, disease, hunger, and despair, they may know full well that the Pacific Ocean is out there all right. The question is, Sam, how can we make them care? That is the problem which faces the educator today. That is the problem he must face, his challenge and call to greatness. Even lots of people here in the US & A, Galbraith's "Affluent Society" (written before they noticed all the poor folks milling & moping around their "pockets of poverty"), even here in the richest country the world has ever known, a veritable Ice Cream Kingdom, a cornucopia of transistor radios, plastic toys and gadgets, deodorants, breakfast foods, hair spray, automobiles, pain killers, appliances, Polaroid cameras, antacids, etc., the only country in the world where you can actually *improve* your hands by washing the dishes, the country with the grossest Gross National Product in history exceeding the limits of anything ever envisioned by the like of Genghis Kahn or Alexander the Great or Lucretia Borgia, even here with the best-informed, best educated public in the world, where leisure is no more an idle dream but a fact of life, even here there must be very few people, aside from surfers, who spend much time worrying about whether the Pacific Ocean really exists or not. Lacking real intellectual curiosity, lacking even the desire or energy to question the validity of maps, globes, books, etc., not even rebellious enough to stand up boldly before their teachers and demand proof of its existence, they frankly do not care one way or the other. They just go around boozing and barbecuing, dancing and wife-swapping, wearing silly or even scanty attire, skate-boarding, roller skating, bowling, fishing, stamp collecting, weight-lifting, playing putt-putt golf, going passively to movies, football games, political rallies, demonstrations, riots and lynchings, or else they stay home hypnotized and brainwashed by the cyclopean boob tube, and *they do not care!* Most of these selfish people would not give a tinker's dam if the Caspian Sea were to dry up tomorrow and thus cause all the maps and globes and books to be outdated and obsolete. They would care, however, if their own personal plumbing backed up or the Utility Company cut off their water. Then you'd hear them holler! Imagine, Sam, if you will, what it would be like if all the toilets in the United States went on the fritz and failed to function for just one full day. Panic in the streets. Anarchy! Lunacy triumphant!

Yet we must not give up on them. Progress is gradual. It goes hand in hand with the long slow process of evolution. We must never surrender our obligation to uplift their hearts. One day, though we shall not see it unless we are permitted to lean down from the golden bar of heaven, bells will ring out wildly against the wild sky announcing officially the opening of The Non-Violent City of Finally Civilized Man. Meanwhile we can keep on teaching them that the Pacific Ocean is out there and that an English apothocary named Keats more than a century and a half ago wrote a famous poem in which he depicted stout Cortez discovering the Pacific; though as we all know it wasn't actually Cortez at all. It was Balboa. However, that is known as "poetic license," justifiable in any case, but further justified in this case because that extra beat, the extra syllable in the word, would have surely screwed up the scansion of the whole line. That being so, Keats could have used any name, provided that it had two syllables and it would have been perfectly all right. He could, with legitimate poetic license have used Milton or Byron, Heller or Mailer, Goldfarb or Jaffe, and it wouldn't have been wrong. Note, though, that once he saw that Balboa was a definite loser, at least as far as his line of poetry was concerned, he did not substitute poetic abandon for poetic license. He reached for and grabbed another Spanish name out of the hat. Not just any Spanish name either. I mean there are lots of two-syllable Spanish names. At least I would guess there are. He took Cortez when he could just as well have used Lopez. Cortez the explorer, the *Conquistadore*, the man who mopped up and wiped out the whole decadent Aztec Empire, thought-fully leaving just enough behind for the tourist trade. Cortez is better than Balboa when you get right down to it. Who knows anything about Balboa? Sure they have named parks and beaches after him, probably highways and schools, but that kind of thing is the kiss of death to a man's historical reputation. They don't name stuff like that after Cortez. Put it in terms of a modern analogy, Sam. Nobody wants to die, of course, but assuming you were dead, which would you rather be—Wilbur Cross with a Parkway named after you, or Al Capone? There will never be an Al Capone Memorial Highway or Airport or High School or Hospital. Not even in Chicago, where he was so widely known and loved. But I say unto you, Sam, that Al Capone will still be remembered when the Wilbur Cross Parkway has crumbled to dust and weeds and wildflowers cover its scar from view.

We call that the irony of history. Every kid on the block knows the name of Napoleon. How many know Jeremy Bentham from the man in the moon? Now that it's all over and done with, and with all due allowances for his frightful excesses, which of the two do you think will be known & remembered for years and years and generations to come: Neville Chamberlain or Adolph Hitler? I see that kids and cutups and kooks are wearing swastikas and iron crosses etc. these days, mostly to bug other people but nevertheless wearing them. I read where it's big business, in fact. Sam, do you seriously think I could make a pot of money by trying to move the *umbrella* as a symbol of Neville Chamberlain? People buy umbrellas to keep the rain off their heads.

The list would go on forever. Which Roman Emperors has John Q. Citizen ever heard of; or, more accurately, which names would pop up first? Nero would be number one on every list. And when little boys come by fits and starts into manhood, whom do they dream of & long for as "the mate that fate intended": the late Marilyn Monroe or the late Eleanor Roosevelt?

Have I made my point clear? Any questions?

Cortez was a much better choice than Balboa. Say the words aloud to myself. *Balboa.* . . . You just can't say it with any conviction or enthusiasm.

However, Sam, before we get off the track, my use of the title is ironic and, really, has very little to do with Cortez or Balboa or Chapman or Homer or even what Cortez's "wild surmise" may have been when, without warning, he saw all that water in everywhich direction. He could have thought anything. Or maybe nothing. Maybe he just shrugged his shoulders thinking: *There goes China right down the Drain. I guess I should have listened to my dear old Mama when she said:* "So you want to go to China? So take a shovel out in the back yard and dig there. And lots of luck!"

As I say, my title is ironic. Intelligent readers will catch on. They are few in number, only a few thou, but this is supposed to be a prestige book, remember?

Okay. Even a prestige book has got to have something going. Maybe not an out-and-out blatant story line, but at least a situation. I've got a character, my protagonist, and a situation. Which is a good beginning.

My hero is a man named R.C. Alger. He is like the last direct descendant of Horatio Alger, the end of that line. His old man, who was a boozer and a wit, named him Royal Crown after the brand of soft drink his wife was always trying to get him to try instead of the hard stuff. It would be bad enough to be named Royal Crown anytime, but it is especially embarrassing now that the Silent Generation and The Beat Generation have been replaced

by The Pepsi Generation. Thus, my hero prefers to use only his initials, which have a certain dignity.

Ironically, *my hero can't travel anywhere.* Except in the Imagination, i.e. "the realms of gold." In fact he can't get out of the bed. I am sad to have to report that he is a shut-in, a bed patient. He is suffering from Muscular Dystrophy (or some other degenerative disease) in a fairly advanced stage. He lies there withering away a little bit at a time. However, and this will be a very important factor in engaging reader-sympathy, he is not oppressed or downhearted. He has inherited something of the cheerful, forward-looking, optimistic spirit of his renowned literary ancestor. Not enough, however, to permit him to view his affliction as, say, an interesting challenge or a test of character. Enough, however, to keep him from just lying there and moping his days away. He keeps busy and creative in spite of it all. He has two major projects underway. One is a major, documented work of history entitled "America, the *Beautiful?*: From Pioneers to Pansies." (More on this project later.) The other is more directly creative. He is developing and expanding the literary *genre* of the poison pen letter to the level of high art. Every day he dictates salvoes and barrages of poison pen letters to various living people. I mention this because he has made a deliberate artistic choice to limit and confine himself to the living, much as he'd like to get off a few well-chosen epistles to the dead. This will help to distinguish him from Moses Herzog of *Herzog.* Which is, of course, where I got the idea, but I don't want to advertise that, now do I? Also *Wake Up, Stupid!* by Mark Harris. Anyway, Sam, don't you worry. My book is fundamentally different from both of these. I only mention my precedents to show I know what *genre* I'm working in.

Here's the deal. Every day a Secretary, who hopes to inherit a pile when the old fart finally cashes in, and she stands a pretty good chance to, too, because he hates his wife and she, poor thing, can't abide him any more, comes in. First they work on the material for "America, the *Beautiful?*" Then, after a recess period, he starts dictating these poison pen letters to well-known people here and abroad. Of course he never signs them with his own name. In fact, she signs them for him using a variety of pens and handwriting styles. They have many different kinds of stationery, hotel and motel stationery, leftover stationery of defunct businesses, political and social action groups etc. They also have a dozen or so different typewriters. And, as a final security measure, the letters are mailed from towns and cities all across the country. Once a month the Secretary spends a few days crisscrossing the whole country in a pattern without rhyme or reason, operating on impulse, feminine intuition and the basic premise to keep moving, by bus, train, plane, etc., dropping off the letters a few at a time in random streetcorner mailboxes. These extraordinary precautions, while they do not insure complete secrecy or security, at least mean that J. Edgar Hoover and his boys will have an interesting challenge on their hands before they can manage to tie in the letters with R.C. Alger.

Sam, the bulk of the novel will consist of a representative sample of these letters, of which, by the way, I have enclosed a few, just to suggest the range and possibilities of the method. However, I plan a more interesting novel than that. As you no doubt know, the key to the successful prestige novel of today, one that can be classified as "controversial" and maybe even make the "People Are Talking About" section in *Vogue*, the rhetorical key is to keep the reader from first page to last asking himself again and again, "What the fuck is going on here?" Your average reader of prestige books is indefatigable. He will never quit reading until he is clear what is happening in the book and what it's all about. Once he finds out, he knows enough to talk about it, so why read the rest of the fool thing? The good prestige novel is never clear or explicit until the very last paragraph and even then it should be highly ambiguous and, ideally, pose a whole series of new questions, possibilities and doubts in the reader's mind. Just when he thinks he's home free, throw a fish in his face.

So, you can count on the fact, Sam, that the reader will not be told right off the bat all the background and details I've told you. In fact some of them he will never be told. That's his problem. I just want *you* to know that I know what's going on. That's where I draw the line. I like to know. Which may be my biggest weakness as a serious prestige writer.

Be that as it may, let me give you an idea how the thing might work. We open with a couple of fairly shocking letters to respected living public figures. That's all. Just the letters. Cut to a pair of high heels coming down the street. At first we don't even know they are shoes, let alone high heels with a girl in them. Just a pair of something, apparently in motion, somewhere. Whatever the two things are, they are moving. What are these two things like? I will describe them at this point by presenting, within quotation marks, a list of the adjectives I have lifted from *a single shoe advertisement* in a hightype ladies' magazine. Whatever else this pair may be, they are "extravagant, graceful, darling, scintillating, poised, delectable, racy, sleek, piquant, sensuous and classic." Some alert readers, willing to take a risk will surmise that the objects in question are feminine. Others, the more sophisticated, will probably reserve judgment, not wishing to be caught in the embarrassing position of making a mistake. In any case, I give the folks a couple of pages about these two things. Then, just when they're about ready to decide that I'm being sarcastic about The Doublemint Twins (whatever happened to them, Sam?) or maybe those two goopy girls on revolving drugstore stools who have a serious, eyeball-to-eyeball confrontation about whether *Certs* is a breath mint or a candy mint, just then, I mention something, nothing explicit mind you, that suggests not an answer, but a question. Is it . . . could it be . . . a pair of shoes?

Meanwhile back in the bed of pain. . . .

You, Sam, you probably figured me to cut back to a couple more poison pen letters. I know better than that, baby. I go straight to some excerpts from "America, The *Beautiful*?"

Now I've got three different things to work with: the gradual revelation of the Secretary going to work, the letters, and the social history. Within those three general areas I can get considerable suspense. For instance, maybe the Secretary is thinking about her most recent letter-mailing trip. Just the places she went to, the order she went to them, the way she travelled, the stationery she scarfed at various hotels and motels etc. Okay, the jerk reader won't know what the hell is going on, whether this is a real trip or an imaginary one, a past trip or a future plan etc. Moreover, since the letters won't be mentioned in any way (being strictly routine to her, so why should she be thinking about them at all? and maybe she'd prefer to forget), this perfectly rational trip will appear to be insane. Is she some kind of nut? What is she trying to prove?

So that's the way I'll handle it all the way up to the very end, when some of the answers will be revealed. Back and forth from present action to letters to "America, The *Beautiful?*", to memories, dreams and dream visions, plans for the future etc.

Being fairly literal-minded and short of time, you, Sam, may be wondering right about now what the simple, straight-forward line of action is, or, rather, would be, if you could abstract, excerpt, and synopsize it. Which, of course, can't be done. But I can try.

The Realms of Gold follows one day in the lives of the Secretary and R.C. Alger (realize that we won't know who he is or exactly what's wrong with him practically until the *finale*). She comes to work; they work on "America, The *Beautiful?*" for a while; then they have a fairly lively recess period, interrupted by the wife who stops in to see if he's dead yet; then they get down to the business of dictation of letters, typing them up etc. The climax comes when J. Edgar Hoover himself and his entourage burst into the room. That may seem weird. Why would Hoover himself show up? Ha! Because, dear Sam, when they at last find out that it's R.C. Alger, the last living descendant of Horatio, a national hero and a symbol of the American Way of Life, they know, baby, that it's one hot potato. What they don't know until they burst in is that he's dying of M.D. That makes it even worse. Bad enough to bring the Last of the Algers to trial, to expose what finally happened to that noble breed! But to have to wheel him in in a bed, from which he cannot, without assistance, raise his poor head? A disaster. . . . By the way, the F.B.I. gives me potentially a fourth narrative thread. They—and we wouldn't know who they were or why—could be making plans for the raid all thru the book. That may really be the element of suspense we need. We'll see.

Anyhow, under the circumstances J. Edgar is prepared to make a deal. No deal, says R.C. As long as he's still able to dictate, he'll fill the mails with poison pen letters. In fact, now that the cat is out of the bag, he can save lots of time and trouble and greatly increase his output of same. A dilemma indeed. Some of the Boys want to rub him out. The Boss, however, will have none of that. That would be murder and there's a witness, unfortunately. They would either have to kill her too or else pay her off for the rest of her life and she looks pretty greedy and expensive.

"Couldn't we frame her or something, Boss?"

"You nitwit! You numbskull! To frame her we'd have to drag her into court. She'd get up on the stand and babble wildly. Of course, nobody would really believe her outlandish story and she would be salted away all right, but during that time the image of our Organization would suffer considerably."

"Yeah, I guess you're right."

"You *guess?*"

"I mean, you're right as rain, Boss."

They decide R.C. has got to go. But how? Cleverly, the Boss calls R.C.'s Doctor to inquire after R.C.'s health. Ordinarily Doctor Smartheim wouldn't violate the confidence of doctor-patient relationship, but knowing who is calling and being vulnerable as hell on tax grounds, he tells all. R.C. is doing okay and will probably last a few more years. Unless, of course, he should catch a bad cold or have some severe shock or emotional strain.

Really?

The Boys go into action. They throw open all of the windows (it being the big middle of winter) and take all the covers off his bed. They make horrible faces at him, point their guns at his head, and threaten to carve him up an inch at a time and other bad things. They bring up his wife and gang bang her. However, none of these things works. Then—inspiration!—they give the Secretary the same treatment. She doesn't mind it too much, but old R.C. does. Because he loves her. The *coup de grace* comes when they break both her hands so she can't type for a good while or even take dictation. R.C. has a stroke and apparently dies. . . .

So we have a near fade out. The wife, at last relieved of this burden, thinking how she's going to enjoy his wealth and live it up a little. The Secretary, the pain of her broken hands alleviated by the knowledge that she recently typed old R.C.'s Will. The wife will get one dollar and the clothes on her back. The Secretary will get everything else. What will she do with it? And with the income from the F.B.I.? Well, here's the kick. Originally she wanted to travel, live it up etc., but now she has become corrupted or inspired, take your pick, by old R.C. and his work. No, she will keep up his good work. She will hire herself a Secretary and continue his work as if he were still alive. Maybe her hands are broken, but she still can dictate. . . .

Back at the nearest Hilton Hotel the Boys and the Boss are throwing a big blast to celebrate the happy ending of "The Alger Caper." Who should drop in but Ephrem Zimbalist, Jr., who is the star of the T.V. series, "The F.B.I." When they proudly tell him of their adventure, he reminds them that they have overlooked one alternative in dealing with the Secretary. They completely forgot the most modern and expeditious method. All they have to do is certify her as a lunatic and have her committed for life. No sweat. No court trial. No blackmail. Nothing. . . . The Boys are delighted. They know how to handle this. They feed enough questions, hints and clues so that the Boss is finally able to think of it all by himself. And next thing you know he's on the phone lining up a cooperative Headshrinker.

But wait! We don't fade yet. We cut to the City Morgue. A stubbly-faced intern is examining R.C with a view to carving him up and learning more facts about Muscular Dystrophy. Lo and behold, there are faint signs of life. He's alive! Naturally he's completely paralyzed by the stroke and will probably never speak or move again. And his days are numbered, though the number can be increased by intensive hospital care. We begin to fade out as they wheel him toward The Intensive Care Unit, planning to keep him alive as long as Science will permit. The last thing we have is the letter to J. Edgar Hoover he's formulating in his mind. We wonder, as he does, whether he'll ever recover enough to dictate it or, perhaps, to wink it out in Morse Code to a nurse. . . .

The End.

That story line may sound pretty pessimistic to you, Sam. Too downbeat. Please do not concern yourself about that. It can be labeled as "Black Humor" and everybody will laugh. Besides, even though you and my so-called editor don't seem to realize it, people know they are only reading a madeup story. They do not actually believe that a book is really happening at the moment they are reading it. That is not the way the imagination works. It (the imagination) is much more interesting than that. Do you remember how that frightened rabbit, my so-called editor, made me go all the way through *Last of Spenders* and cut out all those great and wild and wonderful epigraphs I had so painfully collected? Because, he said, an epigraph was "author intrusion." It reminded the reader he was reading a book. Can you beat that? Of course, I had no choice, so I did it. Then I lost them all somewhere and can't remember what they were. He used to really bug me, you know? He called my writing "scabrous & orotund." I had to look it up to find out if that was any good or not. He used to dictate those letters with a Bennet Cerf jokebook in one hand & Roget's *Thesaurus* in the other. I really developed a strong dislike for him until I met his wife. You know her, Sam? I tell you, *zap!*, just like that, intense dislike bordering on hatred was converted into a neat combination of compassion and contempt. If they ever make the life story of Ilse Koch into a movie *(Return of the Bitch of Buchenwald)* his wife would be natural, type-casting for the lead. Except Ilse Koch was better looking.

But I'm not bitter about all that, Sam. No hard feelings, really. I'm at peace with the world. Willing to forgive and forget.

Anyway, about *Realms of Gold*. It's really a *comedy*. It's an intellectual escapade, a cerebral romp, a regular daisy chain of fun and games. One example. Take the Secretary. Her real name is V.D. Milo, but R.C. never calls her that. He calls her Afra Bane sometimes, sometimes Alpha Payne, and once in a while just Grace. (Because she's got three names, dig?) Since for the longest while we will be uncertain who he is, where they are etc., we also won't know if there are three different girls in the scene or only one.

I want to say a few words about style. This one will be stylish. Admittedly, *Spenders* wasn't written in very high style. It was written in the living and spoken idiom of my native Southland.

It was done that way on purpose, by artistic design and intent. My so-

64

called editor screwed me to the wall with that book jacket prose of his: "Searing honesty . . . crude surge of raw power . . . hardnosed & rowdy. . . ." Frankly, Sam, that is not the way I see myself and it is certainly not the right kind of image for a real prestige writer. Back when *Spenders* was published the pitch should have been: "An elegant and meticulous craftsman, novelist John Towne approaches his bold subject with an almost lapidary *finesse*. . . ." And they tried to hustle me as a "crude surge of raw power"!

Nowdays the pitch has changed a little. Take this example which is at hand, the jacket copy of *The Crying of Lot 49* by Thomas Pynchon. The publishers use the flaps mostly for (a) design and (b) plot summary, but notice they do stress "the same combination of wild hilarity and grim reality that made *V.* so notable." I've never read *V.*, but I can tell you that the combination of "wild hilarity and grim reality" is definitely big shot and the thing to do. However, let's get back to the book jacket for a moment. The back of the book, except for the blank space where his picture ought to be, but he won't let his picture be published (I have carefully drawn a pretty fair copy of Alfred E. Newman in white ink on mine, but every man is free to do as he pleases), is filled up with big, rich, fulsome praise lifted from book reviews by people whose names alone are supposed to give your book class and tone. People like George Plimpton. Okay, never mind that they can't do that on mine, because nobody famous ever reviewed it. Tell you what they could do, though, Sam. They could just print the name GEORGE PLIMPTON in big letters all by itself, no quote or nothing, somewhere on the jacket. Just that—GEORGE PLIMPTON—say it, roll it over your tongue like a sweet lifesaver. Would that be against the law? If so, why? He exists, doesn't he, like the Pacific Ocean. I believe George Plimpton exists. I also believe in the existence of other improbably named people like Mavis Gallant, Calvin Kentfield, Niccolo Tucci, and Speed Lambkin. But then, don't depend on me. I was 21 and registered (a Democrat first and last and always and forever) to vote before I finally lost my faith in the existence of Santa Claus, though I still have some evidence in his favor; and I still have undiminished and devout faith in the Easter Bunny whose name is Donna Michele. And suppose Plimpton exists and sues. I can certainly claim no malice. I've never even met the stud. Even so, though, for insurance, I know of a kindly old gent, a true Uncle Tom of the Old School, who will for fifty bucks and expenses and maybe a six pack of *Dr. Pepper* and a couple of Moon Pies, cheerfully and legally change his name to George Plimpton. Then we could get a direct quote from this new and improved Plimpton. And if the Publisher could see his way clear to backing me all the way, I could go thru "Black Bottom" down home, changing names with reckless abandon and then we could have the whole book simply plastered with names like: John Aldridge, R.W.B. Lewis, F.W. Dupee, Jean Paul Sartre, Hubert Humphrey, and Billy Graham. You name it—any name in the world and, given the $ to work with, I could deliver somebody with that name who would sign aforesaid name to any quote I wrote. A frightening responsibility. Actually, I'm only kidding, Sam. I know you contribute to various Civil Rights Organizations and, thus, so do I indirectly.

I'm just hurrahing you a little, as they say down home.

Back to the book jacket! So in this case the editors didn't need to think up stuff because the critics had already done so. Here's the kind of thing I'd like to see on the back of *Realms of Gold*, quoted from the aforesaid & aforementioned book jacket: "He shows unusual capacities for philosophical discriminations, an astonishing knowledgeability—of history, medicine, geography, sexual love—all expressed with an authoritative ease, especially remarkable in a young writer, and he has the eye and ear of a great parodist."

Okay, Sam, I can see the sad, full-moon widom of your expression. Kids' stuff! If I had any real brains and took any pride in myself I would get on the ball and make a pile of $ and then I could have these guys with all their "philosophical discriminations" and "astonishing knowledgeability" working for me, instead of pining away down here in the remote boondocks, far, far from N.Y., far from George Plimpton (repeat it with enthusiasm; lemme hear you sound off like you got a pair!) and everyone and everything that matters. Agreed, Sam, agreed! I couldn't agree more. Only this *Realm of Gold* may be just the gimmick, ticket, magic carpet to get me right back up there where the action is, trailing my clouds of glory like a peacock's fan, wearing my immortal longings proudly like a medal or a boutonniere, moving across the stage of fame and glory like a guy with a broom and a crossover beard. You get me the contract and I'll write it. See if I don't.

The new and completely different Jack Towne, blackfaced humorist, is going to come on strong, yet with style, discrimination and astounding knowledgeability. You may wonder where I'm going to get this style & knowledge. Don't forget, Sam, I've had plenty of time since that book to think about things, to increase my knowledge, and to improve myself in general. You won't know me. You may not recognize me.

Now, I want to mention a couple of other things.

1. "America, The *Beautiful?*: From Pioneers to Pansies," by R.C. Alger, Esq.

Sam, I forget to tell you the form and content of this history of our times. It's more or less a scrapbook, part scrapbook, part *collage*. He has, with complete disregard of Marshal McLuhan, limited himself to printed words. No pictures, however tempting that might be. He began the collection, never dreaming that it would become his *chef d'oeuvre*, as a little boy. Now, when we find him, he keeps it alive by having V.D. Milo read to him at length from dozens of newspapers and magazine articles.

Of course, her task is made easier because she knows pretty much what to look for by now. In effect, she does the research for him and he passes judgment on the suggested inclusions. Basically a story, to be included in "America, The *Beautiful?*" has to take place in the U S & A or involve Americans or to be an account of some natural disaster or calamity; for example, a very serious tornado or hurricane, or maybe a big fire or explosion or a race riot; or to be a story of monstrous, original, clever or exceptionally diabolocal crime; or to be a "human interest" story in the pathetic vein, for example:

66

SCHOOL BUS DRIVER BACKS OVER OWN SON *or* MAN LEAVES LIFE SAVINGS ON SUBWAY; or to be a prime example of folly & stupidity; or to be yet another *exemplum* of the 7 deadly sins in action; or to illustrate basic blatant hyposcrisy & dishonesty; for instance, R.C. is the kind of cynic who keeps a close record of all the statements of the major politicians and leaders on any given issue. He arranged for them to be pasted into the MS side by side and in neat rows of contradictions.

He hopes his MS will one day become an important document of the history of our times. He believes it will be an accurate picture of the world we live in.

He's wrong, Sam, of course. I know you're a sort of a patriot in your own indefinable way, and you don't want to handle clients who knock America, unless knocking America gets to be a really good business. Okay. Just remember this, Sambo. I love my country. My people had been decadent and degenerate American southerners for many generations while your good people were still running like rabbits from the Cossacks during the annual *Pogrom* season.

Don't get me wrong, now. Don't blow your top yet. I do not feel superior to you in any way. In fact I feel in awe, inferior, if you will, at the rapidity with which you people not only assimilated into this culture, but went right to the top; and in many areas such as the garment industry, distilleries, poetry, psychiatry, sociology, violin playing, and show biz, to name only a few—you actually took over. You have made a real contribution and no denying it. Where would we be without the likes of Albert Einstein, Theodore Reik and Max Baer? Again to name only a few of you.

Moreover American is supposed to be a melting pot, and anybody who even thinks different ought to be ostracized and defenestrated. That's how strongly I feel about it. I don't even like to hear Polack Jokes. All I'm saying is, I have a stake here too and in love for the old land of the free I defer to no man. Furthermore, I served my country in Korea. And, Sam, for heaven's sake, I do not hold it against you that you had bad asthma and were 4-F. They also serve who stand and wait for the others to come back dead or alive.

I am proud to be an American and I like the way things are, just as they are. You won't catch me out there with all the Beatniks, Vietniks, Hopheads, Dropouts & Do-Gooders, putting the bad mouth on anything. I'm for it, man! If I wasn't, I'd be crazy. For this is the only country in the world where a no-account, lazy, shiftless, worthless bum like yours truly could not only survive, but sometimes even prosper. And I'm deeply grateful for every opportunity I've had and every one that comes along.

R.C. Alger is in no way related to me. I'm satirizing him, Sam. He is a mean old, dirty old, cynical old, despicable old man. How could someone like that represent America? No way!

Some may see him that way. Some may misinterpret and say, "Look at old Towne, he's saying this is what happened to the American Dream, to Horatio Alger & all that. He's saying that in a very short time we've become sick & perverted & are a dying civilization."

They will be wrong as wrong can be, Sam. Nothing of the kind.

Permit me to explain. Point one is that my expose of Royal Crown Alger will show how foolish his misanthropic behavior is (look how he ends up; serves him right, too) and is no reflection on the good name of Alger. Did anybody blame Horatio for Alger Hiss? R.C. is a son of a bitch. There are rotten apples in every barrel just as there always are some black sheep in every family, skeletons in closets, and (pardon expression) niggers in woodpiles, flies in the ointment, etc. All I do in *Realms of Gold* is accept the imaginary possibility that a fine and upstanding family could easily degenerate in a couple of generations.

"Ho-ho!" you say. "Aren't you, then, making the same point that old R.C. is in his nihilistic diatribe entitled 'America, The *Beautiful?*'?"

Good question, Sam. It shows you are right in there, brighteyed & bushy-tailed. No flies on you. Precisely. . . .

I may seem to be making that point to the extent that I make the book, according to the best modern rhetorical devices, seem to reflect the Point of View of its protagonist. That certainly is the way the wicked R.C. Alger, hung up in his own subjective closet, views things. That it is an extremely limited view goes without saying. I count upon the Reader to restore order to the universe after the repugnant resonance of R.C.'s negative, anti-social, paranoid, hostile, immature, unhealthy, invalid, and half-assed views has faded into the oblivion they (the views, not the resonance) so richly deserve.

However there is one subtle point I am making about America. A point which I could easily enough ignore calling to your attention were it not for the fact that I believe that complete honesty and trust is absolutely necessary in any viable relationship between Author and Agent; and had I not full and certain confidence that you will understand my position, knowing that though you may find it abhorrent, you will nevertheless defend to the death my right, call it my duty, to express my views freely and openly without fear of in-timidation. For to feel otherwise would be to thumb your nose and give a resounding bronx cheer at and to the sad calm face of The Statue of Liberty herself; she who was first seen through tear-filmed eyes by your parents or grandparents, or whoever it was, where they huddled on the windswept deck, cries of gulls etching the air with a shrill cryptography, salt of the sea mingling with the breeze and with the salt of their pale tears of joy, an almost mystical moment to be savored forever, signaled by the hearty sound of the steamer's whistle (like the carefree fart of a thoughtless giant), while about them hand-kerchiefs dabbed at the tears on a bank of upturned, expectant faces, the faces of other freedom lovers, together, of course, with a pretty fair number of deadbeats, draft dodgers, social dropouts, fugitives from justice etc., all the flotsam & jetsam with which the foundations of the shining tower of American dreams must be built.

In short, you wouldn't dream of denying me the right to have my own opinion, would you, Sam?

The theory I have—and *n.b.* I merely use the theory in the book & am not trying to sell it to anyone—is that the Horatio Alger fiction is not a fair, an accurate representation of the American Way, and that those who accept it as the example & symbol of the AW are doomed from the outset to a disillusionment even more instant/immediate than some of the new instant puddings and custards to which you simply add water, stir 3 times, then jerk the spoon free as fast as you can before it is fixed and frozen there as though set in concrete.

Those who blindly and thoughtlessly accept Alger at face value are clearly bucking for a fat pie in the face.

I can explain on both counts.

POINT ONE: *That the works of Horatio Alger, in spite of their unquestionable & widespread popularity are NOT now nor ever were an accurate symbol of the American Way.* . . .

Historically put it all in context. Era of Robber Barons, of Boss Tweed and all that crowd whose hanky-panky still haunts and indeed informs the whole psychic character of N.Y.C. poltics; era of the fantastically and enormously rich whose power and dominion were practically unrestricted; unshriven and un-ghosted Scrooges beside whose rapacious and whimsical appetites old Nero himself would have thrown up his hands in moral shock and outrage. An era of extreme and brutal poverty, of child labor from dawn to dusk (and if you don't like it you're always free to quit & starve yourself to death) in those proud New England mills and factories; whose owners out of noble and charitable humanity had in the name of abolishing the pernicious evil of slavery, crushed the South forever even as Rome had once reamed Carthage; meanwhile freeing the poor slaves so that slave and master, black and white together, could enjoy poverty equally for three or more generations, these (the mill & factory owners) being rewarded by a grateful Providence with a period of unparalleled growth, boom, expansion and prosperity; and accepting the burden of their good fortune solemnly, seeing themselves as trustees and guardians of the bounty of an abundant Providence and thus, in that role, not so much unwilling as unable to indulge in the sentimental gesture of dissipating that Trust by sharing any of it with any of the nameless and unwashed and unremembered hordes who toiled and spun freely to keep the great Wheels of Progress turning.

I think it must have been just about then that the soft music of cash register bells became consecrated. And to that music great men danced.

Their supreme moment was the great world's fair, The Columbian Exhibition in Chicago (1893? never good on dates) where massive structures imitative of imperial Rome rose in shining whiteness of plaster and papermache from a marshy bog to assert the unquestioned grandeur of our aspirations. A grandeur witnessed by throngs of rubes, hicks, rednecks, tourists etc. who could go back home eye-&-foot sore, yet eternally grateful for the privilege of viewing . . . what? *The Triumph of Shinola!*

Some of them were also lucky enough to have viewed and been briefly mesmerized by the amazing novel of Little Egypt.

O long before Kim Novak!

Some historians (I say this bravely enough though I couldn't name one right now if my life depended on it) see that great exhibition, which, by the way & by design, left even less behind than old man Ozymandias, as a symbol, all right; but of the end of an era at the beginning of a new century, the last panoply and pomp of the old. They're entitled to their stupid opinions. However, I see it as the beginning, a vision of the century ahead. Vision verging on prophecy, augury.

For we do not now live for real and daily in a gleaming phony City of grand pretensions of grandeur, built on a bog, and made of plaster and papermache? Do we not gawk? Are we not so mesmerized by a multitude of navels, these marvelous navels themselves merging into the One Navel, The Absolute Navel, forever dancing in scrimmy light which is somehow so close an approximation of the light of dreams and dream visions that we must constantly pinch ourselves, blink to see, though never to be sure, whether we are awake or dreaming? When I awoke, I cried to dream again, poor Caliban said. Or something like that. (Don't have *The Tempest* handy.) Suffice it to say, we updated Calibans have found a way to keep sleeping and dreaming, to keep the music playing. The music? But, of course!, those dancing navels, mystically becoming the One Perfect and Sufficient Navel, dancing to the mystic beat and belling tones of the aforementioned symphony of cash registers.

Look closely and you see that Navel seems to have two shapes at once. An optical illusion, of course, a trick like those paintings of Jesus where the eyes seem to follow you around the room. (I have this on scientific authority, a source no less than Levy, the Occulist, himself). Anyway, illusion or not, stare at that navel, that soft round place, that cyclopean and completely fascinating eye of the marvelous female body, a circle of joy, becoming in abstraction a symbol and a promise of the total and complete joy of the entire body, forever unified in perfection like a circle is endless. Stare and even as you do you'll see that circle dissolve, replaced with a brief subliminal flash like diamonds or rhinestones of a second, dissimilar shape. That shape, bet your sweet life, becomes manifest, reveals itself in purity even as the navel is revealed. Blink and stare and you'll see it, unmistakably: $$$ . . . !

I'm not complaining. Child of our times, I too think Money & Sex are the twin gods of the household, twin and yet somehow One as well. Just like the Trinity that theologians used to fret about.

I say the works of old Horatio Alger were a phony. Phony then and phony now. I say that his (imaginary) descendant, R.C., has no right to be bitter and that his bitterness is as phony as was Horatio's unbridled optimism. I say Horatio was a lucky fool and R.C. is an unlucky fool, and that's about all there is to it.

Beyond that I make no comment upon The American Way in *Realms of Gold* regardless of what fools may want to read into it. On such a great subject I have no answers. I cannot even settle on a working symbol. I'm tossed and gored by a dilemma. Al Capone or Wilbur Cross? Balboa or Cortez? Kim Novak or Florence Nightingale? Little Egypt or The Singing Nun?

Sometimes it sure is difficult to be a modern man.

Know what I mean, Sam?

Listen, though, Sambo, all bigotry and bias aside, no kidding and no fooling, there are some things I would like to say about my country.

If I were a Big Shot, someone that people would listen to (say, like Nat Hentoff or Tom Wicker or James Reston or Norman O. Brown or Tom Wolfe or Hugh Hefner; you know, someone of that ilk, a Pop Philosopher with an ax to grind and metaphorical heads to cut off etc.), I would write a book. And I would call it *The Triumph of Shinola; or, My Country and Whatever Became of It?*

And I would really try and not be sarcastic or satirical or even smartass. I would try to tell it not "like it is" (who knows, I ask you, how it really is?), but how it seems to me. In doing so I would spare the hides and horns and hooves of no Sacred Cows. I would not shrink from or shirk any legitimate target or antagonist whatsoever even though it brought the I.R.S., the F.B.I., the C.I.A., and, worst of all, the Literary-Intellectual Establishment out in hot pursuit of my lonesome ass.

I would attack all forms of contemporary hypocrisy and double dealing—though it might take as many volumes as the *Encyclopedia Brittanica* to do so. I would even do that one thing which Nobody does any more. I would especially lean on, needle, and poke fun and fury at those with whom I am in general agreement. That is to say, those people and groups whose general aims and goals I happen to share, but whose means to get there tend to make me heartsick, headachey and give me either constipation or the G.I. trots.

Why attack my own "side"? Well, sir, I refer you to Mr. Thomas Jefferson and Mr. Tom Paine and other Early American Antiques. All notions, and especially those which have the greatest apparent surety, as comfortable and correct, all notions need strong opposition. For any Product to be "tested," there has to be a Brand X. If an idea can stand up to inquisition, pressure, scrutiny and even plain old ridicule, then maybe it deserves to. If it can't take it, then who needs it?

You will have noticed the extreme self-control I am exercising, dignifying the thousand and one *clichés* floating around here in The Land of the Big Cliché by calling them "ideas."

My theme—if you can call it that, my hobby horse is better, would reveal itself to be this: that when "ideas" are merely clichés in disguise and when people believe in and commit themselves to clichés, they are surrendering their humanity. Modern man has long since lost his last shattered fragments of divinity. Now he wants to do away with the last vestiges of his humanity. For the whole process of what is called thinking today is, one way or another, a kind of card game with—abstractions. Abstractions are convenient and expedient. They are tools. But all abstractions, it seems to me, become corrupt and vicious when there is no imagination left to check the inevitable excesses.

In our time millions have died and will continue to die, more millions have suffered and will continue to suffer for the sake of abstractions, *i.e.*, clichés. Whether or not they were "good" clichés or "bad" ones seems to me completely irrelevant.

72

The saddest thing of all, since I see it and feel it most, is what has happened to my country. The whole dream has been lost in the shuffle. We live, if you can call it living, by power, pressure, force, and leverage, feeding ourselves daily (as an orchid feeds itself so richly on thin air) on a fattening diet of lies.

I have a friend who is a lawyer. Last time I saw him he was really feeling down and depressed. I asked him what was bugging him, what was the source of his cosmic *angst* & woe.

"Nothing is left," he said. "The whole thing is rotten. You can't get a table and eat in a restaurant without leverage. You can't even get your car fixed without influence. What the hell is the use?"

I have no answer to his question.

Do you?

The trouble is, I think, that something very strange has happened to us, a kind of curious conversion. I can think of no place in recorded human history (excepting maybe Babylon and Sodom and Gomorrah and we know what happened to them) where injustice, inequity, double dealing, hypocrisy, leverage, kickbacks, payola and privilege and pressure have been not only accepted as inevitable but baldly and boldly asserted and indeed often defended under the banners of Honesty and Realism. I sometimes permit myself the reasonable doubt that sin is more abounding and that the ways of the wicked prosper any more in this day and age than any other. But one thing for sure, Sam, this is the first time in our short history that bad people have not been ashamed of themselves.

It would break my heart if I let it and if I permitted myself for a moment to forget that my very survival depends upon the condition and quality of contemporary American life. Where such as I can pass unnoticed, anonymous as any soldier in the ranks. And I don't even have to indulge in vestigial winces of conscience, itself as vestigial as the appendix. For no matter what I do someone else is doing worse.

But I won't bore you with crackpot and misanthropic notions. There is no money in them anyway. In fact there is only trouble.

Besides which I am not brave enough to say what I really think. Not wise enough to know what I really think.

And therefore, good Sam, I put on motley, cap and bells. And I make faces and funny noises. And I hope somebody will toss me a nice bone from the banquet table.

Hey, remember Charles Laughton as Henry VIII? That old boy could really gnaw a bone.

I will continue to play the game, expecting the worst and hoping for the best.

I will believe nothing and will reveal no more than I have to, including my real name.

I shall continue to try to collect my share of kisses and candy, dodging and avoiding curses and cuffs. And I shall devote myself to the lost cause of living (until I die) in an attempt to refute what some character said in

Gentlemen Prefer Blondes: "A girl can't go on laughing all the time."

She was right, of course. But I can see no alternative but to deny the truth of her statement till the day I die, always hoping and praying to be lucky enough to die laughing.

POINT TWO: I know there was something else I wanted to say. But it must not have been all that important. Anyway, I've forgotten what it was.

P.S. I enclose some examples of the poison pen epistles of R.C. Alger.

J.T.

Part Five

Miscellaneous Letters From the Thrilling 1960's

And though the songs which I indite
Do quit thy change with rightful spite,
Blame not my lute.
(Sir Thomas Wyatt—"Blame not my lute")

Some Miscellaneous and Exemplary Letters
from *The Realms of Gold*

Dear President Johnson,

I am only a humble Mexican. My father was a Wetback and I am an unemployed yard man in your native state of Texas, U.S.A.

We are very proud of you and all the good things you are doing. We have your picture in the living room for everyone to see.

I am writing to ask you a favor. I could use some help, but I do not want to ask for something for nothing. Us Mexicans may be lazy and all, but we have got some pride.

Let me expain, honorable sir. Even though he was only a common Wetback and never a citizen of this great land, my father always voted for you many times in every election. Sometimes he was able to vote for you four or five times because all us Mexicans look alike. All he ever knew about voting was to go to the place they told him and give the name they told him and vote for Lyndon Johnson. The last time he voted for you was in 1964 even though he had been dead for several years by then. When they found out he was dead and couldn't vote for you anymore, they copied his name off of the tombstone. They said it was a very high honor. I am sure he was sorry and sad though because he could only vote for you one time that way.

We have always been proud to vote for you in our family. When you think how close the election was sometimes you can see how we feel like maybe we have helped in our own humble way. And we have always been grateful for the little gifts they have given to us as a reward for voting for you. They are very honest men because they could not be positively sure that we did vote for you as they told us to but we did and they almost always took our word for it.

Mr. President, I would like to borrow fifty dollars from you. I need the money very badly.

I know how you feel about lending money to Mexican strangers. I do not blame you. I would feel the same way myself. And I know that it is not possible to be a rich man like you are and get that way by giving money away. So I am not asking you to give it away. It is only a loan.

I will repay you with my vote in 1968. You may think to yourself that fifty dollars is a very high price for the President of the U.S.A. to pay for one Wetback vote even if the Wetback votes many times. That is true Mr. President Johnson but that is not what I am offering you.

First your friends never paid me a dime for taking my father's name off the stone to vote in 1964. I am sure they just forgot but I did not forget. I have not much education but I can always remember a date and names and faces and what is said and things like that.

Second I am now a President myself. I am President of the Pancho Villa Club which is a place where we hang around and drink beer and play cards and sometimes have dances. There are more than 300 members. The President of the Club gets the right to pick who the club will vote for.

Third I have heard that there are bad men who are coming among us and asking questions about how we have voted and plan to vote. It is up to me to tell the Club Members what to do about this. They will answer the truth if I tell them. But please do not worry, Mr. President. I will tell them to forget, even to forget how to understand the language. I will try to forget all the things I remember too.

Fourth is that you are giving away millions of dollars to help Colored People who riot and will not work and vote for who they please. It is only fair to help one loyal humble Mexican who is at least part white and has always done exactly as he is told.

> Sincerely,
> Speedy Gonzalez

Dear Dr. Timothy Leary,

You have brought grief, misery and woe into my life and I don't think that's funny worth a hoot. I don't even think it is very nice.

I am not talking about LSD or reefers or any other drugs you may be pushing at this time. Every man has his own line to sell and far be it from me to knock any other man's product. It's all a case of supply and demand. I mean, if people suddenly took to spreading sh-t on sandwiches instead of peanut butter, there would soon be some hustlers busily bottling and canning it and advertising on the T.V. And no man could dast blame them. Far from it. By all rights they should be praised for their initiative and resourcefulness. That is the bulwark of the Capitalist System of Free Enterprise.

So, if you want to hustle a lot of crazy drugs to dumb pimply kids that don't know any better and couldn't care less, as well as screwed up grownups who would otherwise just be moping around with sad and unhappy expressions on their faces, why I say that is your business. And if you want to make a show out of it with robes and gongs and funny-sounding music and nutty movies and a lot of double-talk, that's all right with me too. If anybody complains, you can always cite historical precedent. Remind the s.o.b.'s of the role played by the Medicine Show in the days of the American frontier. Surely they remember how they used to sell Hadacol only a few years ago. Hadacol must have brought happiness to thousands. I remember they used to have these short radio testimonials to its power. One of my favorites was the lady who said: "For many years I had terrible stomach trouble. The Doctors couldn't figure it out and no medicine would help. Then I tried Hadacol. Now I feel as good as new and I'm proud to say I'll put my stomach up against anybody's."

Seriously, Dr. Leary, I'm sorry about how you and your daughter got busted trying to smuggle stuff in from Mexico. It may have been kind of dumb to let your daughter carry the stuff. It's logical, but it looks bad, you know? Like you were going to let her take the rap or something. Some people say that, but I don't believe it for a minute. I attribute it to plain stupidity. In any case, I don't think it is fair for you to have to go to jail for forty years. That is a long time, Dr. Leary. That's how long Moses wandered around in the wilderness while trying to find Palestine without a map. You've got a very good thing going there and I would hate to see your business interrupted for forty years. Somebody else would probably come along and pick up all the marbles. Somebody else would get the gravy while you were eating beans and sowbelly. I hope you beat the rap, but if you don't, I'm confident that a man of your intelligence will come up with some gimmick to make life in "the big house" more interesting, or anyway figure out something where you don't have to spend all your time breaking rocks and making license plates and such. Maybe you can worm your way into a job in the prison library like Alger Hiss did.

However, as I say, I'm not knocking your line of work or your product. You know what I do? I sell cemetery lots. You might think that's a morbid line of work. Lots of people do, I guess. I prefer to call it a social service. Everybody has got to die. And when they do you can't just stuff them in a garbage can or dig a hole in the backyard. It's against the law. Besides a lot of people don't have back yards. So everybody needs a burial plot, be it large or small, exclusive or crowded. And you can't take care of the problem too early either. Nobody knows for sure when death will come knocking at the door. As the poet says, even the paths of glory are one-way to the cemetery. Think about it, Dr. Leary, any day now you might slip in the bathtub or get runover by some crazy teenagers in a hotrod or even get struck down by a bolt of lightning. It happens. Or maybe sometime by accident you might take an overdose of some of your own stuff and just flip out of reality on a permanent basis. If you're smart, you'll arrange for a burial plot and so forth right now. There's still time to pick and choose. But if you wait, what with the population explosion and all, there may not be any guarantee *where* you'll end up or *who* will be buried next to you. Maybe you really believe all that crap you hand out about escaping into a new dimension and all. I wouldn't blame you if you did. Sincerity never hurt any salesman. It helps to believe in your product. But let me tell you from my own personal experience and observation that when you die you are going to be just as dead as the next fellow. And no matter how hard some highpriced undertaker works on you, sooner or later you will start to rot and stink just like every other corpse in history. Wouldn't you rather have a little privacy during the period of decomposition?

I'm not trying to sell you a cemetery lot. I have all the business I can handle anyway. But if you ever have any questions or need some advice, please don't hesitate to call on me.

The thing I am really writing you about is that interview you had in *Playboy* magazine. You just about ruined my life with that one, Dr. Leary. Let me explain. I have been married for fifteen years to the same woman. Betsy is a very nice looking girl, plenty of curves in the right places and all. We fell in love when she was the head cheerleader at Piedmont High School. I was on the football team and every game I sat on the bench and watched her jumping and jiggling around whooping it up for the team. I longed for her. When she did the high jump right after the Locomotive Cheer and her skirt flared out and you could even see her panties for a second, I tell you I could hardly contain myself. It was the most exciting thing I had ever seen or imagined. You know how kids are. Of course, a man grows up, but you never really get over a thing like that. Every once in a while to this day, when we're both feeling good and nothing much to do, I'll ask her and she'll go up to the attic and get the old costume out of mothballs and put it on and do the Locomotive Cheer for me. Even after fifteen years of wedded life, richer and poorer and better and worse, it still works like a charm. I can still work up a gigantic hard-on without even trying.

That's one reason I'm glad I spent a lot of time on the bench. If old Jay Hooker had ever come out of the game and I had to go in it would have been embarrassing as all get out. Imagine what it would have looked like in those tight football pants. Jay Hooker, he was the first string halfback. A great big guy and a truly fine athlete in every way. I was kind of scrawny in those days. All I could do was run fast and dodge around pretty good because I hated to get tackled. The truth is, I know now, I was afraid. Also I hated all that sweaty old . . . *physical contact*. I only went out for football so I could sit on the bench and watch Betsy. Jay Hooker was good. He made all conference and second team all state. But you probably don't remember that unless you happen to be a real high school football fan.

One time we made an overnight trip and stayed in a hotel along with the band and the Pep Club and the Cheerleaders and all. It was a lot of fun, singing and joshing on the bus on the way there. It wasn't so much fun coming back because they kicked the shit out of us 36-0 and the coach blamed it on attitude and all the singing. But that night in the hotel somebody came tippytoeing around with the message that one of the Cheerleaders was kind of "putting out" for the boys. Not in the gross way you might imagine. It was more of an inspirational thing. For fifty cents you could see her naked. For a dollar you could actually touch her. I had an extra dollar and I figured it might be worth it. I had never even seen a big girl naked except for my sister Lucille in the tub a couple of times when she forgot to hook the bathroom door. And that wasn't such a big deal. For one thing Lucille is plain as pig tracks and has freckles all over her. For another she's bigboned and built like a brick sh-t house. Except for her titties she was built about the same as Jay Hooker. People used to say if I'd of had her build, *even with the titties*, I could have been an All American.

So, frankly, Dr. Leary I was curious.

I paid the guy my buck and went down and waited with the other guys in a dark room. We had to be quiet and all on account of the chaperones on the hall. There was an adjoining room, connecting through the closet, and they let us go in one at a time. And you could stay about a minute and then they let you out the front door of the other room so you could sneak back where you belonged and so none of us would start comparing notes so to speak and make noise. The suspense was almost unbearable, but finally my turn came and I went in the room. There wasn't much light, just a faint glow for a little night light, but it was enough to see that there was surely a naked girl lying on the bed. She had a pillow behind her head and was smoking a cigarette. She was all white and smooth and shiny in the half dark, but I couldn't make out her face at first. I just stood looking.

"Don't just stand there," she said. "It's cold like this."

I could have fainted on the spot. It was Betsy herself! I stumbled toward the bed like a man in a dream.

"What kind?" she said.

"Shoot the works," the guy that took my money said.

"On the tummy," she said. "You can touch the tummy and that's all."

I was weak in the knees and my heart was pounding. I knew I couldn't just stand there or I would faint or something. And I was embarrassed because my palms were sweating.

"Hurry up," she said. "I'm covered with goosepimples."

She was too. All kind of shivering and goosepimples all over. She caught a bad cold that night and was so hoarse the next day she could hardly lead the cheers. I reached out and touched her right about where the navel is and it was the softest, smoothest thing I had ever touched in my life. I came right in my britches, but nobody noticed. I just touched her tummy real quick and then jerked my hand away.

"Who's next?" she said.

And I slipped back to my room and wanted to cry. Partly out of sadness. I mean, it was a sad thing for a beautiful girl like Betsy to be exposing herself like that for money. And it made me sad to think of all those other slobs and studs looking at her too and some of them, the ones who had the money, actually getting to touch her tummy and doing it. But at the same time I was crying out of happiness. Never mind the sad part or the circumstances. I had looked on beauty bare and I had touched her tummy near the navel. And even if I died in my sleep, nobody could ever take that away from me.

That's how I was as a kid—very romantic.

But you know as well as I do, Dr. Leary, that nobody is ever satisfied with what he has got or what has happened to him already. Thank heavens this is so. Otherwise we would just lay around on our ass and live on Welfare and not amount to anything. It wasn't long before I wanted more than the memory of a peek and a touch. But how? I was shy at that age and anyway she wouldn't go out on a date with me or anything. I finally worked up the nerve to ask her and she just laughed. I thought about committing suicide. That would show her. But I couldn't afford any of the clean and painless ways. I tried to improve myself and my appearance. I took exercises, lifted weights, and paid a lot of attention to my personal grooming. All that helped a little, but not much. If I had had ten years, maybe it would have worked. Then I hit on a happy idea. Maybe I could get a job in the summer and save all my money. Maybe she would let me do other things if I had enough money. I worked like a dog all summer and managed to save up more than three hundred dollars. In the fall I approached her and asked her what she would do for three hundred dollars. Again she laughed at me.

"You creep," she said. "I only f-ck my friends. I draw the line."

I must have looked crushed because she told me not to look so sad, that maybe there was a chance. I brightened. I would have done anything.

"I'll give you a piece of a-- for every touchdown you make this year," she said.

Some joke! A fat chance I had of making *any* touchdowns, playing behind the great Jay Hooker. I was ready to use the three hundred dollars to buy some powerful sleeping pills when Fate stepped into the picture. Jay Hooker was showing off on the parallel bars in the gym and fell and hurt his back bad. He couldn't play for the rest of the season. And so on Friday they had to start me. The other school kicked off and I ran it back 95 yards for a touchdown. Then I came trotting over to the bench to catch my breath. I winked at her and she looked terrible. Like she was going to be sick. Little did she know! I made three more touchdowns that game.

I had a great season, an inspired season. I made at least one touchdown in every game. I gave her a pretty thorough going over before the season ended. Unfortunately, by that time she was pregnant and we had to get married. Which might have been a happy ending except that once I got used to her, to the novelty of it, she wasn't all that good. She didn't really like it, Dr. Leary. She was kind of frigid. I hate to admit it, but she was. Well, I read some sex books and decided to try all the stuff they suggested and to be very patient and gentle and all. I'll tell you what true patience is. Seven years it took me. Seven years before she finally had a climax. Seven years of famine. But it was worth it. Because once she learned how she started to enjoy it pretty much and it got better and better.

Things were going great, Dr. Leary, until you came along in *Playboy* and claimed that a woman under LSD could have 100 orgasms. One hundred! I don't blame you for trying to hustle that stuff and anybody except Betsy could see that you were exaggerating a little for effect. But Betsy is very gullible about scientific things. She really believes that. She is mad at me and says I am cheating her out of her rights if I don't get some LSD and try to match your record. Dr. Leary, I am approaching middleage. I come home from a hard day's work and sure I want a little love, sex, and affection. But even if I could get hold of some LSD, I don't think my heart could stand the strain. It's bad enough as it is, because even without LSD she is trying to set records. Inspired by you. I am about worn out. Betsy is threatening to pack up and leave me and seek you out. I say more power to her. You'll be sorry, Dr. Leary, sorry you made those unethical and extravagant claims for your product if she shows up on your doorstep.

Betsy has a very strong sense of honor. She delivers on her promises, as I have noted earlier, and she expects other people to do so too.

I've about had it. One of these nights I'm going to tell her: "All right, go ahead. Go find Dr. Timothy Leary and make him put up or shut up." And she will. And then maybe you won't have to go to jail at all because you'll be dead first.

Just don't say I didn't warn you. And if a goodlooking, well-preserved woman in a cheerleading costume named Betsy does show up at your door, you better get on the phone and order your burial plot. I'll give you a good deal. Because I'm sorry for you even it if is your own fault.

In any case I hope this will teach you a lesson. Think before you shoot off your big mouth, Doctor.

Lots of luck to you. You'll need it.

     T.J. Payne

Dear Bishop Pike,

As a confirmed and dedicated atheist I am so proud of your bold public statements and all the good work you have done to prove that God is not only dead but never has existed.

Keep up the good work!

With all respect & admiration, I remain

     Your friend & fellow unbeliever,

     Jacob Schmertz

Dear Barry Goldwater,

I voted for you in '64 and would vote for you again anytime for any office you chose to run for, from dog catcher to the very top! I was very sad when, after your loss, you seemed to drop out of sight. I was afraid you were going to retire from active public life.

Imagine my surprise and pleasure to read you are back in action, making speeches again. I am deeply pleased.

I have always felt that we needed more comedians and more comedy in politics. Politicians tend to take themselves and the issues much too seriously. That is why I voted for Adlai twice, because of his wit and jokes. And when you came on the scene I rejoiced in my heart. Your superb satire has made the whole business of politics funny.

We are profoundly in your debt. Next time you open your mouth to make a mock of the whole democratic process and to lighten our heart with your amazing levity, please be assured sir, that at least one admirer in hanging on your every word.

> Yours truly,
> Julius Funk

Dear Senator Robert Kennedy,

As a retired carnival "talker" (what rubes call a "barker"), I have lamented the passing of the pitchman's art and craft from the American scene. Intellectual honesty has much to be said for it, of course, but truly it is as tedious as the consistency with which it is manifested. Give me the old double-talking, forked-tongue, straightfaced, doubledealing spiel of an artful pitchman who can sell you you-know-what in a Shinola can and you will even polish your shoes with it before you catch on. Give me that man of the old school who values nothing, not even his good name, above the manly art of the old Pitch! Give me the man so dedicated to the honor of the sideshow itself that he will lie, steal, cheat and do anything to keep the rubes happy.

Rubes are happiest when they are cheated with art and style, since they are born to be cheated anyway.

The world is divided into rubes and freaks, both beyond repair. And then there are a few Talkers who keep the show going, the now-you-see-it and now-you-don't that keeps them as contented as Elsie, the Borden Cow, instead of falling into mischief or at each other's throats. Ours is a noble calling. It is not easy to fool the fools. Sometimes one considers giving up and becoming merely another duped fool oneself. But then the call of duty and the sound of the old razzmatazz wakens the flagging spirit and lifts the heart again.

Good luck. I hope you are President some day.

> Yours truly,
> Jack Spratt

Dear George Wallace,

Although you are villified and crucified almost every day in the pinko, leftist, Yankee press, I hope you can take some consolation in the example of our Lord.

When Christ got tired of carrying His Cross up the hill to Calvary, what did *He* do? He handed it to the nearest available niggerboy and let him tote it for a while.

> Never quit,
> Ray "Rattler" Wheelwright

Dear William H. Masters and Virginia E. Johnson,

As a Movie Producer, I do not believe in "beating about the (pardon the expression) bush." So I will come straight to the point. I would like to take an option on your best selling property with a view to making a movie out of it. I am prepared to offer you a generous deal at top price.

I am delighted that your book has found its way to the best seller lists and looks like a shoo-in to stay there all summer. I am glad to see that all those reviews which knock the book and try to make jokes about the long hard work that went into it haven't had any adverse effect on sales. Critics-schmiticks! The public knows what it wants and gets what's good for it. I hope you don't take to heart some of the mean things those wiseguys are saying about you and your work. But I know you do not. You are scientists and scientists are like priests or something.

Anyway, I see real cinematic possibilities in this property. That will be the gimmick, the story of two dedicated scientists, a man and a woman, who say to themselves, hey, let us try and find out what all this sex business is about. There must be more to it than is in the books.

So, in a way, it will be your story. How you started your research and carried it through to the bitter end, followed of course by a happy ending, like maybe our two scientists fall in love during the process of their studies (in the picture, I mean). There would be some good subplot material in following some of the people who were "studied." Pathos, humor, entertainment and uplifting content. We would probably get big name stars for these roles and "cameo" parts.

For the leads, I see something new and different. No type casting. Maybe Dick Van Dyke and Elke Sommer. What do you think?

I intend to import a good foreign Director, somebody who had a record of handling taboo subjects and "skin" scenes in good taste. Maybe Ingemar Bergman. Maybe Roger Vadim. On a property like this only the best will do and to hell with pinching pennies.

You may feel funny about Hollywood and the movies. Maybe you haven't been to the movies lately because of all your research and making movies of your own. Have no fear. The only way to handle this picture is in the spirit in which you went at it. No cheap sensationalism. No gross-out, no horror shows. Strictly scientific with a human interest story at the heart. Thousands of people will read your book. Millions and millions all over the world can see the flick, be deeply moved by it, learn by it, and emerge from the experience not only better movie goers but better human beings!

For those few fuzzy-heads who go around saying you have written a "dirty" book to make money, I say this: "Fuzzy heads, do you think two reputable scientists with a sincere interest in the subject would do a thing like that. Fie! Do you think that an old and honored publishing firm like Little, Brown and Co. of Boston, Mass. would stoop to publishing a book like *Human Sexual Response* just to make profits and get on the best seller list? Fooey!"

It will be a challenge for us all, good doctors, but I think you got a swell little property there and, done in good taste, it could be boffo. As I said before, Pacemaker Films is ready to offer you "the best deal in town." Furthermore

I am fully prepared to sweeten the deal by buying up any old films you might wish to sell that we could maybe work in as authentic stock shots.

Bless you both and may success smile at you always.

Your friend indeed,
Jerry Wolf

P.S. Is it really true like you say that the "size of the male phallus bears no demonstrable relationship to the degree of sexual satisfaction." If so, I would like to know for sure so I can tell my wife to put that in her pipe and smoke it.

J.W.

Dear Mr. Hugh Hefner,

I have long been an avid and eager reader of your magazine, although probably for many of the wrong reasons. That is why I am so deeply grateful for all the time and energy you have given, together with much space in the magazine, in the careful, step by step presentation of "The Playboy Philosophy." I can imagine what a strain and intellectual effort it must be for you; for I majored in philosophy myself and I know how difficult it is to do. Although I got my college education and degree by correspondence, for pressing personal reasons, I have at least a passing acquaintance with the masters of philosophical discourse down through the ages. I hope you will not be offended if I say that I personally rate "The Playboy Philosophy" very high, and I can forsee the day when it, too, will be a part of any philosophy course worthy of the name, right up there with Plato, Descartes, Locke, Kant, John Dewey, and Norman O. Brown. Your natural modesty will not permit you to agree with me I know, but at any rate even if you think I am a "kook," you will see how highly I regard your contribution to our cultural, ethical and intellectual life.

No doubt you get many flattering letters, and some of them may turn out to be "crank" letters or else request for favors of one kind or another. I would like to assure you at this point that this is a serious and sincere letter, completely honest, as I know you would want me to be, and without ulterior motive save to ask your advice on a personal matter, if that is possible. However, first and foremost, I wish to thank you from the bottom of my heart for all that "The Playboy Philosophy" has meant to me. Perhaps if I tell you a little of how it has changed my life, you will see what I mean.

Until I really got into the "Philosophy," I was a very mixed up person. All my education, though acquired painfully and with difficulty, had not managed to clear my head of the myths and misconceptions which had virtually been branded upon my brain by society, its hypocritical history, customs and mores, and, as well, by my poor, misguided parents who, though well-meaning, were the inevitable product of generations of wrong-headed ignorance and superstition. They thought that any form of gratification of the sex need, however natural both the need and the urge to gratify it might be, outside of the bonds of holy matrimony was a sin. They also thought it was "ugly." About as far as they went was to agree reluctantly with St. Paul that it is better to marry than to burn. They believed in "self-discipline," in the value of work well done, in thrift, modesty, self-reliance etc. All the old outmoded Puritan ideals. They even managed to inculcate in me the idea that happiness and the good life were delusions, simply excuses for swinish self-indulgence. It is truly a wonder I didn't end up in a loony bin. Maybe I might have if I had not read your Philosophy.

Earlier in this letter I admitted to you that I was drawn to your magazine for the wrong reasons. I am ashamed to confess to you of all people, Mr. Hefner, that I would look at your magazine for one purpose—to see the pictures of "naked" girls. I would look at them and become aroused. Then I would look deeply into their eyes (for they all seemed to be looking at me) and in a shiver and shudder of "sin" I would gratify my desires in the way that man has always been compelled to when he is alone and lonely. However it was not that simple. I sincerely believed that I was committing an act beyond any grace or redemption, that I was filthy, rotten to the core and doomed. Doomed and damned. Moreover I sincerely believed that my sins would manifest themselves for all to see: in acne, hairy palms, premature senility, and eventual death by dissipation. I could see my Death Certificate with the dread words written: "Cause of death—Self Abuse." Naturally I invested all sorts of symbolic values in these perfectly innocent, two-dimensional girls. They were more than just filthy temptresses leading me into a pact with the Devil, taunting and teasing and tantalizing me to follow them down the primrose path to shame and complete degradation. They were also tormenting goddesses, supernatural beings, whom I worshipped, before whom I debased and humiliated myself to no avail. In return they rewarded me with guilt and anguish. Finally, at one and the same time, they were imaginary "friends." After such an experience I felt I really knew them personally.

You can see I was really a crazy, mixed-up kid. I cannot tell you how much anguish and remorse I suffered, how many times I tried to "repent," or "improve myself" and failed. Suffice it to say that by the time each new issue appeared, I was as eager to open the pages as some poor junkie is for his fix.

Thanks to the simple limitations of human ability, I was forced to *read* the magazine to kill the time "between times" so to speak. And that is how I found the Philosophy. At first, being sick, I read it skeptically, even contemptuously. I said to myself, "here is a man who is in the magazine business trying to make a lot of money. He is trying to take off the curse of the pornography label by claiming that it is all part of some kind of 'philosophy.' He is a trickster, trying to make a skin magazine respectable. He is also tricking himself, trying to justify and rationalize his own bad habits and dissolute way of life in the Playboy Mansion. He is said to have been married once. If he is so great, how come that didn't work? etc. etc. etc." I am almost ashamed to admit it now, but that is what I thought.

Nevertheless I continued to read your heartfelt words. Gradually cynicism gave way to more objective appraisal. Under objective scrutiny the cogency and lucidity of your arguments, your obviously profound and wide-ranging knowledge and indefatigable intellectual curiousity, and, finally, by the undeniable sincerity that shines through the pages of your work, as a result of all these things I was moved first to admiration and thence to agreement. From the intellectual act of agreement came the concomittant emotional and psychological beginnings of health. A new, bright world dawned for me. All thanks to you. Ring out the old & ring in the new! That's what I say.

Truly you have saved a life and liberated a human spirit, Mr. Hefner.

Ironically, now that I know the truth, I have shed my "bad habits." I now look upon your Playgirls and Bunnies with pleasure all right, but it is a different pleasure. I rejoice in their youth and health and beauty. They are real people somewhere, of course, but truly they also are symbols of the goodness and richness of Life, of the good life. They are the nymphs and handmaidens and muses of The Playboy Philosophy.

Now I know not only that life can be beautiful, when Man sheds prejudice, irrationality, superstition, false gods and religions and thus returns to the state of joyful innocence *and* experience which is his for the asking. Truly, as another great prophet said, the kingdom is here and everywhere, within us and without, always.

You have made life worth living for me. I only hope that in some small way I can do something with my life which will be worthy and commensurate of the great gift of life and joy you have given me, together with thousands and thousand of others.

I do have a small problem, as I implied earlier. I don't know quite how to put my philosophy into practice, because of my personal problem. You see, Mr. Hefner, I am a serious victim of cerebral palsy, what most people crudely and cruelly refer to as being "a spastic." I have got it bad. I have learned to get around a little on my own, I'm proud to say, but I do look terrible to others when I do so. I walk like some kind of a deranged windup toy that has been stepped on, misshapen, battered, but not quite completely broken. I move by jerks, fits and starts. My head rolls. I can't help drooling. My speech impairment makes me sound moronic or dead drunk or both. To type a letter like this one is a tedious experience. First I must manage to grasp my right wrist with my left hand, then gripping as hard as I can to control and steady my right hand, I point my right index finger at the correct key and bring down my hands in one motion like, I guess, driving a nail with a hammer. Between each time I have to rest. It has teken me a long time to do this without making mistakes. I am proud to say that when I send out a letter it is letter perfect. I do not permit myself the luxury of strikeovers. If there is a mistake on a page, I start over again.

I am not asking your pity. I am only trying to make clear that I do have a real problem.

In a larger sense my problem is this. I believe in the "Philosophy." I am your convert and disciple. But what can I do to *live* by it? I can, of course, imagine a good life. I can see myself clearly dancing and singing for joy, hale and hearty, well-groomed, well-dressed, well-mannered and knowledgable. Your magazine with its examples of all aspects of the good life, gives me the stuff to dream on, to build castles in Spain. There is gracious plenty there to keep a full, rich fantasy life swinging and ever renewed. Yet just as man cannot live on bread alone, so he will starve to death if the only thing he's got working for him is spiritual satisfaction.

Mr. Hefner, I need a girl. But what to do? What is right?

I know several spastic girls from the Rehabilitation and Therapy Center, which we jokingly call the RAT center. Frankly, they repel me. And even if I could overcome my probably immature revulsion, it seems to me that the image of two spastics in the sack, trying in writhing jerks and incomprehensible sounds to consummate the holy and joyous act of love is so degrading and unattractive as to defeat the very purpose of the act. That is a risk I dare not run. Perhaps that is all I can legitimately look forward to or have a right to expect. But I must confess that if I really accepted this truth, I should probably try to cut my throat or at least cut off my hungers at their root.

I know how I look to other people. No doubt they share the same kind of revulsion I have for those pitiful and contemptible creeps at RAT. I understand, but I do not *accept* this truth as final and irrevocable. I feel that I am beautiful. My parents would probably say this is merely another example of the supreme folly of and boundless extent of human self-love and vanity. I do not believe that. I believe that nothing human is alien. I also know that no man is loathsome to himself. Or, put it this way, a man can be aware of his imperfections, but he is also aware of his possibility for perfection. He has a profound need to soften the shadows of his imperfections and expose the dream of his possible perfection in the light of a lover's eyes.

I cannot help thinking that somehow I am beautiful and desirable as Man is so.

Must I sacrifice this last illusion? And if I do, will the truth free me or will it destroy me?

To be practical. There *is* one possibility. There is a Social Worker who comes once a week to look in on me, to bring books, records, etc. I suspect she is frightened of me, but only insofar as she is frightened by all human suffering. I know she pities me. She is a cheerful woman and while she is rather plain and not a likely candidate for anyone's imagined desert island caper, she is healthy, has decent enough breasts (about 34's, I'd guess, though you can't be sure) and a genuinely admirable *derriere*. She would be an acceptable compromise, and I believe that if I put my case carefully and in writing, she might respond with at least an occasional toss in the hay. Fear and pity can work wonders and she has a truly remarkable guilt-complex about *not* suffering. I might even be a sort of therapy for her. Since she probably is frightened by sex anyway and may even still be a virgin, doing it with me would be a sufficiently degrading experience to assuage her sense of guilt. Then I might lose her.

However, I would prefer to avoid this kind of seduction. Its duplicity and one-sidedness seems to me completely out of keeping with the premises of "The Playboy Philosophy."

While writing this letter I have come upon what seems to me a reasonable alternative. You are even more dedicated to the Philosophy than I, a mere disciple. I have noticed in reading about Jesus that one of his boldest strokes, one of such savage strength and shrewd vision that it still staggers the offended imagination, was to insist publically that his teachings applied to all, even the least—lepers, cripples, blind people, ignorant children, whores and tax collectors and that ilk. He went out of his way to embrace these people, to include them in *his* world. He embraced the rejects of the world. How that must have begged the "establishment"! And he never stopped bugging them. Right there on the cross, dying for keeps (for I don't believe this resurrection nonsense any more, I think it is symbolic), he bugged them some more, forgiving his executioners. What lofty arrogance! And when one of the criminals up there with him had a nice word to say to him, Jesus didn't even wait to ascertain the nature of his crime or his previous police record, he just said: "Today thou shalt be with me in Paradise." The first admission, number one, was this criminal. Even if Paradise is symbolic, that's a wild stroke of genius and you have to give Jesus credit for it. He kept bugging them right to the last. And that is why, Mr. Hefner, I believe that he is still remembered and talked about two thousand years later which is pretty good, I would say, for an obscure son of a Jewish carpenter in a minor community and completely without benefit of all the modern communications *media*. I would venture the guess that Jesus is the best known Jew of all time.

Now, as I have indicated, I accept Jesus as a philosopher and a man among men. I do not think I am wrong in suggesting that there is much in common between his teachings and "The Playboy Philosophy," except of course that we have had 2000 years of progress and evolution since then. Therefore your teaching is bound to be more sophisticated and relevant to Modern Man. Moreover, your writings are not so cryptic and ambiguous as his sayings, at least as they were reported. And finally you have the marvelous advantage of the availability of all the modern forms of communication. Every time you utter a truth *millions* of people know about it.

I humbly propose that you have reached the position where you can afford to take some big risks in offending the "power structure" by demonstrating the universal application of your teachings to all.

What if one of your nymphs or handmaidens were dispatched to bring Joy, palpably, a real presence, to a poor, unknown spastic who believed your gospel? What if she brought him joy and was joyously refreshed herself? It's a thought.

I see where you sent Jo Collins to Viet Nam to bring the message to our fighting men. That was a fine beginning.

I know that you are sincere, and I believe that those girls who share life at The Mansion with you must inevitably also share a measure of your sincerity. Or, if not, then they must, like all disciples, stand in awe of your dedication. It would seem to me that a word from you would make this creative experiment possible. If it didn't work, you could prevent any publicity, depending on me to keep my lips sealed. If it did work out, it could be, within the context of a human interest story, a major parable of the Philosophy. And, who knows? spastics, after being at best pitied and at worst shunned and ignored, might become fashionable, "all the rage," as they used to say.

Trusting in your good sense, good will, and compassionate humanity, I beg to remain, sir, your devoted admirer and disciple.

As ever,
Buck Harper

Dear James Farmer,

You don't know me from The Kingfish, but please rest assured that I am a Soul Brother; and I know you well from many magazines, newspapers, and on the T.V.

I saw your picture in the paper just the other day, where you addressed some group in Washington, D.C., and tried to see if you could get yet another March on Washington underway. I was very pleased to see you are back in the Civil Rights Business.

Man, you are getting fat, though! Fat as a south Georgia hog! I am glad to see that you are doing so well, but you really must try to watch out for all those hot buttered rolls and biscuits and all that fried food on the celebrity banquet circuit. It is one of the burdens of fame. I know this all too well on account of once I, too, was much in demand as an after dinner speaker. My weight zoomed up to well over 200, which is a little on the heavy side for a man with an average frame who stand 5 feet 6 inches tall. Try to be careful. It is easy to put on, but it is as hard to get rid of as a bad habit.

However, I am not writing you to advise you about your weight problem. Frankly, I need your help in solving a little problem of my own. It is a problem that may be of some concern to you and some of your (distinguished) cronies; for through no fault of my own I seem to be doing great harm to the Civil Rights Movement.

Kindly allow me to explain. I have always believed without question in Civil Rights and Welfare. But the truth is that I never had much time to do much about it. This was mainly on account of the fact that, coming from a culturally deprive background (distinctly trashy if truth be known), I have always maintained as my chief aim the acquisition of the largest possible measure of financial independence and security, together, of course, with such evident luxuries and status symbols as might be construed as an outward and visible sign of my inner drives. I offer no apology for my greedy materialism, except to point out that all of it was, of course, merely another sympton of the disease I had contracted as a result of accepting at face value and without question the dubious values which Whitey offered, nay imposed upon me and my brothers and sisters.

From early childhood it was my ruling passion to seek to acquire large sums of money with what may be described as the minimal amount of sweat and strain. In the Deep South as a schoolboy I delivered newspapers and bootleg whiskey all over town. I fought in many a jolly Battle Royal. I liberated many a hubcap and bicycle. And I advanced steadily up the Ladder of Success. Bellhop, pimp, and finally I emerged at the summit as the sole owner of the only black undertaker's parlor in the whole county. I was anxious to meet greater challenges, to try my dormant wings and cleave the smoggy air in the big world above The Line. Moreover, my wife, a simple country girl named Dalmatia, was herself eager to enjoy the greater amenities of urban living. Our departure would have come sooner or later anyway, but was hastened by a slight misunderstanding which developed between myself and the County Sheriff, a misunderstanding involving four slugs from a .38 caliber pistol registered in my name, found in the body of a no-account nigger named W.W. Jesperson who happened to step into the line of fire whilst I was engaged in a public demonstration of the remarkable accuracy and efficiency of this weapon at Mama-and-Bill's Downhome Honky-tonk one dark and rainy night, where we were seeking some shelter from the inclement weather. This fact was disputed by several so-called eyewitnesses who seized upon the occasion, no doubt wishing to rise to prominence upon the leverage of my own declining good fortune. The Sheriff's personal displeasure was increased by the undeniable fact that the late and lamented Woodrow Wilson Jesperson was his second cousin once removed on his father's side of the family. As you know, Mr. Farmer, when matters involving blood relatives arise in the South, Reason doth flee the scene with eyes averted. . . .

When it became all too apparent that the Sheriff, out of a misguided sense of family loyalty, was not inclined to deal with the matter as a simple misdemeanor and just another Saturday night "nigger killing," as it were, then it was obvious that my course of best discretion was to turn northward without undue delay, beating a less than leisurely retreat beyond the jurisdiction of that benighted racist state. I paused only long enough to pack me a suitcase full of money and to demonstrate once again the amazing efficiency of my Smith and Wesson revolver, firing it in the general direction of the outraged and aforesaid County Sheriff. I left the South without hesitation or regret, vowing never to return of my own free will.

Ah! The idle vows and promises of youth . . . !

Once safely ensconced in the fabulous North, I plunged eagerly into the teeming circus of modern city life, becoming in short order something of a specialist, an expert in the problems of distributing rare pharmaceuticals to the needy. Things were going along quite nicely, thank you, and the future looked about as rosy as the rear end of a big-ass baboon, when two things occurred which suddenly plunged my fortunes to their very nadir. The first was the premature birth of the twins. You see, James, Dalmatia was a great enthusiast of T.V. Quiz Shows in those days. She hoped to make up for her lack of formal education in that way, which was a laudable aim to be sure. She had proceeded to make a kind of household god of young Charles Van Doren. His picture, clipped out of newspapers and magazine, was everywhere one looked. And she quoted him constantly. It was her firm intention that, should we be fortunate enough to be blessed with male offspring, our son would be named after her hero. Believe me, I was fully aware of the absurdity of this desire, but I had no wish to increase the level of her anxiety and discomfort during pregnancy. And I remained ever cognizant of the fact that Dalmatia was an extremely strong-willed woman, able to exert her will by dint of her not inconsiderable, altogether robust and energetic person, standing as she did well over six feet barefoot and weight, dripping wet, not less than 210 pounds, and possessing a truly remarkable coordination of hand and eye which allowed her to dispatch objects and missiles of all kinds, large or small, toward any intended target with a speed and accuracy which surely equalled, if indeed it did not surpass, the celebrated pitching prowess of Satchel Paige.

Therefore, I grinned and resigned myself to the fate of having a son whose given name would be Charles Van Doren.

However, when the tragic scandal broke, Dalmatia's reaction was instant, immediate, and damn near tragic. She went into labor and I feared the worst— the worst that I could imagine, that is. Considering the limitations of the human imagination, how could I ever have conceived that the results would be twin boys, all too healthy, though untimely? How could I have dreamed that in her outrage she would insist on naming the twins *Payola* and *Channel Six?*

However, even before I had a chance to recover from the shock of this startling revelation, I found myself in more serious, not to say dire straits. An envious and unsuccessful competitor in the business of pharmaceutical distribution, out of the depths of his frustration, malice and paranoia, denounced me to the fuzz. Thereupon ensued a series of unhappy circumstances and misunderstandings which, had they not involved my own life, liberty and eager pursuit of the bluebird of happiness, might have been deemed truly hilarious. By following the advice of my counsel, whom I trusted without question, never suspecting the extent to which he was willing to demonstrate his professional incompetence and ineptitude, I soon found myself languishing in a prison cell. It was a condition which I managed to accept stoically enough; for there were some positive advantages, not the least being that my incarceration protected me from the wrath and ravings of Dalmatia whose embittered disillusionment, commencing with the exposure of "dishonest" T.V. Quiz Shows, aided and abetted by the unexpected arrival of twins, had now grown and reached cosmic proportions. King Lear raging in the storm against the cruel absurdities of Injustice had nothing on Dalmatia. Indeed, I should be inclined to give her the edge in sheer volume and theatricality. And whatever she may possibly have lacked in elegance of style and sublimity of language was more than compensated for by the surging power of her quaint folk idiom, bold and primal, projected by a voice which could have drowned out all sirens, horns, whistles and signals greeting a great ocean liner on its maiden voyage.

In short, Mr. Farmer, I was able to accept the ordinary deprivations of prison life as part of the price I must pay for a respite of peace and quiet; and, indeed, it was not long before the thundering resonance of her rhetoric had faded away even from the chambers of my memory.

This is not to imply, however, that everything was coming up roses. Scarcely had I adjusted to prison life when there appeared on the scene, like twin dark clouds on the horizon, two laconic minions of the Law from my native state, bearing with them a warrant for my arrest and, indeed, all the requisite papers to instigate my extradition promptly upon the completion of my sentence. Needless to say, I took a dim view of that. But I surmised that they had me by the short hairs, as the saying goes. I was ready to resign myself to a tragic finale when, lo and behold!, I received my first lesson in Northern Politics. The liberal Governor of the State, bearer of a proud, if not to say honored name, a man with ambitions for higher office and possibly the support, if not the stature for same, looked into his heart and saw with a flash of inspiration the homely truth of all my arguments, arguments which, I must confess, I had advanced without a *soupçon* of real hope or conviction, but rather in an almost Pavlovian reflex and as a matter of pure form and good manners; for it did seem that the nicety of *some sort of argument* was expected of me. I was well nigh amazed when the Governor accepted without question my assertion that the whole thing was a great big "frame." He gave credence to my plea that since all us darkies look alike anyway, we must accept this as a possibly honest mistake on the part of the red-neck enforcers of the medieval laws of the feudal area widely known as the asshole of America.

For which statement he honored my integrity and purity of heart. But that was a mistake and, honest or not, we should not (the Governor and I!) permit this charade to continue without definite clarification and rectification, especially in view of the incontestable fact that the instant I crossed the Potomac and headed into the Faulknerian heart of darkness in that unregenerate region of chaos and old night, I should be subjected to all manner of unconstitutional, unspeakable, unmentionable, cruel and unusual punishments as a matter of course.

Acting then, with boldness and wisdom, the Governor got me off the hook by announcing that he would refuse to honor their extradition papers. And with this timely action he won for himself no little public approbation. I therefore responded with payment in kind. When a spontaneous meeting between the Governor and myself was arranged, gentlemen of the Fourth Estate being present to the point of profusion, I knew what was required of me and I performed my duties to the best of my ability.

I fell upon my knees at the feet of the Governor. I looked heavenward and rolled my eyes with touching reverence and sincerity. I intoned in a voice worthy of the late Dusty Fetcher: "The Lord be praised, Mr. Governor, sir! You have done saved this poor old darkie's life! The Lord bless you and make you the President on the next go-round!"

Dabbing at tears with his monogrammed hankderchief, the Governor then told me to rise. He turned to the assembled group and made a few remarks about how They (meaning me, I reckon), despite all the pressure, anxieties, and hypocrisies of modern life, They had never fallen victim to the headlock and stranglehold of rigid inhibitions and could still somehow express themselves and their feelings with a directness and immediacy like that of divinely inspired little children, uncorrupted, trailing clouds of glory, etc., etc., etc. He allowed as how there was a lesson for all of us in this. He pointed out how We (me again!) had not only made a significant, though largely unrecognized and mostly unrewarded, contribution to American life, but also that in the shining jubilee days to come, sooner or not later, God willing, of full equality, brotherhood and love, We should surely be seen by all as the salvation of the nation from its guilty past and unredeemed present etc., etc., etc. He thereupon cited a few important names such as Ralph Bunche, Sammy Davis, Jr., Nat Turner, Ethel Waters, Sonny Liston, and James Meredith.

And then, save for the briefest of winks which we exchanged, the occasion was terminated and we filed out solemnly, he to his waiting limousine and I to my prison cell, while a Boy Scout Drum and Bugle Corps manfully tackled the stirring strains of "Marching Through Georgia."

After a decent but not prolonged interval, the Governor's Parole Board considered my application for parole and granted it with efficiency and dispatch. Taking the normal precaution of changing my name, I set off at once for the city of Rochester. I planned to arrive there not without some ceremony, but unannounced and unexpected. For Dalmatia, you see, not anticipating my return for some years to come, had moved to that city together with the twins and a colored gentleman friend by the name of T. Roosevelt Jackson. The latter was a Pullman Porter of some distinction who had offered his services as a surrogate father for the twins when Dalmatia evinced the desire to protect them from growing up under the pernicious influences of an exclusively matriarchal environment. And they were as happy as a bunch of rabbits in a vegetable patch, it seemed, at least until I appeared upon the scene.

Realizing that a little humor, like a little wine, is good for the stomach and has a tendency to lighten a heavy heart, I paused at a store specializing in theatrical costumes; and there I purchased the classic convict's striped suit, including the hat, and a large shrill police whistle. Having ascertained the location of the apartment, I waited until darkness had fallen upon the city, then donned my costume and slipped into the alley next to the apartment house. I blew vigorously upon the whistle a few times. Then I mounted the fire escape with stealthy care, and made a dramatic entrance through the bedroom window, puffing and blowing as if the police were only a few steps behind me.

As a comic gesture it was well-timed, well-executed, if I may say so, and effective. Neither Dalmatia nor Mr. Jackson suffered anything more than a severe shock. Here I hasten to assure you that it was never my intention to test their susceptibility or resistance to heart attack, stroke, apoplexy or any other common form of seizure. In truth and in fact I had not intended to frighten them at all, merely to amuse; but when I observed Mr. Roosevelt's large white eyeballs positively fixed, indeed as though mesmerized, upon the small and sufficiently authentic-looking water pistol which I had also had the wit to purchase and was now waving wildly, I could not resist the obvious and obligatory *denouement*. Placing the pistol an inch from the wide bridge of his nose and allowing those amazing eyes to widen and whiten beyond all expectation, I paused, then squeezed the trigger and squirted him fully and firmly.

"Stay loose everybody!" I shouted cheerfully. "Fat Daddy is home for good!"

Since I needed time to readjust myself to all the confusions of freedom, it was agreed that Mr. Roosevelt Jackson would continue to live in the apartment just as before. And he most graciously consented to continue to pay the rent and other miscellaneous bills and expenses as he had done during my enforced absence, at least until I felt myself fully recovered from my traumatic experience and able to resume a more active and positive role in society. A very persuasive argument in support of this civilized solution in our domestic dilemma was the fact that there was a Mrs. Roosevelt Jackson living in Newark, New Jersey; a rather primitive personality, it seemed, indeed terrifying in her authentic simplicity, one who wore a bandana turban, smoked a pipe and dipped snuff, was fond of blackeyed peas and turnip greens, one of that dwindling number of *grandes dames* who will draw their last breath on earth with a superbly keen straight razor always within easy reach. Mr. Roosevelt Jackson had arranged to spend roughly half of his time in Newark and, for various reasons, not all of them entirely selfish, he had not yet deemed that the time was propitious to apprise his wife of the existence of a second domicile and family at the other end of his run. And so it was readily agreed that all would be forgiven at once and perhaps even eventually forgotten, provided, of course, that Mr. Roosevelt Jackson would continue in his present role as an ungrudging and bountiful provider and that, as a testament of his good faith, he would hereafter sleep on the Hide-a-Bed in the living room. Mr. Roosevelt Jackson accepted this solution with alacrity. He was, above all, a most reasonable man.

This situation might have gone on indefinitely. I observed that Jackson *was* a reasonable man, because, I am sad to have to report, a few brief months later he sloughed off the burden of this mortal coil when a serious debate over the ownership of a pair of loaded dice was settled in favor of the opposition by a double barrel 12 gauge shotgun. Which was loaded with buckshot and fired at close range. This incident happened to occur in Newark, and thus it was some time before the unhappy tidings reached us. In perfect innocence, blissfully unaware of his sudden demise, Dalmatia and I and the twins continued to live in the style to which, through his good will and natural generosity, we had become quite gracefully accustomed. Thus when bills and payments due and overdue descended upon us without warning and with the mechanical rapidity of Job's messengers, I was (to put it mildly) not fully prepared for the exigencies of the situation. Of course I immediately applied for Unemployment Compensation and Welfare, but even so, the style of our living began to change dramatically. And I began to be obsessed with our predicament. Prufrock-like, I began to imagine that the total of my days and ways, my life, could be measured out not in coffee spoons, but in a steady stream of repossessed appliances, furniture, clothing and all the miscellaneous items which make for Gracious Living and The Good Life. I was haunted by a vision of us all living in an empty apartment rather like some caveman's domicile, no food in the cupboard, no furniture, not a stitch of clothing or a stick of kindling left. And it is possible that this pitiful vision might well have come to pass had it not been for the celebrated Rochester Riots (oh, long before Watts!) during which I became deeply involved in the Civil Rights Movement at last.

It is a complex story, Mr. Farmer, like all accounts of insight, illumination, and sudden conversion. Yet I shall, of necessity, endeavor to achieve a kind of brevity by presenting the bare facts in sequence and in outline form.

(a) During the first day of the Riots, Dalmatia and the twins were furious with me. All the neighbors except us were watching the Riots on T.V. Our T.V. set had recently been repossessed.

(b) By the second day, their fury mounting and my resistance wearing thin, and hearing rumors of amazing bargains to be had in nearby local stores, I promised to venture forth and try to get a T.V. set.

(c) At an appliance store I found and swiftly liberated a very fine color T.V. set, a first-class piece of merchandise, at the cost, however, of a near skull fracture from a blow by the loaded cane of an elderly colored lady who insisted that she had a prior claim on it. I tried vainly to explain to her that I was only saving her from disappointment, that the set was very large and heavy and so was she. She couldn't have carried it across the sidewalk. It was only in self-defense that I knocked her to her knees with a JFK memorial bookend.

(d) I headed home proudly with the set. My own head, though unbroken, was bleeding profusely.

(e) Suddenly I found myself surrounded by reporters and photographers and T.V. cameras. They ran in yowling packs and mobs and constituted a clear and present danger throughout the Riots. I promptly put down the set and used it to stand upon, hoping to have a little more stature on television. Didn't the late Alan Ladd often do likewise in love scenes?

(f) The reporters seemed to be under the impression that my head injury was the result of police brutality. Rather than waste their precious time and my dwindling energy in an attempt to correct this misapprehension, I fell into the spirit of the occasion. And I made a brief, pithy, and eloquent speech.

(g) I picked up my set and toted it the rest of the way home.

(h) I plugged it in and turned it on just in time to learn that I had now become a Civil Rights Leader.

(i) That's all there was to it.

Those were happy days that followed, Mr. Farmer, brief as they were. I developed a sincere interest in the Movement, an interest which, may I say, remains unflagging and undiminished to this very day in spite of an unpleasant misunderstanding which arose following an audit of certain funds which I was administering on behalf of the Poverty Program. Charity, like Poverty, begins at home, and I waged a vigorous campaign until the audit made it necessary for me, like the proverbial Arabs, to strike my tent and haul ass.

It was not without sadness that I departed from the city of Rochester. It was not without regret that I was forced to leave Dalmatia and the twins behind without word one of explanation.

Taking with me only the pink Cadillac convertible, which had been until then, one might say, my badge and staff of authority in the Poverty Program, I fled southward at high speed, disguised as an African chieftain and taking full advantage of a set of diplomatic license plates which I had exercised the foresight to acquire in advance.

South? you ask. Why South, Mr. Farmer?

My long range plan was to make my way to the Old Country. According to the best available sources, the situation over there remains politically and socially less than stable. Those poor folks over there have got their hands full. It was my belief that a man with my experience, talents, and special interests, might be of real service to the African locals as they moved from trees and bush into a modern life style.

And surely, I told myself, even should my poor contributions come to naught, no real harm would result from trying. Surely I couldn't screw things up any worse than they already are. In short, Mr. Farmer, Africa seemed like a positively heavenly place to be.

First of all, however, it was necessary for me to run the risk of returning to my old hometown and stomping ground in order to avail myself of certain contingency funds, known but to God and me and resting safe and calm at the bottom of an old well. Imagine my surprise and consternation when I discovered, not the old familiar, unpainted tumbledown shack we had all known and loved, but instead row after row of brick ranch style houses, a subdivision indistinguishable from a thousand like it across the land. It was no longer Black Bottom. It was now Lamumba Gardens, a place where Black men in Bermuda shorts, aprons, and chef's caps were busily imitating the inimitable Mr. Charley by cooking old animal flesh over hot coals in their back yards. Then try to imagine my intense relief when I discovered—*the old well was still there!* It had been preserved, oaken bucket and all, as a kind of monument, a sample of authentic local color as it were, a symbol of a way of life which had already gone with the wind.

I waited patiently until the last lights went out and the last stereo playing the music of Andre Kostelanetz and Leonard Bernstein was replaced by the darkness and silence of Lamumba Gardens. Muffled and hooded in my chieftain's robes, I tiptoed cautiously to the well. I dropped a pebble and rejoiced at the sound of a satisfactory splash. I uncoiled a length of rope and was busily preparing myself for my dangerous descent when I heard a twig snap and then a rustle like the rustle of cloth nearby. I froze, becoming one with the night. Somewhere a mockingbird sang. Far off a dog howled. A freight train rattled away in the distance.

"DeLay?"

Recognizing the hoarse familiar tone and timbre of the County Sheriff, I remained motionless, holding my breath, hearing the pounding of my heart.

"You, DeLay!"

"Dano! Baki nali piccolo!" I replied in my best African accent.

"Don't shit me, you ugly black bastard!" he said, and not without a certain kind of warmth and affection. "What the hell are you doing here?"

"Getting a drink of water, Sheriff, sir," I answered.

"Put up your hands and come here before I ventilate your carcass," he suggested, turning on his flashlight.

The upshot of this chance encounter was not altogether unfavorable. True, I had to give up my dreams of an African adventure together with the funds which might have made that pilgrimage possible. But the old Sheriff had mellowed over the years. He acted in a manner which I took to be emotionally mature and highly reasonable. I must add that he was scrupulously honest in carrying out his part of the arrangement. He not only let me go free, and only a little bit bruised, but also he was instrumental in helping me to secure my next position. And, exactly as he had agreed, the very next corpse that showed up in the County Morgue bearing the label "Unknown Nigger" was named after me. He saw it (me) buried with decent, though modest ceremony. He then officially notified the aggrieved widow so that, sad and forlorn as she may have been, she could still collect on my life insurance policy. And with a brisk stroke of his Bic ballpoint pen he closed the books officially on my case.

In the little colored cemetery in my hometown there is a simple granite headstone under the shade of an old pecan tree. It bears my name and an accurate quotation from a famous poem by William Blake, exactly as I requested. Whenever I pass through there now, I take time off to visit the cemetery, to leave a little bouquet of flowers, and to sit in the shade of that pecan tree and meditate upon the transistory values of this world. It is relaxing, not to say inspiring, to sit and look upon your own tomb, knowing that when you are ready you can get up and cut out, feeling good and feeling fine.

Until recently, Mr. Farmer, I was employed by Little David Enterprises, Inc., as a part time Preacher, Public Relations Expert, and General Handyman. I do not wish to impose upon your time and patience unduly by discussing in detail this recent phase of my career except to say that it was at once lucrative and satisfying work. My position with Little David Enterprises itself is now terminated because Little David Enterprises itself is now defunct and *kaput* due to the death by violence of Little David himself. Little David was an ofay midget who passed himself off as an inspired child evangelist. He was murdered by one of his white employees in a dispute over some missing funds. At any rate, we had us a lively and swinging group there, hustling the yokels, and it was good gravy while it lasted. In addition to singing and dancing, setting up tents, etc., I had several specialties. One of my most successful acts, which I performed whenever we were dealing with basically hostile and backward, underprivileged and disadvantaged rural, white, redneck, peckerwood groups, was a soul-stirring account of how I found Jesus and was saved and left a fine, high-paying position in the Movement as *bona fide* Civil Rights Leader; cast the dust off my feet to serve God and to expose the Movement for the Godless, atheistic, morbid, pinko, perverse, Communist-inspired, destructive greedy Thing it really is, admitting out loud that it is almost exclusively controlled by vicious and homosexual Jews who can't speak English without an accent, whose sole aim in life is to repay centuries of largely imaginary slights and petty grudges in the present currency of real trouble; composed also of lecherous, ignorant, libidinous, syphillitic, lazy and shiftless Darkies who do not care if school keeps or the sun comes up or not, whose aim may well appear merely to avoid all kinds and forms of work, but whose real and true purpose is to gratify their jungle lusts upon the defenseless bodies of Whitey's wives, daughters and other female relatives, thus polluting forever the bloodstream of the race, and also, in passing, to burn down Whitey's houses, stores, courthouses and private property, to defecate upon the graves of his parents and ancestors, to wipe themselves on The Stars and Stripes and to give the pledge of allegiance to the Hammer and Sickle.

By the way, Mr. Farmer, these insane and outrageous notions became all too easy to make credible thanks to the big mouths of such Soul Brothers as LeRoi Jones, James Baldwin, Huey Newton, Floyd McKissick, Lincoln Theodore Perry, etc., and the Black Power cries of that ivy-leaguer in blackface—Stokely Carmichael. Do you suppose that is his real name? I think the young man should be advised that though it may be a full and rich name—even better and fuller and richer than a name like George Plimpton—with dignity and verbal texture, and even though it has a certain kind of elegance in print and is memorable as well, it has certain defects for his particular line of work. A bit languid. Moreover it is a name which is difficult to shout with passion and enthusiasm without sounding like a street vendor or some kind of nut. If he plans, as he keeps saying, to overthrow the Government, he better come up with something better than Stokely Carmichael to do it with.

Anyway, I want to say here and now that I am not in the least ashamed of having earned some bread by putting the bad mouth on the Movement. Consider for one moment, with compassion, those poor, ignorant, confused, deluded and rejected rednecks to whom I addressed myself. They sincerely believe all that shit anyway whether I say so or not. Far from stirring them up, I believe I may be judged to have performed a useful social service. It gives any man (if you care to dignify those pasty-faced, white-assed baboons with the term) no peace of mind or serenity to realize that his beliefs are merely the distorted fabrication of his own fevered imagination and have not one ounce of objective evidence to support them. That way leads straight to madness and desperation. My evidently outrageous rhetoric may have made it possible for these otherwise lost souls to think, however briefly, that they were sane and at peace with themselves at last. A man who is at peace with himself is more inclined to be at peace with others. Dig? A non-violent white ape. I dig non-violence as much as you cats. I dig it as much as the late Reverend Doctor Martin Luther King, Ph.D.

But enough of philosophy! Neither you nor I, Mr. Farmer, will ever solve these cosmic problems. To more pressing and practical matters. . . . Now that Little David Enterprises, Inc., has folded, I have been asked by a group of fairly distinguished and well-to-do white apes (albeit they are only one generation away from hookworm, pellagra, cornbread and molasses, the sturdy outhouse and the *Sears and Roebuck Catalogue*—not a decadent blueblood in the bunch) to devote my full time to the Lecture Circuit, giving my heart-felt lecture—"Why I Left the So-Called Civil Rights Movement: An Objective Appraisal"—to interested groups not only here in Hicksville but all over this broad land, wherever the Soul Brothers constitute a sufficient percentage of the population to cause crime rates to soar, Welfare rolls to grow and expand like Yoghurt, V.D. and illegitimacy rates to take off on the charts like guided missiles (straight up), schools to deteriorate, and day-to-day life to become about as safe as an old Tarzan movie; in short, Mr. Farmer, practically everywhere except maybe Maine and North Dakota, which are a bit chilly for the Brothers. The pecuniary possibilities of this line of work, just at this latest time of the "backlash," etc., are not without interest. And I confess, moreover, to a certain understandable professional pride in my growing skill at the art of manipulating mass emotions. Do you know that, while addressing a rally of the infamous Ku Klux Klan recently, I received a ten minute standing ovation? Of course, it was in the big middle of somebody's cow pasture and there wasn't any place for them to sit down; but, be that as it may, it was still a tribute to my performance.

Before I accept this attractive proposition, however, it behooves me to seek out the advice and counsel of some Soul Brother I truly admire. There is no one among the current crop of Civil Right Leaders for whom I feel such admiration and respect, with whom I feel such a strong and innate bond of fellowship as you, sir. I have always marvelled at your instant eloquence and your adroit logical dexterity. They got to jump out of bed early to get anything on you, baby! That's why I am so glad that you are back in action again. For a while I thought maybe they had faked you right out of your size 14 shoes. But here you are, back again, swinging and jiving and militating, and, as always, I am beholden to you from afar both as an influence and an example.

Please give my problem some brief consideration.

Is it wrong for me to continue in the direction I am now headed?

If so, do you think you could see your way clear to finding me a spot in the Movement again, preferably on the executive, administrative level? If you can't swing that, my second choice would be something in the U.S. Government. I will work for practically anybody except Adam Clayton Powell. He may be free and easy with the taxpayer's bread, but somehow I continue to doubt his sincerity.

I look forward, then, to hearing from you at your leisure and convenience.
   Sincerely yours,
   DeLay Rainey

Dear Truman Capote,
 This letter has got to be . . .
 Wait a minute. Begin again.

Dear Gordon Lish,

Just a quick personal note. A word or two of explanation.

Surely you remember that you came to Hollins College in Virginia in June of 1970. And you may well remember (other people do in case you don't) that while you were there you came to an afternoon reading I gave in the Green Drawing Room of the aforesaid college. During said reading (to the best of my recollection and the recollections of others) I read aloud several of these poison pen letters (*including this one to Truman Capote*), and you, sir, in fine fettle, laughed out loud and conspicuously. After the reading you came directly up to the podium (I was still standing there like a dummy) and told me you had very much enjoyed the reading (or some words to that effect). And you asked me if, acting as the fiction editor of *Esquire* magazine, you might have a look at them with a view to possible publication of the same.

Well, sir, I told you that would be really swell, indeed wonderful, but that these letters had been already published in the pages of some rather obscure (read: *utterly unknown*) literary magazines. Therefore, I concluded, they were ineligible for consideration by *Esquire*. You, however, assured me that such was not the case. Or that's how I sure enough remember it. . . .

So, to make a long and typical story short, the pieces were duly submitted to you. And a few months later, just as I suspected but still was green enough to hope otherwise, back came the manuscripts, somewhat the worse for wear (one batch of pages was stuck together with something dark and sticky with a very faint odor of muscatel; did you ever drink muscatel, Gordon, and spill some on my manuscript?), together with a note from some secretary—I'm sure you were much too busy to write—informing me that, as a matter of policy, *Esquire* does not publish things that have already been published elsewhere.

Just like I told you.

Oh well.

I just shrugged and forgot about it.

No, that's not quite true. In private I winced as if somebody had slashed me with a horsewhip. Because it always hurts, no matter how experienced you are in the pain of rejection. I winced and inwardly I cursed your name and wished (justly) bad things upon you and all your loved ones and your kinfolk and your friends, if any. And then, in public, in the presence of *my* friends and loved ones and kinfolk, I shrugged it all off with a smile and said something casual and dumb. Like: "Win a few, lose a few."

And then (honestly), for all practical purposes, I just forgot it.

Imagine my surprise when I walked into Borders' Bookstore in Ann Arbor, sometime during spring 1983, and found your new (first) novel on the stands— *Dear Mr. Capote*. I flipped through the pages and read the bullshit on the book jacket and laughed a little at the blurbs; for I knew these people and why they were saying what they did. Then I (honestly) thought: "Well, it is nice to have been a minor influence in the life of Gordon Lish. Being an influence is a very positive thing. And he has been able to turn a very small, sketchy idea into a whole big novel. Good for him. Creativity is a positive thing too.

True, as an editor, Gordon's reputation is as a ruthless cutter of everything down to the thin and minimal essence. I mean, look what he did with Barry Hannah's stuff. But here he has done just the opposite. He has taken a thin and minimal piece and fattened it up into a fullsize book. Funny, isn't it?, how the critical-editorial impulse so often contradicts the creative . . ." Etc. Etc. Etc.

No hard feelings. Honestly. Not an ounce of malice.

Then I happened to hear you interviewed by Bob Edwards on "The Morning Show" on National Public Radio. Nice long interview, Gordo. Some good and clever salesmanship on your part, too. Frankly, even I was interested in reading the thing by the time you finished. There was, however, one small problem for me. Edwards asked you about where you got the idea, about influences. I was all ready, Gordon, to receive just a teeny-tiny nod of credit. I could have used a teeny-tiny little old nod of recognition and credit at that moment in my otherwise largely uneventful life. The least acknowledgement would have pleased me beyond measure and telling. And you had your chance, too, Lish! Chance came early in the interview. Here's how it went. (May I quote you directly and exactly? Thank you, I think I will do just that.)

BOB EDWARDS
   Where did this come from?
GORDON LISH
   Oh, God! (laughs) Not from my head, I hope. That's a pip of a question, Bob! I think it came from the notion to make a design and to make one as intricately as I could. Then the question was what to lay into the design. I began with a voice, I suppose, a sound I had in my head, a way a fellow talks.

Gosh, Gordon, there are several places in the course of that reply where you could have generously slipped me in there without really losing anything except maybe a little bit of momentum. I felt a little let down. Mildly pissed off.

Then somebody sent me a clipping out of *The New York Post*, a page-6 story all about your troubles at Columbia University. You know the one. You probably saw it. If not, please see "Writing Prof Stole My Stuff, Says Columbia Writing Student," *New York Post*, Friday, September 16, 1983, p. 6. Some student claimed you stole a lot of stuff from him for *Dear Mr. Capote*. And in the course of the article it turned out that the student had taken the stuff, that he alleges you stole from him, from Jack Abbott's lawyer, from a letter of Abbott to Mailer telling all about the murder of the waiter, etc. It is all pretty confusing to us country boys. The best part, for my money, is where you are quoted as telling the *New York Post* reporter (Nicholson was his name, wasn't it?) that he better be careful, that he didn't know who he was dealing with etc. etc. Or words to that effect. I liked that because it shows a certain unsuspected innocence on your part, Gordon, at least where the Press is concerned. You don't try to threaten and intimidate *reporters*, Gordon! They will get your ass if you do. All they have to do is quote you. As he did. The other good part was the end where he quoted you again as saying that you didn't need to read things about crazy people to know how they acted, that you had been in mental institutions twice yourself. (Or words to that effect.) That was slick. Because neither he nor you explain that further. Probably you meant you had *visited* mental institutions a couple of times, dropped in to see buddies from *Esquire* or Knopf, maybe. But the way it was in the papers, somebody might possibly infer you had actually been a patient a couple of times. Perish the thought! But it was funny. You'll have to admit that, Gordo, old buddy.

Anyhow . . .

When I read the story about you in *The New York Post*, I felt (honestly) sorry for you, concerned about you. Even if you are innocent, pure as the driven snow, it is a very embarrassing thing to be accused of stealing stuff from a *student*. That's a bad rap even if you beat it. Know what I mean?

By the way, how did all that work out, anyway? I never heard or read any more about it. I hope you cleared it up and cleared your good name.

Anyway, I figure we are even. I was only a very minor influence, if any at all. And your novel is probably a whole lot better than my little poison pen letter. It's bound to be. I hope you will understand, though, that I have no intention of actually reading your novel. Let it be. I wish you well, Lish. I hope you have a long and happy life. I hope your students and your colleagues, in teaching and in publishing, respect you for the kind of guy you really are.

And if you need any little teeny-tiny nudge to get started on your next novel, please feel free, indeed feel *welcome*, to use anything of mine you want to. We are all in this together, Gordon, and people should be more helpful to each other. At least that's they way I feel about it. How do you feel?

Sincerely,
George Garrett

Dear Truman Capote,

This letter has got to be a pretty short one on account of we aren't allowed to send out but so many pages and only one personal letter to "the outside" each month. And this is it. The wife and the snot-nosed kids can just wait until next month. Besides she can't read too good anyhow. And she is probably still puzzling out the last one.

I'll come straight to the point. Me and my cellmate, Jethroe Pickens, have read your hilarious best-seller *In Cold Blood* and we think it is wonderful. You really have learned how to write good. I don't know who taught you but whoever he is he deserves high praise. We have a lot of time to read around here and both me and Jethroe have read every book you have written. Frankly, until you wrote *In Cold Blood* I thought you were just a silly phoney. I can say that because I know that you are not a phoney now.

You done a good job with that Clutter Caper. It was as good as anything

Dear Mr. Garrett,   8/21/85, 11:30 pm

I'm sorry to have taken so long with the illustrations. Now I'm "burning the midnight oil", as they say, to finish them. Part of my procrastinating has had to do with the money (nuf sed). But another inhibiting thing is, frankly, the writing itself. Some of it is quite raunchy, to say the least. The drawings the text seems to solicit are not ones I'm very proud of. My mother asked to read the ms. & I didn't know what to do. Have you shown this stuff to your family?

I also worry about the repercussions. Suppose one fine day I send a novel off to Gordon Lish at Knopf (Working title: Come On In, The Isolation's Splendid!) Will he make me suffer as your fellow-traveler, your accomplice?

105

I ever read in *True Detective* which is my favorite. Maybe now that you have proved you know how to write they will let you write for that magazine. I sure hope so. They might think *In Cold Blood* is a fluke. They may want to wait and see if you can write anything else that's worth a shit. Even so they'll come around, sooner or later.

Be that as it may me and Jethroe laughed our ass off all the way thru *In Cold Blood*. Hair on the walls! Whee-doggie! You are practically a soul brother. I mean, if you hadn't of made good as a writer you'd probably be in here with us. By the way, if you ever do end up doing time or a stretch in any jail, just mention my name or Jethroe's and the guys won't pick on you just because you are a little sissy. We take care of our own kind of folks.

Anyway, I'm about to run out of space, so I better get to the point. It's Jethroe's idea but he can't waste his letter on you. He's got to write his lawyer about an appeal. The whole thing is, Jethroe has a deal to offer. One of these days, one way or the other, me and Jethroe are getting out of this "Fascist pesthole," as Jethroe calls it for a joke. When we do we will have to do something. Jethroe has this proposition. He knows of this French Canadian farm family away to hell and gone out in the Gaspe peninsula. They are Catholic and very religious. They got fourteen kids including two sets of twins. All the kids are good looking and sweet and the old man is a hardy fisherman. What we will do is drop in out of nowhere and wipe them out. Fourteen, Mr. Capote! And then we will drift around, doing whatever you tell us to do so it will be a good book. Then, when the time is ripe, you can "solve" the case and write it all up and make another pot of money. Jethroe has it all figured how we can beat the rap on appeal. He says that Earl Warren is the criminal's best friend. He wants to put Earl Warren right up there with St. Dismas.

All we want out of the whole deal is 10% of the action, split between us. Which is not much to ask. You probably pay your agent that much anyway. Just give us the 10% your agent would have gotten and tell him if he has any bitch to make he can negotiate with me and Jethroe.

I wish I could send you our picture. But you can take my word for it. I am uglier and meaner than Dick Hickcock. I will be the "heavy." Jethroe is prettier and even more interesting pathetic than Perry Smith. You would like him. He is the best cellmate I ever had. And we both have tattoos and everything.

Just give the word, Mr. Capote, and we'll take care of all the rest of it. You can count on us.

> Yours truly,
> Al Finnoccio

P.S. Is Capote an Italian name? I am Italian myself and I'm not ashamed to admit it.
> A.F.

Dear Ursula Andress,

As a woman myself, I can certainly appreciate your remarks that they quoted in the *Parade* magazine a few Sundays back. I took them down because they are so true, where you said that "Around the corner there is always some other girl—prettier, smarter, better legs and younger. Always younger. And you know how changeable men are . . . beasts!"

I couldn't have said it better myself if they had asked me. Not that they ever will, for I am not a world-famous and glamorous movie star, as you may have already guessed. I am only an ordinary, typical American housewife trying to do the best that she can with the gifts that God has given her.

I see by the articles that you are having troubles with *your* husband too, and I can understand how mixed up and all you must surely feel. It's none of my business and I would never dream of butting in where I am not invited; but if you ask me, I think you are well rid of him. I never liked him when he was trying to be a movie star. I always felt *he* was a "creep," as the children say in their slang. And he certainly did not raise his rating in my estimation when he took out his camera and took your picture—without stitch one on!—and then actually sold those pictures to *The Playboy Magazine*.

I better explain. *The Playboy* is not the type of a lewd magazine I would be caught dead reading. I stick to my Bible and *Good Housekeeping*. But my oldest boy, Holiday (born on Labor Day) he is passing thru Puberty and I have to keep a sharp watch on him so that he does not ruin his health and rot his brain and end up going to hell. I have caught him "in the act" many times and punished him severely, but that did not seem to be any good. So I have tried my best, on the advice of our preacher, to remove all temptation from the house. Imagine my surprise to find a copy of *The Playboy*, the one with your pictures in it, hidden between the mattress and the springs of Holiday's bed. Naturally I took it to my husband Bernard, who goes by his initials B.O. And there never was a better name for him. He sweats like a horse and hates to take a bath and since he is an automobile mechanic this creates some problems. But I guess everybody has their problems.

Anyway, B.O. did not take the matter seriously. I showed him the magazine and asked him to do his duty and punish Holiday for me. I was surprised when he didn't give me any argument. He'll usually argue about anything. And there he was in his easy chair with a can of beer in his hand and his favorite show, *The Flintstones*, on the T.V. He put down his beer can and got up and started down the hall with the "evidence" in his hand, headed for Holiday's room. Here is what happened. I hope you will excuse me if I have to use some bad words, but I want to put them down the way they were spoken and that's the way old B.O. is, anyway—crude.

He jerked open Holiday's door and I was worried that he might be too severe with the boy.

Hey Holiday, he said.

Yassuh.

You little pr--k! You thought you was pretty f--king smart hiding this s--t under the motherf---ing mattress, didn't you?

And Holiday lowers his eyes and says he sure enough didn't think I'd lift up the mattress on account of my bad back.

And B.O. says, referring to *me* mind you, That ole b---h will pry into anything and it's f--king time you learn it, you ignorant little s--t-a-s!

Yassuh.

I am going to teach you a lesson, you t--d.

Yassuh.

I am going to take this here magazine away from you and keep it my own self, B.O. says. Finders keepers, losers weepers. That is the law around here.

Yassuh.

You f--king -a- well better believe it. Maybe that will learn you to be careful the next time you try and hide something from you mother, who is a sneaky c--t!

That is enough for you to get an idea of the cross I have to bear. I have given up trying to improve B.O.'s language. I try to ignore it.

Then B.O. took the magazine and put it under his pillow. He stated to me if I attempted to remove it or he ever came home and found it gone he would do various painful and unmentionable things to me. And that is where he keeps it to this day.

Therefore I feel as though I almost know you like a member of the family, especially because, thru no particular fault of your own, I have had to share the affections of my son and my husband with you. I bear you no grudge, however. I only wanted to explain how it was that I ever came across those pictures your husband took of you "in the raw" and then had the nerve to sell to a magazine.

I see in the same article where he says they paid you 15 thousand dollars for permission to use them. That is a lot of money, but I tell you I wouldn't let them have my picture like that for 15 *million* dollars, and that is a fact. Not that they will ever ask me, but I am ready in case they do.

I do sympathize with your worries about getting old and all. I am older than you are and have had a pretty hard life, what with one thing and another, so I know what it means. I never was what you would call a beauty, but I was always neat and clean and had a clear complexion and a nice smile. And some people said I had a nice figure when I was a young girl. Over the years care and worry and sickness and the children and old "Father Time" have taken their toll. Of course I did not have as much to lose as you do, but, then, nobody can lose any more than what they have got, can they? You will probably have a better life than I have, and I sure hope so, but anyway sooner or later you will have many of the same experiences I have had. You may be able to keep from being pregnant and having to work too hard and all, but no one can hide forever from old Father Time. So you, too, will have to get used to wrinkles and gray hair. But that is not all there is to getting old. Your muscles give out and get soft and flabby. Your bowels and other intestinal organs begin to give you trouble. Likewise your teeth.

Your circulation will slow down and you will have various kinds of aches and pains you never even thought of. Your eyes will gradually get dimmer. Things won't taste as good as they used to and you won't be able to smell things like you did. You will get tired easy but you will have a hard time getting to sleep and when you dream, many times they will be sad or bad dreams or even nightmares. You will wonder if you ever were young and pretty. Sometimes you will go and look in the mirror and pray for a miracle, that maybe you have changed back or something. The only changes you will ever notice will be changes for the worse. You may try to cultivate your mind, but it gets old and tired too and you can't learn as easy as you used to and you will forget even when you don't want to. Other people will not help at all. I mean, maybe if other people would even *act like* you hadn't changed, then it would be easier to get along. But the ones who dislike you will be glad and the ones who like you will be disappointed or even irritated at you, like it was something you had done on purpose. People blame you for the way you look just as they praise you for it. As if you had something to do with it!

You are right, Miss Andress, to worry because time passes by quickly and almost before you know it you will be old and not beautiful any more. You have got a long hard bumpy road ahead of you. Pray you don't end up hating yourself and wishing you had never been born.

Don't think I don't wish you well, because I do. I wish you every happiness there is, but nevertheless I know exactly what is in store for you.

I hope you do not have to have major surgery like I have, both inside and out too. Awhile back I had to have one breast removed. In a way I was relieved because I thought now B.O. would leave me alone. I have, *had* I mean, rather a large, well-developed bustline and B.O. used to be very crude with them. He liked them. He said they were the only half-decent thing about me and if there was any way he could enjoy them without *me*, he would certainly take advantage of it. You might think I would be glad I had something he liked about me or maybe even be proud, but that was not the case at all. I did not care ever to be toyed with or to be the object of his lewd and animal desires. Sex is unfortunately necessary if you are dumb enough to want to have children but that is about the only use of it even under ideal conditions like I have never had. Sleeping in the same bed with B.O. is not ideal conditions. Besides the fact that he is dirty and has bad breath mixed with beer breath (I do not touch a drop of alcohol) and always needs a shave and scratches you, besides that he is big as a horse and heavy as a ton of lead, besides the fact that he is rough and crude and very unrefined and says awful things, besides all that, he is very energetic and it seems like he can never get enough. He only has to rest a few minutes and he is ready to go again. I had been told that if he got drunk enough, that would help. It didn't.

But I will not bore you with my "intimate" problems. I only wanted to explain why when they had to remove one breast I consoled myself with the thought that at last B.O. would leave me alone. I thought surely he would be repulsed by me and even upset, for he had been very fond of them. He even had a habit of talking to them like they were different people from me. He called them "the twins," and named them Darlene and Delphine. Sometimes he said rude and awful things to them right in front of me.

Surely, I thought and hoped with all my heart, now that Delphine is gone for good, B.O. will leave me alone.

Well, I was as wrong as wrong can be. It did not change B.O. a bit. He is the same as ever which is worse and almost more than a body can bear.

First, he props up in the bed and looks at your picture while. Then he yells at me.

Come here, you one-b------d b--ch, you! Get in this f--k--g sack before I break your nose and give your soul to God, cause your a-s is all mine!

Miss Ursula Andress, I don't blame you for the indignities I suffer. I do not blame you either for helping to turn Holiday into a sex fiend like his father. If it was not you it would be somebody else.

My purpose in writing to you is not to complain or to ask you for help or money or anything like that. I only want to tell you how I sympathize humbly with your problem about getting old and all, even though it has only just begun and you will have to live with the problem (just like a husband, ha-ha) for as long as you live. I want to give you some free advice, Miss Andress, make your peace with God and trust in Him. God will love you just the same when you are old and ugly. And God is not impressed with you now, just because you are a big Movie Star and have lots of money. Maybe God has some real test planned for you in the future, did you ever think of that? You better get down on your expensive knees and pray to Him to give you strength before it's too late.

I trust in the Lord and it keeps me happy. It even keeps me glad, for one thing I am sure of is B.O. is going straight to Hell and every mean thing he does just adds more to his infinite and eternal torment. I would only like to see what they do to him "down there." That may seem like an unChristian thing to say and maybe it is but it is the truth. B.O. is going to hell and in a funny way you are helping him to go there. So you are an instrument of the Lord even if you don't know it. Some good can come from everything, you'll be glad to know.

I only hope B.O. dies and goes there soon enough so that I can save Holiday before it is too late. But, if Holiday has to go to hell too, it will be the will of the Lord and His will be done.

I must close now. B.O. is due home any minute and I would rather he did not read this letter.

Remember, Miss Andress. "Vanity, vanity, all is vanity, sayeth the preacher."

Your fan,
Idabel Brunk

P.S. Please do not feel you have to answer this. If I do not hear from you, I will understand.

Dear Jean Shrimpton,

The real reason I am writing you is, of course, about the dreams. You know all about that already, but even so you probably do not know the background leading up to them or all of the surrounding circumstances. Dreams are all very well and terribly important, and without them we would all probably wither and fade away like cut flowers in a vase. But there are facts too, hard facts (if you will pardon the expression), and sometimes they cannot be denied. Things between us have gone on long enough without my going to the trouble of writing you to let you know exactly who I am or what my situation is in "real life."

It takes a lot of courage to write you like this because you may not like everything you hear about me. Yet that is a risk I must take. It may be a blind act of faith, but I am certain that somehow you of all people will understand, and if forgiveness is called for, you will be as generous with forgiveness as you are with your other qualities.

You probably have noticed already, I imagine, that the style, syntax, grammar, punctuation, word choice etc. of this letter indicate that the writer possesses a certain educational polish and, insofar as may be surmised, is of higher than average intelligence. Certainly this letter stands head and shoulders above your average crank letter or fan letter. It must surely seem to be of a distinctly higher order.

Miss Shrimpton, if you have surmised that the writer of this particular letter is a person of high intelligence and superior sensibility, you are exactly right.

My intelligence and sensibility have been the source of considerable difficulty, however. I have always been, by nature and constitution, a rather frail and languid chap, bookish you might say, preferring solitary pleasures to more active and rowdy group pursuits. And even though this natural inclination on my part pleased Mother—a true saint if there ever was one—it sorely distressed and, indeed, p--s-d off my "Old Man," who was a gregarious and boisterous fellow, fond of such things as hunting and fishing and playing poker with the boys, taking his pleasures and solace from beer and John Barleycorn. More out of deep disappointment in the nature and character of his only son than out of pure sadism, Daddy was forever making derogatory comments about me and holding me up to public ridicule and humiliation whenever possible. For example, I cannot help recalling the time a friend of his inquired of me which sport I preferred. Before I could frame a suitable answer Daddy leapt into the conversation.

—Sports! Games! he roared at the top of his gravel pit voice.—This puny little s-n of a b-tch couldn't even work up the energy to play "Drop The Soap!"

Miss Shrimpton, I am fully aware that you are not only very ladylike, but refined and British to boot. You probably don't have the faintest idea, the least (pardon expression) conception of the activity to which he was referring. Suffice it to say it was not a complimentary remark.

It is a strange thing how after all these years one should still remember, indeed still *hear* a single remark like that. His words are fixed forever in my mind as clearly as the chiselled epitaph upon a marble tombstone. With my luck his words may very well end up being my epitaph.

But I do not want to bore you with the shabby, paltry details of my so-called real life. In general my life can be described as a sequence or series of sordid disasters. Adding up to a total, though inconsequential failure when judged by the standards and wisdom of this world. Next to me, Lee Harvey Oswald looks like a born winner. And, I suppose, in one sense he was. After all, disregarding the singular circumstances of his fame, one would have to admit that he got his picture plastered on the front of all the better magazines.

In any case, until I really understood and mastered the art of Dreams, I led a more or less uniformly unhappy life. For, as it happened, I am an odd mixture, having inherited my Mother's frail, light-boned, unemphatic delicacy, together with a real strong dose of my Daddy's baboon-like hungers for the rough and ready pleasures of life. My parents probably reached some sort of conjugal compromise in their lives, but within me, in my very makeup, their differences settled into a continual and brutal war of nerves and attrition. I was rather like poor old Poland back in 1939 when Hitler and Stalin, having shaken hands, proceeded to carve it up like a Turkey in late November. This analogy has a certain aptness, for my Daddy was the archtypal Polack long before the advent of Polack Jokes. (Which, by the way, are less than amusing to me.) If only my Mother, in perfect innocence, had not taken up the sport of Duckpin Bowling!

A tough thing it has been, Miss Shrimpton, acutely uncomfortable, to be blessed with the physical constitution and makeup of, say P.B. Shelley or Rupert Brooke, and at the same time to be possessed by the hungers of Attila, the Hun. This "combination" drove me to do any number of desperate and foolish things. Needless to say, as I was to learn unforgettably, joining the U.S. Marine Corps was not the solution to all my problems. Nor, for that matter, was my impulsive marriage to Wanda Kazinsky, star Jammer of the Teaneck, New Jersey Terrors, a Roller Derby Team of some local notoriety. Actually, I must here confess to you that Wanda and I are still married in a strictly legal sense of that word. I share a roof and one half of a double-bed with Wanda. But, in a larger sense, our lives are now (fortunately!) separate. She has her hairy hands full raising our three sickly, puny kids. Who are, if anything, worse off than their poor *pater*, suffering as they do from weak eyes, bad teeth, tired blood, countless allergies, and, as well, being rather "slow" learners in school.

I actually thought I might die of simple exhaustion before the kids came along, bang and one, two, three, to save me. Wanda, full of high fettle and fresh from the rigorous active life of the Roller Derby, had an incredible surplus of energy and zest far exceeding the limits of my own ability. In her homespun way she explained to me on our wedding night that her sole and only purpose in marrying me (or anybody else, for that matter, she having previously determined to marry the first sober man who asked her) was "to get laid regular." By which she meant more than regularity, implying instead the maximum conceivable frequency with the aim of possibly setting new records. I was rapidly wasting and withering away, and, indeed, I might have been at best an invalid now had not fate come to my rescue. Nothing that I could think of to do, none of the ancient and honorable marital dodges, could spare me. If I feigned deep sleep, she roused me by the application of a cattle prod which she had acquired while working as a Specialty Performer at an American Legion gathering in Wheeling, West Virginia. I have never inquired of her precisely what her "specialty" may have been. She sings like an intoxicated crow heard over a wornout public address system. Though agile and muscular she dances like a hippo in quicksand. The thought of Wanda popping out of cake—even then before she threw her girdle away and decided to see how much beer, popcorn and pretzels she could consume in a lifetime—staggers the imagination. I suspect that whatever she did may have involved roller skating in scanty attire or, perhaps, none at all. For, given the fact that the bold Legionnaires were probably drunk out of their minds and the fact that Wanda could have been no more than a vague blur as she sped past on skates, it might possibly have worked. At any rate, her cattle prod inevitably and abruptly ended my feigned and heartfelt snores, and the threat of its further application to reluctant flesh spurred me, as it were, into action. Soon however, my sleep was urgently real. And nothing, neither the cattle prod nor a lighted cigarette, could (pardon the expression) raise anything from me save a piteous groan or two. Implacable, Wanda tackled this problem by slipping benzedrine into my evening Ovaltine.

It was during this period that I first discovered the untapped powers of my imagination. Now that sleep was out of the question and in order to perform my conjugal duties, I found myself concentrating very strongly upon the image of some very well known movie star or other celebrity, imagining, for example and partly for the sheer and reckless irony of it, that I was sharing a blissful experience with Grace Kelly or Deborah Kerr or, for that matter, anyone a little more refined than Wanda. (I should add, at this point, that even though Princess Lee Radziwill would seem to be a natural for this sort of imaginative exercise, I have never once included her because it is, after all, a Polish title. There are limits to irony too.) This method worked very well, so well, in fact, that as my imagination began to bloom and thrive Wanda became suspicious. By threatening me rather drastically with a sharp but rusty pair of hedge clippers she was able to force me to admit to the details of my strategem. Lucky for me, it only amused her. Each evening, after cutting off the Late Show on T.V. and killing the last can of beer in the house, after shucking her clothing with such insouciant abandon that it seemed as though a hand grenade had exploded in a lady's suitcase, she would strap on her roller skates and, getting a good running start from the far corner of the living room, come sailing toward the bedroom and the bed, a wild glint in her bloodshot eyes and a hearty "Okay, Pipsqueak, who am I going to be tonight?" trumpeting forth from her lips.

That daze of lost nights ended when the kids came along. Now completely maternal, she has left me my privacy at least. As she herself has put it: "It wasn't exactly a gas getting them and every damn one of them looks like you, only strained through a silk handkerchief, but they're all mine!"

Having, by accident and out of necessity, discovered the wondrous world of the unfettered imagination, I then continued to pursue my researches, arriving gradually at my present (pardon the expression) peak of refinement. I have absolute control over my dreams. Of course anyone can daydream and fantasize while wide awake. That is a crude and common pleasure. But I have moved steadily into a more mystical realm. I will not bore you with tedious detail. It is enough to say that by contemplation of, for example, a photograph of the "intended," and then by imagining a basic setting and situation, I can prepare and then set in motion a perfectly controlled dream. At these moments I am, I sincerely believe, in touch with *The Dream*, that vast reservoir of the collective unconscious where there is neither time nor space, where we are all beautiful and shining and happy without even a fig leaf of inhibition, where we are all loved and loving. In short, Jean, I have succeeded in transcending the hangups of so-called reality.

Out of a sense of justice and fairness and because I wanted to share the joys of my discoveries, I made every effort to explain all this to Wanda. But even though she could be presentable if not beautiful in that realm, she is so caught in the vise-like clamp of heredity and environment that she is unable to accept the credibility of my experiences. As she puts it: "You little jerk, you are so full of sh-t I ought to send for the Department of Sanitation to cart your -ss away."

She even threatened to send me to the (pardon expression) booby hatch.

I put up with these things not only because Wanda is my lawful wedded wife but also out of an understandable expediency. You see, after that unhappy incident at the high school where I served as Custodian (a misunderstanding involving a young drum majorette who was practicing for the Annual High Steperama in the Boiler Room), after that unpleasant *contretemps*, I was forced to seek employment from my father-in-law who owns the U-Do-It Wishy Washy Launderette. One badmouth word from Wanda and I could be lining up and waiting for a Welfare check.

I am the night man at the U-Do-It. Which suits me just fine. Plenty of time to sit around and watch dirty clothes go round and round and plan some good dreams.

Oh how I wish I were a real poet with words! In a way those washers and dryers, whirling like oriental prayer wheels, are an adequate and functional symbol for the power of the turned on human imagination. We put our poor and shabby bodies and souls into the machine of imagination. The little cupful of detergent represents that *soupçon* of reason which must be admitted to the experience lest it spin off into sheer surrealism. And water from the pure and depthless well of the human consciousness flows in, itself reflecting the bright essence of the divine just as a calm clear sea captures and reflects the glory of the sky. The end effect is cleansing. Whatever was soiled and spoiled emerges, however briefly, as clean and fresh, of sweet odor, renewed, and without stain.

Oh, but it is redundant to tell *you* all this. For of all the creatures with whom I have shared my dreams you are the most sympathetic and understanding. You know how it is.

Fate must have intended it that way. It was only by the purest accident that I first met you. One night a lady left behind her paperback copy of your autobiography—*My Own Story: The Truth About Modelling.* I added it to my collection of trashy reading material gathered against ennui; for a man can't spend all his time dreaming or getting ready to dream. And so it was that, lacking anything better to do, I glanced through the book and, captivated by your expression of bright-eyed, perfectly symmetrical vacuity, I decided to let you join me in the traditional South Sea Island Shipwreck Dream. From the beginning you were so extraordinarily kind, gentle, eager to please, understanding and, let me admit, satisfactory, that I automatically cast you as the captive Saxon Princess in my Roman Emperor Dream. Now that it's all (pardon expression) behind us I confess that this was a test of character to see how you would act under somewhat more strained circumstances. You came through with flying colors, and even though the Orgy may have been somewhat degrading for you (especially that part involving the Nubian!), you never lost your natural pride or aplomb. The ultimate test, then was the Auschwitz Dream, the one where you are a highborn Jewess and I am the Nazi Stormtrooper. I must apologize for subjecting you to that unpleasant experience. I'll never do it again. Unless, of course, you are a (ha-ha) naughty girl.

After that final test, I sensed a permanency in our relationship, an almost mystical wedding as it were. You were simply fabulous that night, Jean. All I could do to repay you and to prove my good intentions was to reverse our roles. So I let you be the Bitch of Buchenwald and I was the Polish Prisoner with all the fascinating tatoos. You played your part magnificently, and even though I ended up as a lampshade in your living room, you can be sure I was the happiest lampshade in the whole world.

And we have been living happily ever after ever since. Now that I have a certain someone to share my dreams with I find I am able to return to the "real world" with renewed zest and vigor. I spend a lot of my free time doing intensive research at the Public Library trying to find new and interesting roles and situations for us to enjoy. I am trying to improve *myself*, thus to extend the powers of my imagination. By the way, if you have any good ideas for some swinging dreams, don't hesitate to let me know. Two imaginations are bound to be better than one.

Wanda, of course, thinks I am a fool and some kind of a nut.

"Look at that crummy little b-tch!" she cried, pointing at your photo on the cover of *My Own Story.* "She may have a nice tight little c-nt, but you can tell from looking she's got sawdust in her head instead of brains."

Who is Wanda to comment upon anybody's I.Q., presumed or otherwise, I ask you!

Another time she brought home a copy of *Pageant* magazine, swiped during one of her very rare trips to the Beauty Parlor. She pointed out, in a thrilling article all about you, where you said, "If you take off all the makeup, I'm ugly." I tried my best to explain to Wanda that this was a subtle philosophical comment on the ageold mystery of appearance and reality. I will spare you her reply. Never forget, though, Jean, when you're feeling lonesome, lowdown and blue, that in dreams it doesn't make any difference. I mean, I am not exactly a beauty myself. That used to worry me. So much that I would waste time and energy in my dreams transforming myself into somebody more attractive and desirable. How little I knew! In dreams you have to (pardon) take me as I am and like it.

More recently Wanda got hold of a copy of *Look*, the one with the article "Jean Shrimpton: The Star Model Makes Her Movie Bow." It had many good photos and quotes. I was deeply pleased. But Wanda, being crude, wanted to know what I thought of the photograph of you in a bikini bathing suit standing there with that creep, that cross *you* have to bear, that so-called actor Terrence Stamp.

"Look at the skinny thing!" Wanda suggested. "She might as well be a boy. I doubt she's even got a real p-ssy! etc. etc."

I controlled myself. After all, I know better.

At any rate, it was Wanda who urged, or better say *dared* me to write this letter. She insists, in unprintable terms, that you will never answer my letter. She says that if I do get a reply it will be in the form of two men in white coats with a straight jacket and a one-way ticket to the nearest Funny Farm. (Just for that I have made her be our slave in a couple of minor dream episodes. That will teach her!)

I have complete and absolute faith that you will answer my letter. Then I will wave it (the letter I mean) proudly in her face.

However, let us assume that I am wrong and she is right. Let us assume that you are nothing more than "a scrawny little Limey c-nt who thinks her short hairs are made out of mink" etc. Even if that should turn out to be true, I have no intention of cancelling our relationship and arrangement. Admittedly, in a pique (I'm only human), I might subject you to The Spanish Inquisition Dream, but that would only prove how much I really care.

Or, dreadful thought, let us assume that for some reason you are offended by this letter. Let me assure you, from the (pardon) bottom of my heart, no offense is intended. But should you insist on taking offense, frankly I couldn't care less. Who the f-ck do you think you are, anyway? Sure you are a big Success and a Celebrity. That's the whole point. Anybody who is, in the modern sense and meaning of the term, a *celebrity* is fair game. That's the whole idea of celebrity. Right now you can bet your boots that some pimply kid somewhere is bringing you a bouquet of roses in his romantic imagination. Some potential or would-be Jack-the-Ripper is busily trussing you up and carving you like a Christmas (pardon) goose. You name it and ten to one it's probably happening to you right this very minute. Not the "real" you, of course. The "real" you doesn't matter and, for all practical purposes, may not even exist. I have an interesting theory about this. If you have ever glanced at *The National Geographic* or any other publication, popular or scholarly, dealing with far away lands and people, you will have run into the fact that really primitive folk are very difficult to get pictures of. They are terribly afraid to have their pictures taken. Have you ever stopped to wonder why, Jean? Superstition? Oh, yes, it's a superstition. It seems that most primitive people sincerely believe that if one is photographed enough times, three or four being a gracious plenty, one's image being seized and carried away as the private property of some stranger, one is in dire peril of losing one's soul. Crazy? Maybe. We all know, though, that if your insides are photographed (i.e., x-rayed) enough times you will probably get cancer or have some kind of a mutation for a kid. Right? Celebrities are all the time p-ssing and moaning (on the way to the Bank) about how (a) they have no privacy and (b) how "the real me" is nothing at all like the public image. An understandable state of confusion to be sure. Any celebrity is somebody who has been reduced to two dimensions and then parcelled out like the loaves and fishes to the starving multitudes. As a celebrity you have no life and no "reality" except what *They*, each one separately, choose to give you. Ergo, as celebrity you belong to each one of them separately and distinctly and absolutely. You are at once the creation and the slave of each and every one. The so-called "real" you, which exists only and solely for you, is purely and simply a very slight occasion, a mere stimulus to and for the imagination of total strangers. Precisely in proportion to your "success," the extent of which you can be said to "capture the public imagination," you are hanged, drawn, quartered and subdivided into millions of parts. In short, Miss Shrimpton, the primitives are quite correct. In something very near to the "literal" sense, a human being who is photographed too much *does* lose his or her soul. You are a *photographic* model! These are the saints and martyrs of the new Faith of Celebrity. They offer themselves up with careless abandon.

I am sure that the "real" Jean Shrimpton, whoever and wherever she may be, will understand. Furthermore as long as I continue to realize that whatever has happened between us in my imagination took place only there, in "un-reality," then whatever you may do elsewhere is neither praiseworthy nor blameworthy. I won't hold it against you. You can be sure that I have no (pardon expression) hard feelings.

Well, it's about time to lock up the U-Do-It Wishy Washy, to turn out the lights and drag home. The kids will be sound asleep. Wanda, can of beer in hand, will be fixed in front of the Boob Tube watching "The Late Show." I'll sit down and watch with her until they play "The Star Spangled Banner." Which is only fair. Then we'll slouch off to the sack, to sleep and to dream separately, she hugging her pillow as she dreams (no doubt) of oceans of beer and acres of pretzels. I will close my eyes and drift off. . . .

Tonight to a Carribean island where you and I live in a lovely stucco house surrounded by palm trees and facing a beach as fine and white as flour. Needless to say I have some surprises, some jolly fun and games, planned for tonight. But I'd better not spoil it by telling you in advance. Be ready for anything.

So, until later, dear Jean, I wish you well. Don't let all those faggot photographers bug you. Just remember somewhere there is someone who treats you like the grownup beautiful woman you really are.

Love & kisses—
Mike Lipinsky

Part Six

Intermission

Say he is rude that cannot lie and feign, ·
The lecher a lover and tyranny
To be the right of a prince's reign
                    (Sir Thomas Wyatt—"Satires")

Interlude or Interruption or Intermission or Intrusion

[Hi, Sam!]

1.

Much as I hate to butt in again, this seems like as good a place as any to do it. And it is better than some.

Before you innocently go ahead and read further, I feel that there are some more things you ought to know, for your own good, about this "John Towne," his life and "art."

It may be that, despite my scrupulous efforts to maintain editorial objectivity and critical neutrality, I have slightly prejudiced you against the author. Perhaps his own words, taken out of the context of his much larger design, arranged and edited by me, have been unfair, indeed even hostile witnesses against him. I certainly hope not. And I reiterate that you must judge for yourself. I, for one, am convinced that you have the capacity to do so if you will really try. For unlike the more active members of the Publishing World who must deal more or less directly on a day to day basis with the Public, unceasing and unflagging in their continual effort to con you out of your money and make ever more luxuriant profits, I can afford the luxury of continuing to believe, despite all evidence to the contrary, that the Reading Public is not completely made up of fifty-seven varieties of Fools whom it is the duty and calling of the more fortunate (Knaves) to preserve in that blissful state of ignorant self-deception which is called "happiness."

It is possible, in spite of all my good intentions, that I may not have been perfectly fair with you or to John Towne either. If I were arrogant, I could shrug or thumb my nose at your objections and point out that nobody is perfect and you probably deserve a sound thrashing for some of the things you think, feel, and do every day. Most of you probably deserve hanging. But I recognize that I am also involved in "the human condition," mixed up in the same mess, so where do I get off feeling morally superior to the average reader?

In my own defense, however, I should like to point out modestly that objectivity is impossible and "fair play" is an obsolete, outdated, WASP concept if there ever was one. Especially when it is applied to someone like John Towne.

And I would strongly urge you not to be fooled or foxed by his occasional brief moments of apparent seriousness and even signs of "sincerity." He may fool himself from time to time. To the extent that he shares in the general characteristics which we euphemistically call "human nature," it is likely that he does enjoy moments of self-deceit. But there is no earthly reason I can think of why you and I should passively accept his illusions.

In any case, I feel that I should fill you in on certain details of which you might not otherwise be aware. Thus you will have more evidence upon which to reach your own conclusions. Some few of you may find factors and circumstances which seem to be extenuating or mitigating. Others, probably the consensus, will find that everything serves to confirm what you already think about Towne. In which case, allowing for the tedium of redundancy, you can at least enjoy the undeniable pleasures of self-esteem and self-righteousness.

It would be ever so much easier for one and all if you have a copy of the completed MS of *Life With Kim Novak Is Hell* in front of you. Then, performing the proper function of a critic, I could cite chapter and verse, point out the obvious and speculate upon the obscure and the enigmatic. I am sorry that that cannot be arranged at this time. Perhaps at a later date the MS will be finished or, anyway, in a sufficiently coherent state to be presented to the Public. However, I do have in my possession the rough and incomplete MS from which I may quote and to which I may refer.

I ask that you trust me to be accurate. On the "honor system" so to speak. The world is bad enough without adding suspicion and mistrust to our share of mortal woes.

Anyway, it looks like you'll have to trust me whether you like it or not.

2.

A Brief Description Of The Papers of John Towne With Special Reference To The Manuscript Entitled *Life With Kim Novak Is Hell*

The contents of the duffle bag and the wardrobe trunk include a wide variety of papers of all kinds: incomplete poems and stories and articles, miscellaneous chapters from abortive novels, laundry lists, letters and postcards, bills and advertisements, cancelled checks, several menus, old magazine and newspapers, student term papers and bluebooks, match covers, Kleenex, an expired Driver's License, snapshots of unknown persons, aphorisms, lists of figures, and miscellaneous items including a Texaco road map of the southeastern United States.

The chief item, however, is the manuscript entitled *Life With Kim Novak Is Hell*. It is a typescript of roughly 1000 pp. The final page is numbered 989, but there are many errors in pagination.

This MS is identified by the author as a "Confessional Novel." The author calls himself John Towne and lists as his published works in book form the following titles: *Live Now & Pay Later, Mondo Teeny Boppo,* and *Goldwyn Boy: A Hollywood Novel*.

Frankly, I have never heard of any of these books. Which, of course, proves nothing. He openly admits that each of them was an unsuccessful book. There are literally dozens and dozens of novels published every year that nobody ever hears of. However, it would be easy enough to check out Towne's claim to have written these or any other published books. A brief visit to any public library would suffice. And I firmly intend to look into this matter one of these days. Meanwhile perhaps some enterprising or energetic Reader will do his own sleuthing.

Some of you may suggest the telephone as a possibility. But I dislike the telephone with an almost pathological intensity. If you can stand to use the phone, then more power to you.

In any event the truth or falsehood of his assertions seems entirely irrelevant. We can take him on faith or we can ignore him, and with impunity either way.

Alas, the manuscript is real enough.

In a draft of a brief preface, handwritten on yellow legal size paper, Towne states that this novel is intended "to give a true and naked picture of myself and that it is specifically (and ostensibly) addressed to my best friend, Ray Wadley as I shall call him." He points out that the structure of his book is composed of ten "sections," each representing what he wrote while under the influence of a powerful "goof ball," an amphetamine pill of some kind. It seems that he had only 10 of these "beauties" left at the time he began writing and that there was no possibility of getting more. He adds that he did not wish to acquire more of the potent drug; for he has "gone off the stuff," not without pain and difficulty, as a literal testimony to the sincerity of his confession.

Though the entire MS was written "under the influence," Towne vigorously denies that it is "automatic writing," no matter how free and easy and at times illogical it may appear. "The taking of ten pills, one at a time over a period of time, is a planned act if there ever was one." Moreover, he contends, during the interim between the taking of the pills he gave considerable thought to what he would write in the next section, next time he got high.

John Towne defines his method of composition as "the calculated cultivation of spontaneity." Though he permitted himself to plan ahead, he insists that he never allowed himself to re-read anything he had written nor, above all, to revise anything. "And accepting the truth of this is terribly important to the whole sense and purpose of a confession. If we could correct things done or left undone by simple imaginative revision there would be no need to confess anything, would there?"

He states that it was all originally written in longhand "with a number of multi-colored, felt-tip, Pentel pens, all made in Japan." The MS was then typed by a kindly young student of his named Linda. She is responsible, then, for the state of the typescript MS. He swears "upon a good Gideon Bible stolen from the Chase-Park Plaza Hotel in St. Louis, Missouri" that he has never so much as glanced at the typescript despite occasional temptations to do so.

He fears that Linda, "trying to be helpful in her inimitable chuckleheaded way," may have silently edited and/or corrected the MS in an attempt to make it more "consistent." Nevertheless he is content in his ignorance. He suggests that for the sake of "artistic integrity" the MS should be published exactly as it is, including all typos, misspellings, mistakes, strikeovers etc.

At the bottom of this preface he notes that he can be reached under the names of John Towne or Radio P. King, c/o American Express. London, England.

Here it behooves me to point out certain discrepancies and errors of fact in the relationship of this handwritten prefatory note and the typescript. There are many others which I do not mention, but never mind about them.

Item. The "structure" of the book is said to be in 10 sections. And so they are numbered. "Section 4," however, is either missing or has been deliberately or accidentally skipped over. Which leads us to. . . .

Item. The Goof Balls. A Psychiatrist, with whom I am acquainted on a purely social basis, has examined the MS and informs me that it is his opinion that the whole thing was written under the influence of something, and something more potent than coffee or tea. It is quite possible that it was written under the influence of some fairly strong amphetamine combination as Towne claims. Judging by the length of the individual sections, by the style and the contents, the good Doctor is inclined to guess that the MS was written while the author was under the influence of 25 milligram spansules of a commercial drug called *Desbutal*. The Doctor also points out that the prefatory note, despite its brevity, is so close in style and spirit to the text of the MS as to indicate that it, too, was written under the influence of the same drug. If so, then Towne lies outright and is still "on the stuff." And he has not "offered it up" (*his* phrase) in witness to the sincerity of his repentance. Or, to be more charitable, not to say credulous, the prefatory note was written under the influence of the last of the ten pills. A fact which Towne has childishly attempted to conceal by omitting "Section 4" from his 10-part structure.

Item. Method of Composition.

Although there is an apparent amphetamine-consistency in the 9 sections, each section is itself a diminutive version of the duffle bag and wardrobe trunk, *i.e.* "padded" and fleshed out with a great deal of extraneous and irrelevant material.

124

These may or may not date from the ostensible time of composition. Which, as Towne asserts in the prefatory note, was "strictly limited to a few weeks in the spring of 1966, so that both time and place would be fixed and irrevocable."

Then there are (again) parts of letters, fragments of verse and stories, plays and film scripts by Towne or others. There is one laundry list and one cancelled check which is made out to The National Rifle Association. There is a postcard, blank, with a young lady portrayed, nude as an apple, advertising "Chuck Landis' Largo, 9009 Sunset Blvd., Hollywood, California." A second postcard displays "Maud, The Famous Kissing Jackass from Mackey's Animal Farm on U.S. 17, 23 miles south of Savannah." The address and name of the addressee have been blurred beyond recognition, but the cryptic message remains readable: "Now Rugby Man knows everything, so I guess you'll have to do without 'Happiness' for a while at least. Think pure & clean for a change./ Love/ Bunny Margaret."

Finally, among the papers of "Section 7" there is a 2500 word term paper entitled "Point of View in James' [sic] Portrait of the Artist as a Young Man." It is signed with the name "Scooter Snell" or "Schnell," dated May 10, 1956" [sic] and on the cover in red crayon directly below the title is scrawled "VARSITY FOOTBALL!!!" This paper, in my opinion, is highly inaccurate, nearly illiterate in style, and utterly puerile in content. There is no mark or correction of any kind on the paper, excepting an "A" written in green ink and circled in the upper right hand corner of pg. 1.

There are many yellowing newspaper clippings mixed in among the pages of the MS. They have in common only a uniform quality of pointless and irrelevant absurdity. In no case are major national or world events referred to.

Typical is the following, here offered complete:

Mourners Flee Fiji Geyser

SUVA, Fiji (AP)—Hundreds of mourners fled as a geyser spouted from the grave after the burial of a local farmer on Labasa Island. The watery mud spout subsided and the dead man was laid quietly to rest again.

This clipping and many others like it, clearly reveal a grotesque and morbid turn of mind, totally divorced from the serious and challenging issues of our times.

Item. Method of Composition, Cont'd. . . .

More damaging by far than the many odds and ends, which may have been mixed with the MS of "Kim Novak etc." accidentally, are some serious matters of internal inconsistency. In view of Towne's claim that his "Confession" is set in the spring of the year 1966 and his insistence that he had

125

not so much as glanced at the typescript, let alone revised it, for fear of destroying the "purity" of it, attention must be called to the fact that there are a great many references and allusions to events and personalities of the years 1967 and 1968. And these are freely drawn from all four seasons of the year. A few typical examples will have to suffice here:

(a) It is a fact that nobody had ever even heard of Penelope Tree in 1966. She had not yet graced our public scene. Nevertheless the author refers to this delightful young lady (of distinguished lineage) several times and always in rude and derrogatory terms.

(b) He refers to "The Pentagon Peach [sic.] March" (1967) in a number of places, calling it "farcical," "hilarious," and "strictly from The Keystone Cops."

(c) At the same time he often goes out of his way to ridicule Dr. Spock. It should be remembered that in 1966 Dr.Spock was still very much of an American hero and a celebrity in good standing.

(d) A further example of crude bigotry and prejudice is to be found in a number of references to Nat Turner as "a bad Nigger," "a sassy Jungle Bunny," and "an uppity Jigaboo," In context there seems little doubt that Towne is reacting to and referring to *The Confessions of Nat Turner*, a novel by that distinguished American author, William Styron. Styron, himself, is referred to as "that *Connecticut* Southerner from Arthur's Discotheque." It is possible that Towne, ever alert to the publishing scene, may have been aware of the fact that Styron was hard at work on his timely and relevant best-seller in 1966. Certainly Mr Styron made no secret of his intentions or of the importance of his work-in-progress. And members of the Literary Establishment would have known of this and been waiting for the appearance of the book with baited breath. But John Towne can by no stretch of the imagination be called a member in good standing of the Literary Establishment or, indeed, or any Establishment, then or now. There is every reason to believe that, racked by his own selfish concerns, Towne would have been completely unaware of Styron's work-in-progress.

(e) Similarly there is a gratuitous and vulgar attack upon the work of that distinguished stylist—Mr. John Updike. Whom Towne called "John Pipsqueak." In this outrageous display of envy and bad taste Towne lists some of the works of Mr. Updike, distorting the titles, to wit: *The Whorehouse Fair; The Sordid Prose; Rabbi, Run!* and *Cripples.* The latter, of course, is a childish pun upon Mr. Updike's distinguished and in-depth examination of the complexities of suburban sex life—*Couples.* Which was not even published until 1968!

(f) There are several obvious allusions to Antonioni's film *Blow Up.* Most frequently recurring references concern a single memorable scene in that film, which Towne calls "the purple paper caper." In another place, apropos of nothing much, he writes,: "Vanessa Redgrave won't show us her tits!" Apparently referring to a scene in the same film where that actress appears topless but decently modest. The point is that it would have been impossible for Towne to have seen *Blow Up* in spring 1966.

(g) There are many other examples of discrepancy and anachronism through-

126

out the MS. I leave the pleasure of discovering these to the alert Reader.

(h) In short, the evidence is overwhelming that Towne *has* revised the MS of *Life With Kim Novak Is Hell*, albeit in a careless and desultory manner.

(i) So much, then, for his vaunted principle of "spontaneity."

Item. Linda, the typist.

This is a very complex and curious matter.

There is a young lady to whom Towne refers in a number of places in the MS, not without some feeling and, upon occasion, some intimation of intimacy that goes beyond the usual teacher-student relationship. She is called "Linda Coffey," "Linda Cafe," and in one place, apparently a typo, "Linda Kinky."

There is to be found here a brief document, a letter signed "Linda" and addressed to him. Evidently she has been doing some typing for him in return for some unspecified promise concerning her final grade in a course she is taking under him. In this letter she offers a *critique* of all that she has typed so far. Her criticism is so rational and well-organized as to be clearly the work of someone else other than John Towne. Indeed, it is a devastating and accurate indictment of the grammar, style, form and content, and the immorality of the MS.

In the last section of "KIM NOVAK" we learn, with sadness but no surprise, that Linda will flunk his course and not graduate. Disregarding the effect of this doublecross upon the sensitive young girl, Towne gloats and chortles at his own "triumph" over her fiance, "a smartass from Yale." For, as Towne puts it (and only he would do so): "All through the beautiful springtime I was pulling off her plain white cotton panties and slipping old Happiness to her while Smartass, the poor clown, was probably straining his brain to write her all the exciting news from New Haven."

More pertinent, many different typewriters have been used in preparing the MS of "KIM NOVAK," and the quality of the typing varies from excellent to execrable. The typing of the document, the letter signed "Linda" and sub-titled "One Reader's Reaction," is uniformly neat and precise.

In sum, then, any thoughtful reader will be aware that in matters concerning John Towne we are dealing with an individual whose "credibility gap" approached Grand Canyon proportions.

    L.H.

Part Seven

Exhibits in Evidence: Or,
Happy Times at Nameless College

None of ye all there is that is so mad
To seek grapes up on brambles or briars . . .
(Sir Thomas Wyatt—"Satires")

A. Draft for a Lecture on How to Achieve and Maintain A Modern Prestigious Literary Style

Now if you want to sound poetic and literary all at the same time, never forget to get the show on the road with a big, fat, easygoing dependent clause, holding off the subject for a good while and letting your participles and your adjectives do the heavy work for you. Hold back on the verb for as long as you possibly can. Otherwise it can end up being as embarrassing and disappointing as premature ejaculation. Moreover this particular method serves to generate a certain suspense. Which can be a great help. Particularly if your story doesn't really have any in the first place. Also it sounds like you have read a truck load of foreign books in their original languages.

Here I have put together a very stylish sentence as an example. Of course, it suffers from being no more (and no less) than a hastily constructed *pastiche*. But nevertheless I reckon it will have to do.

Here's how it goes:

"Bemused and even perhaps vaguely mysterious behind the smooth *café au lait* of an unseasonal suntan, the Colonel, clutching his invisible but nonetheless palpable enigma gracefully about him like a marshal's splendid cape. . . ."

And next, right here, is where the verb should come along.

Let's take a look at it. Point of view. We are observing the Colonel from the outside, from a sort of camera angle. That's good. And there is an ambiguity about this civilized lens. Which is also good, in fact very good. Ambiguity is almost always a good thing in this line of work. In fact, the narrator-observer merely tosses these perceptions gracefully aside. He's got a million of 'em. Or so it seems.

Notice the use of *café au lait*. Words in italics which, upon closer inspection, turn out to be words or phrases in some foreign language which the average lazybones may fairly be expected to know (or anyway recognize) at sight tend to look good on the page and add some status and snob appeal. They serve to join the reader and the observer-narrator in a spontaneous, yet exclusive club for slightly world-weary world travellers.

"Unseasonal suntan" is a stroke of genius, if I do say so myself. There it is, just lying there in the big middle of the sentence like that, like a candy wrapper or a crumpled kleenex by the roadside. Yet it contrives to tell us a whole lot about the Colonel. To begin with, consider this: *he has got a tan at the wrong time of the year*. He probably uses a sunlamp and probably looks in the mirror a lot. Or maybe he is always sneaking off to Florida or the Virgin Islands or Barbados or somewhere else like that when he ought to be home and working for a living like everybody else. In any case, he is either a victim of his own stupid arrogance or bad taste or both. Metaphorically, which is on the all-important second level, this teeny-tiny little clue lets us know that he may very well be a bad guy. I mean, he is not natural. He is a phoney. Sun is good and good for you. Everybody knows that. People who love the sun and get good natural suntans—excluding, of course, all those peoples and races of mankind who seem to be stuck with permanent suntans of one shade and the other and who, in most modern and contemporary fiction are definitely to be presumed to be good until it is irrefutably proved otherwise—people who don't blister or peel or ever have to rub themselves with Noxema, sun people are good people. We all know that. It is an article of faith.

But mark this well, readers. This cat, this dude, this jive turkey Colonel with his suntan, he is coming on like he is one of the good people. Like your real, honest-to-God fun-loving, mankind-and-nature-loving, liberal, right-thinking, sun-loving people. And chances are we might not be able to distinguish him from the real distinguished thing. Except, dear hearts, for that jewel of an adjective—"unseasonal." Which our otherwise more or less neutral and objective observer-narrator has tossed like a gold coin or a piece of cake into the unruly mob of words. And by that adjective alone we who know our modern lit. from peanut butter are at least entitled to suspect that he may be a bad guy who has swiped somebody else's white hat. Oh, he will probably fool some of the characters in this story, especially among the slow-witted ones; but we, as ever alert and suspicious readers, shall remain faithfully on our guard.

Now notice some of the other key words—"bemused," "mysterious," "enigma" etc. While receiving the observer-narrator's basic signal—"Beats me what's bugging the Bird Colonel," we are also getting a side dish of literary class. And we can relax and be safely assured that our observer-narrator has at least carefully gone through *Thirty Days To A More Powerful Vocabulary*. He is definitely a literary kind of a type; for (ask anyone) "bemused" is one of your gold-plated, definitely okay literary words.

Note the adverbs. Which are sparingly and judiciously used. Frequent use of adverbs implies a very high degree of intelligence and sophistication. For example, in fiction your average upperclass British character may be expected to throw his adverbs around like they are fixing to go out of style the day after tomorrow. This is also true of those Americans who have been to school at Oxford or Cambridge or would like to sound like they might have. As a practical exercise you should count up the number of adverbs found in any *New Yorker* story or article, picked at random. You'll see. Chances are you'll find a swarm of adverbs anywhere you look. It is smart and chic to use adverbs a lot.

But let us not sit here smugly and rest content with this easy observation.

132

After all, no matter how stylish and decorative it may be, an adverb is still a functional part of speech. Among a number of other things, an adverb usually qualifies the action of a verb. To qualify something is to divert attention away from the thing in and of itself; that is, away from the action. An abundance of adverbs can bring all the action to a screeching shuddering halt. Please remember that all action is, *per se*, vulgar and commonplace. Or put it another way. You may pick your nose in public if you must. But always try to do it with style. Do it with an adverb.

Moreover, since adverbs are, in a sense, the traveling salesmen of style, they tend always to make a persuasive case for style even without seeming to be hustling. Let us suppose, just for the sake of example, that you were a writer with absolutely nothing to say—John Updike, for instance. Would you just confess to your problem and quit writing? Hell no, you wouldn't. By the shrewd and judicious use of all the shellgame devices of style, you could give content and substance the middle finger and just keep on writing the same old crap forever and ever.

Be that as it may, please permit me to call your attention to another artistic touch, almost the equal to the brilliant use of "unseasonal." I am referring to the clause which reads "clutching an invisible but nonetheless palpable enigma gracefully about him like a marshal's splendid cape. . . ." Now that one is a honey, a real humdinger. That one little word, "clutching," speaks volumes. Let's be honest with ourselves. Let's face it. To clutch anything is to be very crude. Clutching, like a number of other forms of grasping, is associated with greed. Also with all kinds of unseemly urgency and boring desperation. It conjures up a sordid world of ridiculous social climbers who are not to the manner born. If you get my meaning. Don't be fooled for even a minute by all that "invisible but nonetheless palpable enigma" stuff. This Colonel is not only most likely some kind of a phoney, he is also running scared. He is obviously terrified of something. On the other hand, please do not feel that the other characters in the situation are necessarily low grade morons or retards just because they can't see through the Colonel. You shouldn't expect them to be as smart and as sensitive as our narrator-observer, who appears to be willing to share some of his *apercus* with us. Art isn't all that simple. Many times Art will fake you right out of your shoes. Art will leave you standing there, sucking wind and wondering how you ever got into this mess.

Sure he is "clutching" his "enigma." Why not? Wouldn't you be if you had one? But never mind. The really important thing is, of course, how he is clutching it. Like a lady with a towel when the friendly plumber barges into the bathroom without knocking? Like an old man with a shawl when he feels a chilly draft? Like a miser with a dollar bill? Like a jackpine high up near timberline on the sheer edge of a cliff? Like Harold Lloyd on a window ledge? Like King Kong holding Fay Wray? No, no, a thousand times no! I mean the man tells us how—"like a marshal's splendid cape." Not Herbert Marshall or E.G. Marshall or R.G. Marshall or General Marshall. Just a marshal, any old marshal. "Gracefully," too. Graceful is good. Clumsy and awkward are bad. Graceful is what your basic good, natural, suntanned people usually turn out to be.

Now, then, the cape.

Ask yourself—and I mean this seriously—when is the last time, outside of some old movies, you have actually seen a marshal's cape. For that matter, when is the last time you have actually encountered a marshal. (I here exclude Federal Marshals.) There are marshals and marshals. Know what I mean? There is old Marshal Tito, for example, an ambivalent character. There are Hitler's marshals. They were very bad. Except some people like Marshall Rommel, the Desert Fox. Napoleon had marshals, too. Who cares if they were bad or good? Nobody really knows or can remember. Nevertheless they were French. And they are now long since dead and gone to dust or glory. So, as dead Frenchmen, they can now be glorious, romantic, dashing, brave, doomed, impeccable, "splendid" etc.

And thus we are getting the old double whammy. Maybe this Colonel is the Hitler type. Or maybe he is Napoleonic. Frankly, I incline toward the former view on the strength of that "Unseasonal suntan" and the "clutching" going on. But only time and a couple of hundred pages will tell for sure. And during that time and those pages we must always allow for the possibility that the aforesaid Colonel may change for the better or the worse; or stay pretty much the same; or get dropped out of the story and forgotten about. Anything (or nothing) can happen.

I shall not trouble you by calling attention to such minor and felicitous technicalities as rhythm, assonance and dissonance, alliteration, symmetrical balance, parallelism etc., except to point out that they are all in there and plenty of them, too. Notice that you are approximately halfway through the sentence (go right ahead and count if you want to), all the way up to that word "suntan," before you even have a clue what the subject of the sentence is.

It is a bird?

Is it a plane?

Is it Vanessa Redgrave?

Suspense mounts steadily to reach a peak at "suntan."

"Ah! It's the Colonel," we say. "I wonder what the old fart is up to."

Then you have to wait all the way through the second half of the sentence to find out.

Don't hold your breath.

Sooner or later a verb will come winging on in and land safely. Just like in German or Latin. Do you remember those good old high school Latin exercises? "Then having saluted and having bade farewell to the centurion, from the north gate riding forth, the south gate being sorely beset by the barbarians, the messenger the letter from the commander's hand to the Emperor bravely sought to carry."

Or let's try one in Kraut: "Hans Schmerz in the Black Forest during April near the charming village of Horsford was born."

Point is, see?, if you can screw up an English sentence sufficiently, you can pass for a college graduate.

Although it is absent from my own sentence, the verb nevertheless important and relevant will prove to be. Now then, your average writer, who might be called a run-of-the-mill, blue collar stylist, could probably get that far, huffing and puffing. And then he would probably blow the whole thing skyhigh by introducing an inappropriate verb. Consider what things the Colonel may possibly do and still not violate the context, decorum, dramatical architecture and syntactical construction.

What if he:

(a) took off like a big-ass bird?

(b) burped, belched, barfed, and blew lunch?

(c) whistled "Pop Goes the Weasel"?

(d) farted as loud as a slide trombone?

(e) made himself a peanut butter and jelly sandwich?

(f) grinned and whinnied like a jackass chewing briars?

(g) crossed his eyes and fluttered his tongue in a loud Bronx cheer?

(h) lit up an exploding cigar?

(i) picked his teeth with a rusty nail?

(j) dropped his trousers and threw a bald moon at everyone standing behind him?

I shall spare you by ending this list which is already threatening to grow to epic proportions. From here on you will just have to take my word for it. In point of fact, there are only two things in the whole world which the Colonel can actually do.

He can cough discreetly.

Or he can smile.

I like to think that under the circumstances he may have smiled. Because smiles are more ambiguous than coughs.

The point is that real style is very hard to do. And it gets harder and harder all the time. Everybody keeps jumping in and trying to get into the act. For instance, all the good shiny prestige words keep getting snatched up by politicians and newspaper writers and cheap and grubby advertising types. Why, those people can take anything, even a nice, clean, crisp, ordinary word, one that we all know and love and use all the time, and in no time at all it will be filthy and soiled beyond any saving.

Faced with the pitiful and constant corruption and debasement of his native tongue, the average American writer can only do what he has always done before and emphatically return to the strength and energy, the indecorous and often unbalanced vitality of the living and breathing and spoken vernacular. And just hope for the best. . . .

(From here on just keep winging it until the bell rings.)

    J.T.

B. Miscellaneous

MEMO
TO: Professor Louis Rosen
FROM: John Towne
SUBJECT: Your recent request for list of publications by members of Department for information of President and the Board of Trustees.

(1) As you well know I am engaged in intensive research on a number of important scholarly projects, including my dissertation. Which, I am happy to report, is almost completed.

(2) Moreover, in my spare time ("Idleness is the Devil's workshop.") I have finished a draft of a novel and am now polishing and revising. Several publishers have been besieging my agent for the opportunity to publish this work.

(3) However, due to my concentration upon these large, long-term projects, I have not had time to produce more than one little scholarly article so far during the year. I'm sure you will see that this fact in no way represents the extent of my efforts to make a contribution to knowledge.

(4) Publications of John Towne during academic calendar year: "*The Red Badge of Courage*; or, Famous Authors in the Sun," *The Urban Nudist*, XXIV, no. 3, Winter, 1964, pp. 10–13, 71, 74.

> Respectfully,
> John Towne

MEMO
TO: Prof. Louey Rose
FROM: J. Towne
SUBJECT: Plans and ideas for new courses.

(1) Sorry to be late turning this in. Don't, please, let my tardiness be misinterpreted as a lack of interest. I, too, feel deeply that we need to update the curriculum.

(2) Sorry, too, by the way that I became slightly ill at the Departmental party at your house last Friday. Just for the record, even though I know *you* wouldn't imagine what some may think, I was not drunk. I can hold my liquor as well as any of the faculty and some of the students. However, I occasionally suffer from a recurring intestinal thing, which I acquired in the service of my country; and I never know when it is going to hit me. When I discovered the bathroom was occupied, I had no choice but to rush into the backyard or else barf all over your wall-to-wall carpet. Sorry about the azalea bushes. I couldn't see them in the dark.

(3) I also agree with you 100% that we must "encourage more students to take English courses and, if possible, to choose English as their major subject." And we must do this not alone for *their* sake, though we all believe strongly that there is no finer discipline in The Liberal Arts. We must consider practical matters as well. As I understand it, the Departmental Budget—including all salaries, mine and yours, petty cash and other funds—is directly proportional to two figures: (a) the number of English majors, and (b) the

number of students taking English courses. Of course we must maintain the high standards of our Department and our profession. But we would be crazy to scare students away with dull or difficult courses, excessively demanding reading lists, severe and inhumane grading, etc.

(4) I should therefore like to propose a number of possible new English courses which I feel will help sucker more students into our clutches. I will not tax your patience with details, but should you wish a fuller outline of any of these, I stand ready to deliver.

A. "A Phenomenon of Recent Culture: 'Camp'."

Would begin with scholarly approach. Take off like big-ass bird from Susan Sontag's celebrated essay.

Would deal with all forms of camp literature: *King Kong*, Tarzan, nurse stories, Norman Mailer, etc.

Deal with great camp works of the past. Spenser's *Faerie Queen* as high camp. Poetry of Stephen Duck as low camp.

Watch T.V., seeing such camp shows as "Batman," "Captain Kangaroo," and "The Huntley-Brinkley Report."

Examine camp periodicals from *Mad* to the *Partisan Review*, from *True Screen Romances* to *Harper's Bazaar*.

View camp movies at the Drive-In.

Take camp field trips. For example, visit a shopping center, attend a meeting of the United Daughters of the Confederacy or the N.A.A.C.P. Drive to Lynchburg for the Annual Hi-Steperama for Drum Majorettes.

I am sure you can see the possibility of this wide-ranging course.

B. "Pornography: From the Greek Anthology to the *Story of O*."

No, I am not kidding.

I feel in all sincerity that thanks to the new liberal interpretations of the Supreme Court and the demonstrable interest the distinguished Judges have evidenced in the subject, pornography is now firmly entrenched in our literature and life. It may turn out to be the significant *genre* of our times.

Anyway, it behooves us to prepare these young ladies, the future housewives of America, to be able to cope with the literature they will all be reading. I believe that they should learn to develop the same kind of knowledgeable critical powers of discrimination and to demand the same standards of excellence in the pornography they will read as in the poetry which they will never glance at again.

As I see it, this course would be objective and scholarly, placing its emphasis upon the growth and development of the literary conventions of the prurient. Always, of course, in good taste.

Rather than ramble on at the expense of your time and energy (and mine), I will now merely list some suggested courses, all more or less self-explanatory:

C. "Cowboys and Indians: Growth and Development of an Indigenous Form."

D. "The Detective: From *Oedipus Rex* to Mickey Spillane."

E. "Black America: Studies of Significant Writing Of, By, and About American Darkies."

Please give the above suggestions your thoughtful, serious consideration. If you have any questions, don't hesitate to call on me.

> Respectfully,
> Jack

MEMO

TO: Prof. Louis Rosebud, Chairman

FROM: John Towne, Instructor

SUBJECT: Reply to your peremptory request for a tentative reading list for courses during next academic year.

(1) Since I haven't had the courtesy of hearing word one from you regarding my creative plans for future new courses, I can only assume that at least for the time being we are condemned to continue under our present crummy and unimaginative curriculum and course plan.

(2) Even though your request was mimeographed (in purple ink yet!) and addressed not to me personally but to "All Members of the Department," I am assuming quite naturally that the fact that I received the request is evidence that my contract will be renewed and that I will be here next year. Otherwise it would be a sadistic joke to ask me what I plan to teach next year. And whatever else our little differences may have been, I never took you for a comedian.

(3) Your silence on the subject shall be construed as assent.

(4) At this point, Louey, I'm submitting a few changes in the Reading List for one course only, my Seminar in Contemporary Fiction. Am planning to replace some books, which don't work out as well as they ought to, with others which, it is hoped, will more engage the students' interest. Also, as will be obvious, I'm trying to update and improve the course, expanding the boundaries to cover a somewhat wider area of interests and concerns.

(5) The choices speak for themselves. It would be an insult to your intelligence to *explain* what I am up to.

(6) Replace Mary McCarthy, *The Group*, with Jean Shrimpton's *My Own Story: The Truth About Modelling*.

(7) Replace John Cheever, *The Wapshot Scandal* with Winston Lyon's *Batman Vs. 3 Villains of Doom: Batman Battles Penguin, Catwoman and Joker*.

(8) Replace Ralph Ellison, *The Invisible Man* with Booker T. Washington's *Up From Slavery*.

(9) Otherwise the course will be pretty much the same. Same old crapola.

(10) As indicated above I do not wish to clutter a brief memo with lengthy individual explanations of why these changes are necessary and advantageous. Suffice it to say, my criteria are:

(a) relevance to artistic concerns and directions of our society and the cultural *milieu*

(b) relevance to the interests and needs of our students

(c) consideration of serious gaps in their education and experience

(d) and an attempt to give the course as a whole a proper balance.

(11) You may have noticed that 2 of the books I plan to add are what might be called "non-fiction." You may ask, and not without a modicum of justice, how the hell such works can legitimately fit into a course which is supposed to be devoted to the study of fiction. Good question, Lou.

(12) I answer that the artificial and arbitrary lines between "fiction" and "non-fiction" are breaking down. Just as in a larger sense the old, outdated, obsolete and unworkable distinctions between "truth" and "falsehood" have long since been dispensed with in this society by everyone from Presidents to drunks in the gutter. Naturally the arts are not immune. And, in fact, the boundaries of "fiction" and "non-fiction" had long since blurred and dwindled before Truman Capote came along and made a pot of gold by creating mischievous fun and games out of the violent deaths of six "real" people, all jazzed up for the titillation of the so-called civilized and non-violent readers of the *New Yorker*.

(13) Which reminds me. Replace Truman Capote, *In Cold Blood* with Paul Holme's *The Candy Murder Case: The Explosive Story the Newspapers and T.V. Couldn't Tell*.

> Respectfully,
> J.T.

C. A Letter to Towne

Sunday night

Dear "Prof." Towne,

Here is the typing, finally finished. I sure hope it is all right. I had some difficulty getting used to your handwriting, but I have been very careful and I hope you will not find many mistakes.

Actually it was no trouble at all. I am a fairly fast and accurate typist. Maybe I can be a good Secretary or "Girl Friday" if the right man does not come along.

The truth is I am very grateful for the opportunity of being able to help you even in a small way. It lets me feel that somehow I am involved in the "creative process."

As far as "reward for services rendered," please do not feel you owe me a thing. I certainly will not accept any money. That would not be fair at all. I realize that a professor's salary is woefully inadequate, and, as you may know, my parents are rather "well-to-do." For you to give me *money* would be like carrying a cold to Newcastle or something. Just consider it as a favor to a "friend in need." At least I would like to think that you are my friend as well as my teacher. And if I am lucky enough to graduate this year, then I hope we can be real friends, outside of all the phoniness of the Teacher-Student Relationship.

By the way, I know you were only kidding around about my "grade" in the course and all. You have a truly wonderful sense of humor and that is one of the things I admire about you so much. Some people might not understand that. They might misinterpret you and even question your motives and your sincerity. But I can always tell you are making a joke, even when you have "a straight face."

So, again, please do not feel in any way obligated or beholden to me. Maybe some day I will need a favor too, and I will ask you. We can call it "Payment in Kind," as they say in Economics Class.

Reading and typing this has been a fascinating experience for me—like "peeking" through the keyhole of an artist's studio! Some things shocked me a little bit, and there were others which surprised me. But we are all grownups together, despite the slight difference in ages.

You can depend on me never to discuss or to reveal anything about the contents of this manuscript to anyone. I would never dream of taking advantage of your confidence.

I ought to warn you, though, not to be too trusting a person. There are plenty of girls around school who would cheerfully "spill the beans" just in order to have something to say. There isn't *all that much* to do around here, and some of the girls gossip like a bunch of old hens. You don't have to worry about me, though. I value your friendship too highly for that.

I will be very interested to see how it all turns out as a book. It is hard to imagine but I guess you know where you are going and I probably won't even recognize the "finished product."

As you know better than anyone else I am not a Literary Critic by any means. However merely as your friend and student and typist I have put down a few brief notes of my reaction to the work so far. I hope you will not mind. I just thought you might be interested. And you know you can take anything I say with a "grain of salt."!!

Thanks again for letting me type this and *bon chance sur votre livre*!

> Your friend,
> Linda

P.S. You said something about how maybe you will dedicate the book to me when it gets finished and published and all. I do not think that is a very good idea. I myself would not be embarrassed at all. In fact I would be secretly pleased, but daddy is a big square and very old-fashioned. He does not know a thing about the Modern Novel. It might hurt his feelings and he would probably get the wrong idea. I would not like to hurt his feelings and besides he handles the "purse strings." There is no use *looking for* trouble!

> L. . . .

140

D. One Reader's Reaction to the Incomplete MS Entitled *Life With Kim Novak Is Hell* by Professor John Towne

1. I do not understand your title. It is kind of cute & catchy but aren't you afraid she will sue you?

2. You use too many commas. Maybe they are correct where you use them but they do clutter up the pages and make it hard to read.

3. Also, unless I am mistaken, you are guilty of the error of the "Run On Sentence." Maybe not, but some of your sentences go on and on and are hard to follow. Couldn't you break some of these down into short and direct sentences that would be easier to read?

4. I know that you plan to change most of the names etc. but I do not like calling our school Nameless. Some people may make a mistake and think it is Hollins or Sweet Briar. That would be a wrong impression.

5. Too many adjectives and adverbs.

6. Too much repetition and redundancy. Brevity is the sole of wit.

7. Some of the naughty words and vulgarisms are in bad taste and should be excised.

8. I know you are just "feeling your way," sort of "groping" at this stage, but anyhow I hope you will not mind if I make some more general and serious comments below. If you mind you can always skip them.

9. Your main character that you are calling by your own name in this "rough draft" is not very clear to me. I keep thinking he is you, and then he is not you. (At least I hope not!) I think you are going to have to make up your mind what kind of a person he really is and then stick to that.

10. Another thing is it is very hard for the reader to decide what is really true and what really happened. In the first place the way you let your hero tell it is very confusing. And then your hero, he seems to make things up and tell lies too. And he judges people all wrong and lots of times he judges himself wrong, too, it seems to me. I would not say he is a very reliable person that you could depend on.

11. There is a lot that is unattractive about him too that will put people off. He says he want to "confess," but he does not seem very sorry about the bad things he has done to other people. *Inconsistency?* Sometimes he really acts and thinks so bad that I have to remind myself that this is only a "story" and not really you. Of course the average reader won't know you from Adam so maybe that won't be a problem.

12. Another thing I don't like about your hero is he seems to be so bitter about everything. All he can do is "knock" things. He does not make any constructive criticism. He does not offer any alternative. I think I am typical and many readers will not like this about him. They will think he is emotionally immature.

13. He seems to think he is some kind of a "joker." At least he tries to make jokes all the time. Some of them are not very funny. Some of them are in very bad taste and some of them are just plain sick jokes. Sick jokes are not "in" any more, and besides many readers will be repelled by this. Can't

he even see that the only person he is kidding is himself? Some people would say that he is guilty and is trying to blame his guilty feelings on the world and other people and the Society and all. That may be true. But I think that he is so insincere that he could not even feel the "pangs" of a real guilt. I think he is a person who has been hurt a lot maybe and has failed at difficult things and does not want to admit to himself that he is a big failure. So he goes right ahead kidding himself and making these bad jokes and hoping that nobody will notice that he is just pathetic.

14. He certainly is "horny." You try to explain that away by saying that he is making himself be pure while he writes his confession. I am not sure that that isn't phony. He certainly does not have pure thoughts all the time or even try to keep from having naughty thoughts. You do not tell whether or not he is really and truly pure during this time. The modern reader who knows about these things might imagine that he is only technically being chaste. He might be indulging in "autoeroticism" or some other unhealthy substitute for sex.

15. Speaking of sex. . . . There is much too much of it in the book. That is a little old-fashioned. They have run the subject in the ground. Henry Miller and William Burroughs and Terry Southern and all those others have pretty well "covered the subject." I am not sure there is much new information to be added. Besides which there are other things he could be thinking about. He doesn't only have to think about sex and money. We know there are other things and things on a higher plane. It is hard to be sympathetic with a character who is always so base and low all the time. There is a time and a place for everything. Doesn't he have any interesting hobbies you could write about? Doesn't he care a little about the real social problems and issues of our time like Viet Nam and Integration and the God is Dead theology? He might even care about The Sexual Revolution. Intellectually I mean! Certainly that would be "in character." Maybe his whole trouble is that he doesn't care a hoot about these things. If that is so, I believe he does not care because he is afraid of getting hurt. You do not want your hero to be a coward do you?

16. Another thing that concerns The Sexual Revolution. I do not know how much you know about the New Generation's habits and customs. It has been written up in many magazines and books, but maybe you have been too busy to keep up. Sometime you should take a look at *Sex and the College Girl* which everyone agrees is very true. Anyway you should know how they feel and act in general. That will be important if you plan to go any deeper into this "romance" between your hero who is a teacher and this student you call "Linda."

17. If she is supposed to be a typical college girl of this era, she will be a little more "liberated" than, say, the girls of your generation were. With the pill and all she will not think sex is such a big thing. Some girls will do real sex and some will not. If she is one of those who will do it, she will do it for fun or out of friendship or maybe even intellectual curiosity. Anyway it will be healthy and wholesome and sometimes even beautiful when every-

142

thing works out all right. Or maybe you want this girl to be a bad type. There are plenty of those around. They are the kind who will use sex to get what they want like a high mark in your hero's course or something. You probably won't believe me when I tell you this, but there are plenty of girls right here at College from good families who would do a thing like that. They would actually offer themselves if they thought it would help, and they wouldn't give it a second thought. There are teachers here, too, who would not hesitate to "take advantage."

18. I do not know how you plan to end this relationship in the book. Maybe you plan to save everything with a happy ending where they at least fall in love or maybe get married after she graduates. Many college girls like older men and creative types. If you plan to do that it might be better if you let the girl be a typical "good" girl of the New Generation. She might or she might not be a virgin, but any way she probably would not go "all the way" with her teacher at least until they had declared their love to each other and it looked like they might get engaged. That does not mean that he would have to go around all hot and bothered though. Just because she will not go "all the way" without a good reason does not mean that a girl has to be inconsiderate and no fun at all. She can keep her self-respect and still practice other forms of pleasing a boy or man.

19. So your hero does not have to go around feeling so horny and hard up all the time, especially since temporary relief is "just around the corner" anytime.

20. By the way. That scene where he hides in the dark and is a *voyeur* looking at the character "Linda." I hope you just heard about that or else made it up. There really was a window-peeping problem over at Martha Washington Dormitory, and one night I really *did* get peeped on. I complained and thought it was the Night Watchman who had been looking at me funny anyway. They had to fire him of course. But I am sure he was the one. It just worried me a little when I read that part in your book. Not that I am ashamed of my body, but I would have hated to have blamed the wrong person. He was not a nice man anyway however. If he was not peeking that particular night it was probably the first time.

21. I guess that's all. Please do not misunderstand my criticisms. They are well-meant. I enjoyed every minute of it.

     L. . . .

E. Seminar in Contemporary Fiction

Final Examination
"Lechery, lechery, still wars and
lechery; nothing else holds fashion.
A burning devil take them!"
Shakespeare—*Troilus and Cressida*, IV, ii

Directions

Read the questions carefully. Take your time. Try to think a little. You may find it a novel and interesting experience.

Do the best you can and try not to cheat.

Ready?

Question One—One Hour

Below are a number of significant and representative quotations taken from works which you are supposed to have read this semester. Please *identify* each quotation by giving the full and correct title and the name of the author of the work.

(1) "A sea of faces, some hostile, some amused, ringed about us, and in the center, facing us, stood a magnificent blond—stark naked."

(2) "No book she had ever read, no story she had ever been told could equal the terror which swept her in increasing waves. It was a terror which made her feel that every inch of her insulted body was alive with unmentionable things."

(3) "She wore a plaid shirt, blue jeans and sneakers. Every movement she made in the dappled sun plucked at the most secret and sensitive chord of my abject body."

(4) "Apropos of this, it is lamentable but a fact, nevertheless, that inferior races greatly desire the women of their superiors. That is why the Negroes rape so many white women in our southern states."

(5) "Both her legs and arms were tied down with rags, a gag of rags was in her mouth, but otherwise she was stripped like the car we had left in the ditch."

(6) "He got out of his clothes hurriedly in order to display his youth and his brawn, but he asked her earnestly if she minded if he took off his underpants."

(7) "In my heart I know she isn't a virgin, but perhaps childless with pink buds for nipples or even if they're sucked and dark I don't mind."

(8) "Her underwear felt sticky from the lubricants the doctor had used, and this nasty soiled sensation made her fear she had got the curse."

(9) "Eyes on her white, plump, quaking buttocks, he raised the belt high; and then, in another frenzy and in another nightmare, he beat her unmercifully."

(10) "He lay back, the sky bright with moonlight fell over his eyes, and he closed them, stretched out his legs, unbuttoned, out of breath, barely murmuring 'you're disgusting' and then he was silent."

(11) "The more loathsome parts of the dream—the dried-up female organs, the yellowed scabrous flesh, which looked only too much like pictures she had once seen in a medical book—these faded away quickly upon awakening, leaving her with just the breath of the dream, the peculiar smell, and with a vague feeling of triumph."

144

Question Two—Two Hours

"A woman does not want to be punished, abused, tormented or flagellated, but wants to be loved."

Theodore Reik—*Masochism in Modern Man*

Reik, of course, is a very distinguished Head-shrinker. Do not let that snow you. Apply his outlandish statement to any three of the books we have read and *to your own personal erotic experience*. Test the validity of his claim. And please do not ignore the experience of the Imagination—of dreams, day dreams, and dream visions—in dealing with this matter. "Fantasy life" is certainly relevant. Be honest, straightforward and uninhibited.

And don't forget to sign the pledge!

(Editor's note: A separate scrap of paper, containing the "key" to "Question One" is stapled to this copy of the exam.)
Answers to One
  (1) *Invisible Man*
  (2) *King Kong*
  (3) *Lolita*
  (4) *A Cool Million*
  (5) *Love Among the Cannibals*
  (6) *Wapshot Scandal*
  (7) *The Ginger Man*
  (8) *The Group*
  (9) *Eternal Fire*
  (10) *New Italian Writers*
  (11) *Lie Down in Darkness*

F. Two Letters to His Agent

Dear Sam,

I haven't heard a word from you and I am still waiting. My reason for waiting to hear from you is simple. I've been out of touch for so long, and even if the letters haven't been returned, that's no sure sign that you have received them. Did you get my previous two letters? If not, let me know.

Also, it is just possible that you may be out of town, taking a hard earned & well-deserved vacation. A man needs, from time to time, to get away from it all, all the nagging little problems & responsibilities, to throw care & caution to the wind, and just . . . relax. Like you did in April of 1962 in Haiti. You and Jane. She wrote me a nice letter about the good time you were having, mentioning the trip to Trinidad the year before which apparently had been at least equally amusing.

So, you old scamp, you may be up to your old tricks & soaking up sun in the Carribean. Or maybe it's the Riviera this year. You could always put it on a credit card. Fly now & pay later. Live now & pay later. I envy you, Sam, but without any bitterness. It couldn't happen to a better guy.

I know I still owe you money, but I can't send a negotiable Money Order thru the mail unless I know that there's a fair to middling chance (considering the sad state of the U.S. Mail, Zip Code & all) you will safely receive it.

By the way, the first payment will be a bit larger than I originally anticipated. Had a couple of real good nights of poker recently. Good nights! Folks down here may be simple and rural, but they're sharing in the general affluence & they will gamble on anything.

Anyway, the sole purpose of this letter is merely to add two more examples to the epistolary novel I have in mind, examples which will further indicate the possible range and variety of the form and, as well, illustrate another side of my protagonist. Who, I feel, lacks a certain "edge," needs more dimension.

Hang in there, Sammy, and do let me have a word or two at your earliest possible convenience.

> Sincerely,
> Jack

Enclosure #1
Letter #
To: Director of Internal Revenue
    Federal Building
    New York, N.Y.

Dear Sir,

Far be it from me to snoop or pry into anyone else's affairs. I always try to mind my own business. "Cultivate your own garden," Voltaire said, and when he did, he said a mouthful. My Philosophy of Life is to live and let live.

Frankly, sir, I have never approved of the I.R.S.'s way of encouraging one citizen to rat upon, yea even to squeal on another citizen, by offering a monetary reward to those who can give tips which result in convictions for tax fraud. I have always believed that such a method, even if it works, is unworthy of the Great American Government, particularly in this new era of The Great Society. It appeals directly to those qualities of envy, malice, and greed, qualities which there is already too much of. Everywhere you look there is envy, malice, and greed. Also lust which seems to be widely prevalent.

I believe Government shouldn't encourage these things. I believe Government should set an example, a noble example the like of which our forefoathers envisiged many decades and scores of years ago.

Be that as it may, there are times when even a man of principle must compromise in favor of some larger duty. Duty is the sublimest word in our language. When Duty calls, a man has got to get up and go, whether he likes it or not. I have thought and thought about this, and my duty seems clear.

In order not to compromise my principles completely, however, I have decided to remain anonymous. Therefore, if my suspicions about a certain party prove to be well-founded, I shall not receive any reward at all. Except the highest reward of all, the sense of a job well done, irregardless of the profit. No, I shall not ask for a reward. The Government can have it all.

I know that you all can't take an anonymous letter seriously, not as seriously anyway as one signed in a bold John Hancock which turns out to be legit. You will probably consider my letter to be "a crank letter" and will file it in File 13, as they call the wastepaper basket, where it belongs. If you haven't done so already, though, permit me to make a modest suggestion in all humility. You have the manpower and equipment to make a great many investigations and audits. From everything I read and hear, it seems like you have to create a certain amount of busywork for these highly paid, full-time employees. And you have to keep the public honest, on its moral toes, so to speak. Which I gather, you do by the time-honored methods of snooping, harassment and fear. Blind fear, in a way, for, if what I read and hear is true, you routinely make a large number of investigations and audits at random. That makes good sense and is fair enough. For if the random party in question is completely honest in every way, he or she has nothing whatsoever to fear. And sometimes you probably do catch real crooks in addition to those folks who have made an honest mistake.

You will notice, sir, that I am not saying word one about those abuses which have been exposed as a result of investigations of the I.R.S. by other impartial investigators. There are always a few bad apples in every barrel. If there have been cases of bribery, payola, kickback, blackmail, and malicious harassment etc. it's only human.

Like the yokels say in my part of the world, "One swallow don't mean it's going to rain birdshit before sundown." If the I.R.S. has occasionally been involved in political activity, lining up support for this & that, shaping up and silencing opposition, why I say it is those people who are "influenced" by such tactics who are to blame for their own trepidation and weakness. After all if the individual is not a crook, he has, like I said before, nothing to fear. You are not a Gestapo. The analogy is grossly unfair. All you have the power to do, within the law, is seize a man's records, close down his business, put his funds and property in escrow, bother his family, friends, and neighbors, and then tie him up in toils of litigation for months or years, litigation which, even if he is proved innocent and clean as a hound's tooth, may be prohibitively expensive, it's true; but what is money when a man's pride and good name are involved? And, assuming that there is no evidence of deliberate fraud, all you can do if judgment goes against him, is to take the money that is coming to you, plus a fair interest. Besides, he need not let it go that far since the Law, in its wisdom, permits the two interested parties, the U.S. Government and John Q. Citizen, to settle out of court, to negotiate a deal fair to all. So, if John Q. Citizen can't stand the pressure, for example, or perhaps is unable to bear the expense of litigation, why he is still protected. He need only come to you and negotiate a settlement. Nor need he unduly fear your prerogative to conduct similar investigations of his affairs every year to follow, year after year. In the future he can just be more careful, that's all. No, sir, I say to those who fear the powers inherent in the I.R.S. are a threat to free and democratic government, I say to them "Fooey on you! One thing they can't do, not yet anyway, is slap you in a concentration camp like in those totalitarian states. And they wouldn't do it, even if they could, because you see, the beauty of it is that the I.R.S. has only one goal—*to raise revenue*. When they slap you in jail, that costs a lot of money, to feed you, clothe you etc., even in a most rudimentary manner."

Together with F.D.R. I say proudly: "The only thing we have to fear is fear itself."

I have already made clear the reasons I'd rather remain anonymous. But, like they say, there is no use looking for trouble. It is for that reason that I have mailed this letter in a city far from where I live. I have typed it on a public, rented typewriter, with my gloves on the whole time. The only way you can really nail me is on the basis of internal, stylistic evidence, a form of evidence not highly regarded in the scholarly world today. From what I hear tell.

So all I'm asking is that you read what I got to say below about a certain party in your fair city and then, if your curiosity is aroused, just add his name to your list of random checks and let the chips fall where they may.

As a gentleman named S——, by trade a literary agent, I'm sure his income is modest enough. I think, however, that his business expenses and deductions might be justifiably scrutinized. For example, it is a matter of curiosity to me how a former Belly Dancer at the Port Said Restaurant, now unemployed, can also be listed as his Secretary when, in fact, she cannot type or take dictation, has at best a marginal interest in literary matters, and, so far as I can ascertain, has yet to enter his office. Maybe she works at home or, more accurately, at his second business address. I do know that he types his own mail and employs a young high school girl to answer his phone. I wonder if she, the nymphet, is paid the minimum wage and if he is keeping up with her Social Security etc.?

I do not understand how an M.G. sportscar driven almost exclusively by the aforesaid "Secretary" could legitimately be classified as a business car, in both depreciation and running cost and maintenance.

Moreover, although it is certainly true that the business of a literary agent involves considerable travel in the endless search for new talent, I fail to see how annual month-long trips to the Carribean, in the company of the aforesaid Secretary, are legitimate business trips. Unless, of course, he can show that in the course of these annual jaunts, he has met with writers and perhaps even added some new clients to his list.

Finally, there is his practice, almost unique among literary agents, of arranging various contracts so that the money will go directly to a client; the the client can pay him his commission. While this appears generous to a fault and expedites the payment to the client, it does seem strange that he prefers to receive at least a large part of his commission in cash or in a series of small U.S. Postal Money Orders mailed at irregular intervals.

Perhaps I am unduly suspicious. If so, please excuse me. I mean no harm.

148

I only want to serve. They also serve who stand and wait around.

     Yours truly,

     "John Q. Citizen"

P.S. His address is:

_____

_____

_____

Enclosure #2

Dear Mrs. S——,

The last thing in the world I want to do is to make trouble for you in any way or to cause you to worry. I *am* worried, however, about your husband. He is a man whom I deeply admire and respect, and I know how much you love him and how very much your love and his family mean to him.

That is the reason I am writing to you. Because I know that your immediate reaction will be the unselfish desire to help him in his hour of need.

Something bad has happened to your husband. At first I thought it merely fatigue and overwork, but more recently I am convinced that it is more serious than that. Mrs. S——, I believe your husband may be being blackmailed, probably for some minor indiscretion and peccadillo which he is too ashamed or proud to tell you about. Men are sometimes foolish like that. They fear to hurt the ones they love, not realizing that their loved ones have been made strong by their love. Not realizing that their loved ones are there ready, willing and able to help.

I do not wish to indulge in idle gossip nor to speculate, on the basis of very limited evidence, as to the details. All that I can say for certain is that for the past couple of years to my knowledge, and perhaps before that, your husband has been paying considerable sums of hard-earned money. To someone. I have no idea why. All I do know is that it hurts him deeply, it wounds him to be giving up money that by all rights should be forming a nest egg for his retirement years and, even more immediately, could be of real value in enabling your fine children to attend the college of their choice.

Of course, I know your husband too well not to realize that he would never let you be in real need. Even though there was hell to pay, he would see that his family is taken care of. But I think it is a shame that at a time when his business has never been better, when he is at the peak and prime of his profession, he cannot enjoy the fruits of his labors by sharing them with you.

For instance, I know that for years he has planned for the day when he could afford to buy a nice piece of property in the Catskills. Not that he loves the country, but you do and he has always been very proud of your "green thumb." It hurts me, almost as much as it must hurt him, to think that now that it would be easy for him to give you the place in the country he has always promised and planned, he cannot do so.

149

Maybe the situation he is involved in isn't as serious as he thinks. And, if it is, he needs your love and help as never before. I know that, come what may, you will stand by your husband. Though I have never had the pleasure of meeting you, I feel as if I know you from him. A lady of the old school. Someone wholly admirable, a model of courtesy, class, and courage.

I wish I knew more to tell you, but I'm sure when he knows that you are standing by him, he will share his troubles with you, just as he has always—until now at least—shared everything else.

It is entirely possible that Jane, his very personal Secretary, might know something about this unfortunate business. She worships your husband and it would be difficult for him to keep it a secret from her. Loyal to the last, as any good Secretary should be, she would never speak out of turn; but I believe she would be greatly relieved if you contacted her directly and asked her what the score is. I may be wrong about this. Having been with him so long, as you no doubt know, she may very will feel compelled to "play dumb," until he decides in his own good time to tell you himself. In any case, should you wish to talk to her privately, her unlisted phone number is: _____ She can usually be reached there any day between, say, 4:40 and 6:00 p.m.

I do hope that my "educated guess" turns out to be wrong. However, I know that *something* fishy is going on and the longer it does on, the worse things will be. Mrs. S——, I did not have the good fortune, the blessing to woo and win a lovely wife like yourself. I married for all the wrong reasons and I have lived to rue the day that I let impetuous attraction lead me to folly and sadness like a sheep to the slaughterhouse. I do not have a happy family like yours. I have only memories, most of which are regrets. I'm not complaining, though. Most people lead lives of quiet desperation and regret like mine. But you and your husband have something so fine and so special, that it simply *must* be preserved.

With deep admiration and the sincere conviction that all will be well now that the matter is in your lovely hands, I beg to remain

>Yours truly,
>A Faithful Friend

Dear Sam,

A friend in need is a friend indeed. Your most generous advance "against any future advance, royalties or earnings" came like a bolt out of the blue, a real and generous surprise. True to character all the way. You won't regret it, believe me. It's an investment in your future. And far more eloquent than any words you might have written. Just a check. It speaks volumes.

So it's full steam ahead for me. I'll be working like a madman from here on in. Actually I'm hard at work already on a project which I think you'll find highly original. Originality is "in" these days, and I think I have hit upon a gimmick that will really surprise you.

Not a word more, though. Not until the happy day (soon I hope) when I bundle off the MS to you.

Your belief & trust in me is better than a goof ball or even a shot in the arm.

You won't hear from me until my present property is ready. And please do not feel compelled to write me. Ignore my many questions & queries. Just relax, live a little, and wait and see what you're going to get in return for your faith & your $.

All the best, Sam. If I am brief, it's because I'm saving all my words & energy for the job at hand.

Your buddy,
Jack

P.S. You did me a big favor. So let me do you one. Here's a photostatic copy of a certain letter I received from Haiti. Just thought you might like to have it as a souvenir.

J.T.

Copy of Letter

My Darling Jack,

I bet you are plenty surprised to get a letter from me after all this time. And just look at the postmark and the fancy stationery. We are living it up down here in the best hotel and everything.

I am sitting by a window that overlooks the swimming pool. I have this great new bunch of bathing suits & am getting so tan I could pass for a native. The natives are mostly Jigaboos down here. They go around jabbering French for some reason. A lot of good it does them. I don't care what they are saying anyway. They are all the same, you know what I mean?, even if they are "well-hung."

Old Santa Claus, which is my private nickname for Sam, is flat on his behind in the bed, lying there like a big pig, snoring to beat hell. When he takes a nap, he takes up the whole bed. So I couldn't take a nap even if I wanted to. Not that I care. I encourage him actually, to tell the truth. What I mean is, I know if he eats a big lunch on top of a few drinks, he will go out like a light. I'd rather have him asleep and snoring than wide awake and raring to go. If you get what I mean.

Jack, you will never know how much I have missed you. Honest! Sure I was mad when you had to take off for Hollywood. Mad as hell. And jealous too, thinking all the time who you was with and what you two were doing. And I didn't really appreciate too much being set up with the Kike Santa Claus either. That was before I knew he was a Yid Santa Claus. I thought he was just repulsive. Well, he is still repulsive, but you get used to it in time. And I can't say he hasn't been very generous because he has.

Anyway, I'm not getting any younger you know. I wasn't exactly a "springy chicken" when you knew me. But, oh my, you sure made me feel a lot younger. It was like every time we were together you took years off my heart and miles off my feet. I like to have went nuts right after you left town. Like the song goes, I couldn't get no "satisfaction."

For quite a while there I hated you because I thought you had ruined me for everybody else the way they say Frank Sinatra does all those girls. I was so pissed off at you. I wished you every kind of bad luck.

All that is behind me now. I realize we could never have married each other. It wouldn't have worked. We would never have gotten out of the bed and we might have starved to death or been evicted or something (ha ha). Not that it wouldn't have been "a wonderful way to go!"

I saw this program on my new color T.V. (that Hebe Santa Claus gave me) all about Johnny Appleseed. And all of a sudden I burst out laughing out loud because I thought of you Jack and that you were a kind of Johnny Appleseed too. Only different.

I swear to God no man ever was or ever will be so "intimate" with me again. I mean, to be a little crude, we did it all. "That's all they is, folks. They ain't no mo'," as the Jigaboos say.

You know what? Now I'm grateful. It was quite an experience!

I know what you're thinking. I know you and your "dirty" mind. You are wondering about me and my old Jew-Santa. You would love to hear all the "gory" details. Don't deny it. Well, that will have to wait until the day when we meet in person. I feel kind of shy in a letter. All I can say is it doesn't bother me. It's usually over before it even gets going good. I don't take advantage though. I mean, some girls, especially if they had my kind of training in Middle Eastern Dance, could shorten the "experience" even more. I believe in giving him at least a fair chance. I believe in keeping the man that pays your bills happy. And if he's happy real quick and easy, then that's his problem. It suits me fine this way. If he was more "amorous" he might die of a heart attack or something. And then where would I be?

When I need a few "kicks," I can get them and he'll never know. What he doesn't know doesn't hurt him a bit. And I have a right to be happy too, don't I?

If you can take a hint, it would make me real happy if you would drop by the next time you're in New York. You're probably set up for life though. Teaching in a girl's school! There ought to be a law!

Maybe I can make you jealous. There's a waiter right here in this hotel who has got "equipment" you would have to see to believe. I didn't believe it myself, and I have "been around" a little. If I get real bored or fed up, all I got to do is snap my fingers and my French-talking Jig comes running.

This place is a drag though really. I am fed up with looking at Jigaboos and the pictures of their Jigaboo President everywhere. It just isn't neat and clean like Trinidad was where we went last year.

Well, I must close now. Sheeney Santa will wake up any minute and I will have to go back into the old act. You know what he calls me?—"Rosebud."

Maybe if I hadn't of gotten mixed up in show biz, I wouldn't of ended up like this. Nothing but a fat ugly old man's "Rosebud." The way to look at it though is it could've been even worse. You know?

Jack, baby, if you'll come and see me sometime, I'll prove to you everything I've been saying. Or if you can't make it maybe I can figure a way to come

152

to where you are. Ha-ha! Maybe Longnose Hymie Santa will send me.

Take care. Don't do anything I wouldn't do.

> All my love always,
> "Body & Soul"
> Jane
> XXXXXXX

G. Another Memo

MEMO:

TO: Lou Rosenfartz, So-Called Chairman

FROM: John Towne, Esq., Former Instructor

SUBJECT: Reply to your forthcoming silly and curt letter terminating my contract.

(1) I am not in the least angry or disappointed that, against all the ethics and customs and traditions of the academic profession, you are planning to "fire" me during the final week of school. It's typical of you and the way you do things—cowardly, sneaky, and halfassed!

(2) I am pleased to "beat you to the punch" with a letter of resignation. I have already seen your letter, in draft form, laying around the typing pool, waiting to be typed up. If you weren't so lazy, Lou, you could have typed it up yourself, saved time (College time) and spared those poor overworked, underpaid women, two-finger typists one and all, the effort and eyestrain of trying to make sense and order out of your absurd chicken scratchings.

(3) I'm not going to dignify your ridiculous "charges" with an answer. By and large, they are ridiculous. As the great Sam Goldwyn said, on another occasion, "It rolls off my back like a duck." Couple of things I can't let pass, though, trivial as they may seem. You make a big thing out of my misunderstood remarks at the Vietnam Teach-In. You refer to my offer, from the podium, of a five dollar bill to any student at Nameless who could properly locate and identify Laos and Cambodia on an unmarked map. That was not intended to insult anybody's intelligence or sincerity. It was frankly and honestly intended as an incentive. I wanted to make a contribution, and that seemed a polite way to do it. No irony intended. But, of course, I *was* being ironic when I suggested that, in any event, this war, just like mine in Korea, was a big waste of time "because no matter how many gooks and slopeheads we waste over there, these people multiply so fast that it will have no effect one way of the other on the Population Explosion. The Yellow Peril is here to stay." Or words to that effect. I was trying to shock those kids with the harsh realities of War. Of course I made a mistake. That kind of subtle irony is wasted on students. They are so literal minded. But I would have thought better of you. Reckon I was wrong. Reckon you wouldn't know subtle irony if you stepped in it. As for the damage resulting from the excitement following

my appearance at the Peace Podium, *I* didn't break up any furniture or windows. *I* didn't write obscenities on the walls of the Dolly Madison Room. *I* didn't take a crap in the wastebasket etc. I left the room immediately following my statement; in fact, I didn't bother to finish my statement. As soon as I saw that they were likely to misinterpret the tone of my remarks, I quit talking and left at once through the rear window, hoping that that would prevent them from becoming rowdy and riotous.

(4) As per the difficulties of Miss Linda Kelly. You refer to her "unpleasant medical problems." Which sounds a lot worse than it was. Somebody might think she was pregnant or something. In point of fact, as I understand it, Miss Kelly had the bad luck to come up with a little dose of clap and a pretty busy clutch and itch of the crabs. Miss Kelly was a good student, even if her record of absences during the last six weeks made it necessary for me to flunk her. So? She can graduate next year. Her old man can afford it. But I deeply resent your implication that I might have had something to do with her "difficulties." In a moment of hysteria and despair she might have said such a thing. If so, I forgive her. In a sense it is flattering, and, out of gallantry and good manners, I would cheerfully accept the blame if that would help her in any way and would serve to preserve her reputation. But it would serve no useful purpose. If you want to know how Linda Kelly got in trouble— out of a misguided social conscience, as it were—why don't you ask one of the Darkies (any of them) who mow the lawns and rake the leaves for Buildings and Grounds?

(5) But all of this is quite beside the point. The point is that I can no longer in good conscience work for a man who has repeatedly said that the American Association of University Professors "is entirely composed of dirty communist traitors, crooks, perverts, faggots and rat finks." And who has threatened to "ruin" anyone in our department who would join this distinguished organization.

(6) You say in your letter that I don't quite "fit in." You can say that again. I could never "fit in" with a department whose chairman continually makes crude and vulgar jokes at the expense of the beloved President of our college. Example: "What did our President do with his first fifty cent piece? He married it."

(7) Further I just can't cotton to your advice about how junior members of the department should add to the inadequate earnings. I guess I am just too old-fashioned to believe in padding expenses accounts with bogus items, or, for example, putting in for train or jet travel fare and then taking the Greyhound bus and pocketing the difference. Not only is this unfair to our College, but also I believe a man might get into serious trouble trying to cheat the Internal Revenue Service. Especially by deducting $25.00 for "Entertainment" every time some visiting writer or lecturer pokes his head on the campus.

(8) I was dismayed at your "personal advice" to me, as one of the few bachelors in the Dept. I certainly agree with you that self-abuse can have serious consequences. And I agree that adulterous relationships with faculty

154

wives is a bad idea, though I see it as a matter of morals, whereas you call it "bad taste." But where I have to draw the line, where I simply cannot go along with you is with your often repeated, one may say *obsessive* notion that young *students* are the obvious answer to any sexual problem. They pay a very high tuition to attend this institution. They come to acquire knowledge and one hopes, wisdom, not to be debased and degraded and abused and maybe even have their feelings hurt. I cannot agree that we ought to take advantage of the faith and trust of the Dean of Students. And upon the basis of a few meetings with that gracious lady, I cannot agree with you that she is "an old witch, half-senile, blind as a mole and deaf as a gate post."

(9) I can, of course, sympathize with your attitude when I stop to consider that you are bound by marriage contract to *Mrs.* Rosen. Still, sir, I do believe that a man of your age and education and experience should make some effort to try to control the bestial promptings of his *libido*. I am aware, naturally, that you have attempted to sublimate your abnormal sex urges by the solace of strong and secret drinking. But, my friend, that can only lead to more trouble. I agree wholeheartedly with your wife in her desire that you should swallow your pride and contact Alcoholics Anonymous. They can help you if you will let them.

(10) For all these reasons, then, together with many minor ones too tedious to enumerate, I hereby resign.

(11) Please do not trouble yourself about my future. You probably do not realize it, but I am a devout Catholic. I have been considering joining a Trappist Monastery for some time.

(12) I hope you can "pull yourself together" before it is too late and enjoy a happy and profitable future of teaching here at the College.

> Sincerely,
> John Towne

cc:
The President of the College
The Bursar
District Director of Internal Revenue
American Association of University Professors
Alcoholics Anonymous
Dean of Students

P.S. About my entirely and completely inadvertent public use of a number of vulgarisms and of several four letter words in swift sequence during the final Departmental Meeting. . . . Let me assure you, sir, that it is neither my habit nor custom to indulge in the use of vulgar or obscene language at any time, let alone in public. I tend to agree wholeheartedly with Sir Walter Raleigh (or was it Guy Fawkes? would you believe Henry Percy, Earl of Northumberland?) that style is what makes the man. I would never engage in ugly talk of my own volition. Unfortunately, at the precise time of the aforesaid meeting, I was under the influence of a strong tranquilizing drug, prescribed by the brutal and inept College Physician to enable me to meet the heavy obligations of grading final exams, term papers etc. The combination of that pill and the horrible Gallo sherry, which you insist on serving at Departmental Meetings, seems to have reduced my natural inhibitions and to have dredged forth, from the depths of my innocent unconscious, some dim words and phrases which I must have heard long ago in the barracks of the U.S. Army or the dormitories of Princeton University. However, under the circumstances, I must apologize. Still, I remain puzzled at your reaction. You stated to me, at the time and in the presence of the entire assembled Department, that it would be a capital idea if I excused myself to wash my mouth out with Octagon Soap. What the fuck is Octagon Soap????

J.T.

Part Eight

Saint John's Epistles to the Filipinos: Some Nasty Letters From 1980

Though falsehood go about
Of crime me to accuse,
At length I do not doubt
But truth shall me excuse
(Sir Thomas Wyatt—"Mistrustful minds be moved")

Saint John's Epistles to the Filipinos
1980

Dear Bo Derek,

Well, it has happened to me again. I have gone and slipped a disc in my back while raising up the mattress on my son Quincy's bed. Partly it's because I am old-fashioned enough to believe a body's mattress ought to be turned over every once in a while. How do you feel about turning mattresses? Anyway, all snooping aside, it is very very important for mothers to know what growing boys are hiding in different places of which under the mattress is one. Well, there I was, hoisting up that heavy mattress when, lo and behold!, there you were, smirking and nearly about as naked as an apple, right on the front cover of *The Playboy Magazine*. "Lordy, Lordy," I thought to myself, "last time it was 'Suzanne Somers' Nude Playmate Test: Ten Glorious Pages of TV's Hottest Sex Star' and now this!" I stood there holding the mattress up and trying to catch my breath when all of a sudden my back went out on me. It is positively ironic. As a Big Success and a child bride to boot, you probably haven't had a lot of time yet to learn about irony and arthritis and constant constipation and lower back pain and all the other things that life brings to all of us. But you will. You can bet your sweet little bootie on that! Meantime, however, the irony is all on me. Because, see?, last time I hurt my back was the time I lifted up Holiday's mattress (Holiday, that's my lazy, no-account, worthless, lowdown, brutal and bestial husband, who was born on Halloween which is how he got his name) to find the same thing—a bunch of bareass, buck nekkid pictures, taken by and sold for money by the same man, your husband, of one of his many earlier wives—Ms. Ursula Andress. Frankly I have come to feel pretty close to you Derek people. First and foremost there is the steady pain that's in my lower back, and the fact that I can't stand up straight any more, to remind me of you all. And that's one of those ironies, too. God doesn't give folks gifts equally. As you probably learned, yourself, in school when you tried to memorize the Gettysburg Address or how to do compound equations in Algebra. Anyway, the one good physical thing I had going for me was my posture. People used to compliment me all the time on my posture. And that made up for some of my minor problems.

159

But now thanks to you and your husband—say, is he as jealous and bad-tempered as they say in the fan magazines?; if so it may be better not to share this letter with him; a man of his age might have a fit or a stroke or something—and the other old wife, thanks to all of you, I've got a constant shooting pain and I can't stand up straight. That's bad enough, don't you think? But how about my men? They are like any other normal men. They look at your pictures and it excites them and they can't resist temptation. The net result is that they are completely corrupted, body and soul. You probably never passed a basic Sex Education Course (and not just because you couldn't memorize all the different complicated names of all the parts) or you wouldn't be so blithely doing what you are doing. You probably have heard of the Tragedy of Psoraisis. What the heck do you think Self Abuse is—a *comedy?* A bundle of laughs? On the contrary, it causes severe skin blemishes, it makes hair grow on the palms, and it causes the Syndrome of Progressive Brain Rot. Some authorities say that if you do it 1000 times, you die. When I informed Holiday of that medical fact, he just laughed and said in that case he has been a walking and talking ghost ever since the age of 12. Well, he can laugh all he wants to, but it is just plain sad to see how his brain has become . . . well, non-existent. Quincy, on the other hand, still might be saved if he could only break the habit. And I was doing pretty good, scaring the poo-poo out of him, even allowing for the Suzanne Somers lapse, until the March 1980 issue of *The Playboy* came into our house. Of course, I hid that copy that I found under the mattress. But, like a drunkard or a dope fiend, it turned out that he has copies stashed all over the house in many secret places. So does Holiday. He claims I can never find them all and they will never run out. Holiday says he wants at least one copy to be buried with him in his coffin. "Just in case I can still get it up in the next world," as he crudely puts it. Holiday is truly crude. So there's another one of those ironies. In a very real way, Mrs. Derek, we have both of the men in my life and house in common. Whether you are aware of it or not. But I want you to know that I bear you no grudge, Ms. Bo. You have your problems, I guess, and I have mine. Tell you the honest truth, all things considered, I would prefer even old Holiday to yours; even with his skin problems, hair-covered palms, and mushy birdbrain, he is at least . . . well, more, pardon the expression, *masculine* looking and acting, it seems to me. But what I'm really writing you about is this theory I have come up with that I want to share with you. I don't know if you, too, read a lot of books about espionage and the Monolithic International Communist Conspiracy. Come to think about it, I don't know if you read any books at all. I kind of doubt it, being as you have such a busy career and social life. But I have a lot of time on my hands and I read, and it came to me recently that it is just possible that your husband is some kind of Saboteur or Secret Agent. Maybe. Maybe his mission is to corrupt the health and welfare of the American male. So, while all the American men of military age are locked in the bathroom, looking at pictures of his wives and ex-wives and playing with themselves, the Commies can just walk right in and take over without firing a shot.

If that was to happen, it would make you the greatest American traitor since Benedict Arnold. But then, off course, the Commies would put statues of you all over in the parks and public places. Then the dopey Russians would see you and get all excited and tempted, too. Then they would be corrupted, and everybody on both sides would have equally no brain left (except us women and then we would take over at last!) and you would turn right around and be the biggest patriotic hero since Molly Pitcher.

Wow! That's a real irony for you. I bet it would make a swell drive-in movie.

Well, Ms. Bo, I must close now and get back to my "domestic chores." Lots of luck to you. May you keep your looks and your shape for as long as it is physically possible. Then you can cultivate your mind. Meanwhile, try and be real careful. Never lift up your husband's mattress. You might slip a disc, too. And who knows what you would find there?

All the best—

    Sincerely,

    Idabel Golk

Author's Intrusion

Look, man (and you, too, ma'am, if any) I know, oh yes, I know very well that a modern author is not supposed to (pardon the expression) *intrude*. Not in his own fiction or anybody else's either. It is very bad form. It is dumb. It will get you nowhere in the world of Modern Literature to go around intruding. It will give you a bad name.

I know better, but I have got to do it anyway.

You want to know what I think? It's Towne. It's got to be. Towne is back. It's the only reasonable explanation for the rash of poison pen letters recently reaching various distinguished, highly regarded, prominent public figures and, in some cases at least, hurting their distinguished, highly regarded, prominent, public feelings. It has been more than a decade since Towne did this kind of thing. He seems to have honored The Genteel Seventies. Of course, it could conceivably be somebody else, but the weight of evidence is against it. Everything has the Towne touch: all done on different typewriters and different kinds of stationery; all mailed from widely different regions, areas, and cities; none with even a hint of a fingerprint on it, which also indicates a highly developed sense of paranoia. Remember Towne feared and distrusted the F.B.I. long before it was fashionable. But the inferential evidence is even stronger. Style—nobody, at least nobody I know of, thank God, writes with such reckless disregard, if not invincible ignorance of unity, decorum, the amenities and good taste. Substance—beside the aforementioned incredible bad taste, Towne also has no sense of the difference between the sacred and the profane; he does not easily shy away from the unthinkable and the unacceptable. A few examples of his misanthropy will suffice. He does not take Leonard Bernstein seriously, in life or art. He thinks Gloria Steinem and

Phyllis Schlafly are "equally half-assed and ridiculous." He says William Sloan Coffin is "a howl" and has referred to him as "the Oral Roberts of the Old Left." Towne has been overheard telling Amy Carter jokes. He once referred to the Reverend Jesse Jackson as "the Leon Spinks of the Civil Rights Movement." In short, he is a living argument against a too strict or literal interpretation of the First Amendment. He is beyond redemption. Of course, you can bet yours that, like any bad-ass, he has a theoretical base for his unconscionable actions. First of all, he likes to cite *literary precedent*. He claims he is working in the genre of Satire, and he quotes *The Oxford Classical Dictionary* to support himself. He always quotes the general description, to wit that Satire (*Satura*) "may be broadly defined as a piece of verse, or prose mingled with verse, intended to improve society by mocking its anomalies, and marked by spontaneity, topicality, ironic wit, indecent humour, colloquial language, frequent use of dialogue, constant intrusions of the author's personality, and incessant variety of tone and style." Towne claims, therefore, to be in the ancient traditions of Lucilius, of Persius and Juvenal, of Joseph Hall (1574-1656) and his "byting Satires," of Pope and Swift and Defoe in *The Shortest Way With Dissenters*. He also offers the metaphysical argument that celebrities and public figures are not *real people*; that is, insofar as they are "images," and all that we really know is the image created by themselves or by the friendly or hostile media, they are not entitled to privacy or any special "rights." He of course maintains that he doesn't know any of these people from Adam or Adam's Housecat; so there is nothing personal at all in his insulting satires. Here (going too far!) he claims the support of the late Will Rogers, when he says—"All I know is what I read in the papers."

Who is this guy? You ask. I wish you hadn't. He started out simply enough as the protagonist in an unpublished and unpublishable novel of mine, called, after a headline in the *National Enquirer*—"Life with Kim Novak is Hell." In that role, briefly in the Sixties (and long before *The National Lampoon* got going) he was to be found in the pages of some wonderfully obscure little magazines. Maybe you ran across him in *Rapier, Latitudes, Per/Se, Contempora, Fly-by-Night,* or others of that fine ilk. If you did, you already know he is a Bad Human Being. And one of the nasty things he used to do was to write these poison pen letters/satires to public figures. His letter from an Illegal Alien, President of the Pancho Villa Club of West Texas, to Lyndon Johnson was considered a minor classic in some circles. The letter to Hugh Hefner was a hideous exercise in brute misanthrophy and bad taste. His letter to Ursulla Andress actually got the *Author* in trouble! "Enough is enough," I said, and abruptly ended the novel with Towne in real trouble, trapped in a hospital having an emergency appendectomy while cops, creditors, lawyers, and even the outraged parents of an underage young woman, who was a little bit pregnant by Towne, waited outside for him to try to leave.

"Get out of that, smartass," I said. "If you can. . . ."

Well, he sure did.

Disguised as a Black clergyman, under the improbably and probably insulting name of the Reverend Radio P. King, armed with false documents and a clutch of stolen credit cards, he walked right out the front door, escaped to London, England, and vanished. "Good riddance, creep!" That's what I said. So imagine my surprise a couple of years ago when Towne surfaced, in a photo in SOLDIER OF FORTUNE magazine, beating a big bass drum in the International Mercenery Marching Band. "Well, you have finally found your niche," I said. "Lots of luck." How could I have dreamed that he would demonstrate the gall, the brass, the *chutzpah*, the crazy courage (if you insist) to come back here to the scene of the crime and start in again? Well, he's out there somewhere and up to no good. Here I present some brief excerpts and highlights of the kinds of insulting things he has been writing. But first I'd like to assure everybody—and especially all the prominent and powerful people he hereinafter mentions or refers to—that Towne's opinions and feelings are strictly and entirely his own, not mine. (Of course, he would claim the same, since he has created fictional characters who write the letters.) I would also like to promise that as soon as I can locate him, I will stamp out and suppress forever his perverted idea of fun and games.

Towne, wherever you may be, enjoy it while you can. Your days are numbered. Soon your you-know-what will be sucking wind. Meantime, here are some random and representative examples of your recent work.

Dear Ronald Reagan—
You really look terrific these days. Who does your hair? Who is your Makeup Person? I, myself, am a Mortician by trade, and I can tell a really good job when I see one. . . .

Dear Livingston Biddle—
Hey, I would just like to congratulate you on all the really swell things you are doing to shape up the Fine Arts in America. I am especially pleased that you are making some real progress in closing down New York City as a so-called cultural center. They have had their chance, those lazy, overpaid, no-talent creeps! Most of them are illegal aliens or minority freeloaders or just smart-aleck kooks anyway. It's important to spread the wealth and culture around a little more, anyway. Here in Vermont we have a wonderful group of which I have the honor to serve as President—The Lewis Carroll Chowder and Nymphet Marching Society. With a grant from you guys we could buy some cameras and work a tie-in with local Girl Scout and Brownie Troops. And everybody would be happy. . . .

Dear Governor Jerry Brown—
Me and my good buddy, Leroy (we work together as the ha-ha "tail team" on a garbage truck) are really great fans of your philosophy, your career, and your way of life. We would sure enough like to see you win the election, or, anyway, win *something* before you die. But the main reason I am writing

is that Leroy and I have had a great big argument that has turned into a serious five dollar bet and is now a (pardon the expression) Mexican Standoff. Can you settle it for us? Leroy says that Linda Ronstadt was the star in the cinematic classic—DEEP THROAT. I say no, it was Linda Kasabian of The Charles Manson Gang. Who is right? If it turns out that Leroy is right, I can sure understand why you took her over to Africa with you. . . .

Dear Linda Lovelace—

I happened to be home with the 'flu the other day and saw you on the Phil Donahue show. Wow! I can't wait to read your new book—*Ordeal*. I loved DEEP THROAT, but I couldn't figure out how you could ever really top that one. Well, this whole new gimmick is just brilliant. By saying the they *made* you do it, *forced* you to against your will, you get what amounts to a re-run on the whole thing with a new wrinkle—the kinky stuff. Meanwhile you get to go around to all the talk shows, dressed real modest and matronly, like somebody's sister or mother or something. And that's pretty sexy, too. There are no flies on you, girl! Do you mind if I ask you a question? That guy Donahue, did he, you know, *after the show*. . . ?

Dear President Carter—

I finally figured out the whole thing and I want to offer my congratulations. It never occurred to me, not until last night down at the Tavern, how you and that crazy Ayatollah rigged this whole thing from start to finish. Brilliant! Eat your heart out Tricky Dick Nixon! I mean, you diverted everybody's attention and you fixed it so nobody can really run or campaign against you. So *that's* what you meant about whipping Teddy's ass! And the beauty of it is that no harm has been done. I mean even the Hostages have no real complaint coming. They are salaried government employees and have to be in Iran anyway. This way they can get their back pay and probably bonuses, plus anything they can raise for writing about it. When it all came clear, I told the guys at the Tavern, and I added that the Bert Lance trial is probably a Publicity Stunt also. "That shows how dumb and innocent you are," my friend Rodney ("Rosebud") Flowers said. Rodney is a real cynic. *He* claims that dumb Lance may think it's a publicity stunt, but that what you really have in mind is getting out from under the huge personal debt you owe him. What is it—five million? In a way, I hope Rosebud is right. It proves you don't have to be well-educated or even very smart to be real shrewd. . . .

Dear Senator Teddy—

Your campaign is the funniest thing since the late Barry Goldwater ran back in '64. You are just too much! You and your whole gang. You have cleverly managed to offend nearly about everyone. Is it true that your old Mama is writing your speeches? And she never wanted you to run in the first place? Don't answer that unless you really feel like it.

The main and real reason I am writing to you is to suggest a brand new approach to the so-called Chappaquiddick problem. I am not at all sure that the arguments suggested by your highly paid advisors have been very helpful. I mean, I know times passes swiftly and all that, but, even so, it seems to me a little too soon to pretend you've forgotten all about it and couldn't care less. A lot of people seem to take umbrage at that. Why not turn the thing around on them? Next time they bring it up, just put it to them this way: "Look, what if *I* had drowned and *she* was the one who had managed to escape? Would you still be picking on her after all these years? Would people hold it against her and not elect her the first woman President of the U.S.A.?"

If you will only try that, you will stun them into complete silence.

Hang in there and never quit.

> Yours,
> Joe ("Snake") Timilty

Not even the minor decorative arts, like contempory poetry, are safe from Towne's nihilistic japes and pasquils. Here, for instance, is a proposal evidently intended for the very distinguished John Frederick Nims, Editor of *Poetry: A Magazine of Verse*. The idea, in a longwinded letter, was that to increase the circulation of POETRY and, as well, to cut down on the number of pages filled with "Neo-surrealist mumbling," Nims should begin to include games and contests and even gossip columns about living poets. He suggested that one "game" could be based on the idea of finding an analogue in real life (actually, Towne said "a real human being") who is in some way *like* a contemporary poet. To show what he meant, Towne included a sample list. I have no idea who any of these people are, so I can't judge the wit and/or wisdom of his comparisons, but perhaps somebody else can.

Diane Wakowski is the Martha Rae of American Poetry.
Charles Wright is the Bill Blass of American Poetry.
James Dickey is the Idi Amin of American Poetry.
Robert Bly is the Torquemada of American Poetry.
Carolyn Forché is the Ann-Margret of American Poetry.
Daniel Halpern is the Sol Hurok of American Poetry.
Louise Gluck is the Greta Garbo of American Poetry.
Stanley Plumly is the Tommy Manville of American Poetry.
James Dickey is the Idi Amin of American Poetry.
Donald Justice is the Bobby Fischer of American Poetry.
Charles Bukoski is the John Belushi of American Poetry.
Lyn Lifshin is the Typhoid Mary of American Poetry.
Michael Harper is the Emperor Bokassa of American Poetry.
Mark Strand is the George Bush of American Poetry.
Dave Smith is the Robert Penn Dickey of American Poetry.
James Tate is the Steve Martin of American Poetry.
W.S. Merwin is the Bo Derek of American Poetry.

Joyce Carol Oates is the Shelley Duvall of American Poetry.
Galway Kinnell is the Smokey the Bear of American Poetry.
Charles Wright is the Bill Blass of American Poetry.
Carolyn Kizer is the Carol Doda of American Poetry.
Fred Chappell is the John Boy Walton of American Poetry.
Brendan Galvin is the Seamus Heaney of American Poetry.
Howard Moss is the Pope of American Poetry.
F.D. Reeve is the Superman of American Poetry.
Dabney Stuart is the R.H.W. Dillard of American Poetry.
Gertrude Schnackenberg is the Sally Rand of American Poetry.
Charles Bukoski is the Joe Cocker of American Poetry.
John Ciardi is the Godfather of American Poetry.
Helen Vendler is the Joan Rivers of American Poetry.
David Huddle is the Warren Beatty of American Poetry.
Charles Wright is the Calvin Klein of American Poetry.
George Garrett is the Don Rickles of American Poetry.
And so on and so on. Keep it up and you'll soon have yet another anthology. . . .

Part Nine

Exemplary Letters From the Exemplary 1980s

I cannot honor them that sets their part
    With Venus and Bacchus all their life long;
    Nor hold my peace of them although I smart.
I cannot crouch nor kneel to do so great a wrong,
    To worship them, like God on earth alone,
    That are as wolves these seely lambs among.
        (Sir Thomas Wyatt—"Satires")

There are cozeners abroad; therefore it beehooves men to be wary.
        (Shakespeare—*The Winter's Tale*, IV, ii.)

A Few Final Letters
from the 1980s

NOTE: It appears that he's still at it; for the following letters, selected from among many tasteless and foolish and unpleasant items sent to celebrities, dignitaries and various and sundry Sacred Cows— Hey, speaking of, you know, sacred cows, I wish I could publish the text of his letters to Farrah Fawcett and to Princess Caroline. Boy are they something! In the Farrah Fawcett one he actually tells the old joke about the monkey and the lion marooned on an island by a flood. But there is, even in the US&A, a limit to candor. There are things better imagined than talked about. So, just imagine Towne letters to these two, together with such political types as Jesse Jackson (a letter which sets back race relations even more than the Kerner Report and the Bakke decision), George McGovern (a letter which includes some horrid references to Alzheimer's Disease as a possible explanation for the conduct of this distinguished and perennial candidate), Gary Hartpence and Fritz Mondale, the latter of whom Towne, in his invincible ignorance, assumes to be *Italian*, thus allowing himself occasion to tell Mafia jokes and to make cracks about modern Italian military history etc. Anyway, it looks like Towne is still alive and up to no good. Or that he *was* alive and up to no good at least as late as late 1983 and early 1984. Of course, there's always a possibility that these poisonous communications are not by Towne at all, but, rather, by some imitator or literary clone or copy-cat. Internal evidence suggests otherwise, but (see the letter to Truman Capote) there are gifted cozeners abroad. There is also the distinct possibility that we stand at the threshold of a new age in which the PEOPLE, fed up with the veritable Herpes-2 rash of celebrities we have to live with, will take up the art and craft of the poison pen letter and fill the mails with their venomous words and phrases. What I guess I mean, folks, is that anybody but me (oh no not I, not I!, NOT I!) could have written these things in the Towne manner. Perhaps already there is a Pseudo-Towne out there doing his thing. Time will tell. Meantime it's better not to think about it.

So here goes. A few final bits of documentary evidence to round out this so-called book. Laugh or avert your eyes as it pleases you. And, please, don't blame me. I only work here.

Hail & Farewell—
Lee Holmes
Professor Emeritus, Nameless College

Dear Brooke Shields—

As an old alumnus, myself, I would like to take this opportunity (belated as it may seem; after all, you have been there a year already) to welcome you to Princeton University. I guess it is a lot different now. In fact, I *know* it's a lot different now what with not only broads in the classroom as well as the bedroom, boys and girls actually *matriculating* together, if you'll pardon the expression, and with funny-looking people of every race, creed, religion and national origin wandering around in their designer jeans and sleeveless down jackets and their little back packs for books and stuff, every kind of person, a veritable rainbow coalition of students, swarming all over Cannon Green and McCosh and the Firestone Library, freed forever of the quota system, liberated to come to Princeton and study their Freud and their Nietzsche and their Marx, their Camus and Sartre, their Plath and Rich and Sexton . . . .

(Say, did you ever see that joke poster they had a couple of years ago at Yale? I think Princeton was too insecure to allow it. Anyway, it showed this great, big, humongous Spade with a head like a cannonball, wearing a letter sweater and carrying an armload of books—Freud, Nietzsche and Marx, Pound, Eliot, and Yeats etc. And the caption was: A STRONG BACK IS A TERRIBLE THING TO WASTE. Get it? My idea is to update it. We make a poster of you in your underwear or a string bikini or something eye-catching, carrying a bunch of books—stonedead female poets and famous feminist literary critics, that kind of crap—and a sad, perplexed look on your face. Maybe you are wearing reading glasses. Anyway, the caption would be: "It Is a Shame to Waste a Sweet Ass!" Ho-ho-ho. Only kidding, Brooke.)

Anyway, it must be a lot different now what with all those kinds of kids you never even saw in my time unless you had to go over to Rutgers for some reason or else made a trip to the Empire Burlesque Theater in Newark. Where, coming and going and in the theater, you could see all kinds. A regular zoo of God's mistakes and low rent models, as we thought of them then, in those lost and happy days.

Hey, you could see some splendid stuff, firstclass quiff and nooky, on the stage, too. My favorite of all time was Winnie Garrett, The Flaming Redhead. Gosh, she was nice! Chunky, but very, very nice! I can still get an erection just remembering her. (Do you ever wonder, Brooke, if there are guys out there who can get it up just *remembering* you? That is the true test of stardom.

Maybe there would be some way to make it scientific. Where you could get a crowd of guys, say, in an experiment; and then just flash a name on the screen, that's all. That way you could probably rank the stars very accurately. Don't mention this idea, though. Or next thing you know they'll be doing it at some place like Chapel Hill or the University of Texas in El Paso.)

Hey, I hope you aren't going to let your mother read this letter. She is closer to my generation and she might not understand, you know? If she does happen to get hold of this letter, you can reassure her that I mean well. After all I have a daughter your age. Of course, she's not as pretty as you are (who is?). In fact, she's about as plain as pig tracks and not too smart either. Princeton wouldn't touch her. (The only quota they have now is *against* alumni children.) But there are compensations, Brooke. She is rich, very rich, richer than you ever can or will be. I'm rich, of course. But my wife, actually my ex-wife, an equally plain lady from Providence, Rhode Island (actually she looked and still does sort of like Senator Claiborne Pell in drag. Or vice versa), my ex-wife is so fucking rich you can't begin to comprehend it. She can make private loans to Developing Third World Nations (what we used to call Banana Republics and *National Geographic* countries in the good old days) and never even feel the pinch of it. And she does, too. It's one of her great weaknesses. I mean, Idi Amin turns her on. She would like to get it on with Robert Mugabe. Except he isn't really primitive enough for her. Of course, she has this huge weakness for Black guys. All except American Blacks. They bore her. She thinks they have been corrupted by hanging out with white folks for too long. Be that as it may, she has been a great help to certain *bona fide* Africans and certain crummy little countries which have come to depend on her. I mean, if she lost her checkbook for a week, you would read in the paper about the fall of various and sundry governments on the Dark Continent. (I bet they don't call it the Dark Continent at Princeton any more, Brooke. They probably don't even refer to Medieval times as the Dark Ages. Say, does the expression "Wogs begin at Calais" mean anything to the youth of your generation?) Anyway, my wife is much involved in the aid and comfort of Developing Nations and Developing Peoples. (Actually the guys from over there are pretty well *developed*, if rumor be truth. I mean, those coon studs are hung. Am I right? What is your opinion, Brooke? Do you have the experience to back up your opinion? I'm only kidding. If Jean Seberg was still around, we could ask her. But she isn't. And I'm sorry about that, to tell the truth. I always liked her in the movies. Especially in *Breathless*.) Anyway, my wife is very generous to these folks and their fly-by-night governments. Meanwhile she is very tight, not at all generous with her old friends, ex-lovers and ex-husbands. She won't even lend me money these days. The last time I tried to borrow some $ off her, I got all dressed up in a *dashiki* and did myself up in blackface like Al Jolson and tried to get her attention at the Country Club. She wasn't amused. Not even a little bit. Well, she was never famous for her sense of humor. Except cruel humor at other people's expense. Her idea of a funny joke was, just before we were supposed to have sex, to point at my tumescent you-know-what and chortle and say "What's that?"

"A penis," I was supposed to say.

"That's not a penis," she would then remark. "A penis is black and nine inches long."

Then she would laugh her ass off and keep on laughing the whole time we were doing it. You might wonder why I went along with that (and others as well) degrading and humiliating practice. Well, you may not believe this, but that plain-faced, skinny woman could move like a python and was, all things considered, the finest piece of ass I have ever known. I mean, she was incredible. I have no doubt, indeed I have every confidence that both Idi Amin and Robert Mugabe would agree with me if they ever got a chance to make it with Priscilla. (That was her classical, WASP-o name.) WASP girls are often decadent, even degenerate at times, but the novels by ethnics have it all wrong. They are very physical and enjoy a good toss in the hay as much as anybody—even Hungarians.

I can tell you this much, Brooke, from a lifetime's experience. When it comes to fucking, looks aren't everything. In fact, making it with some pretty girls is like making it with a tackling dummy. Do they still have tackling dummies? Does Princeton still play Tackle Football, or have they changed over to (pardon) Touch?

Listen, on second thought, I think you better not let your mother see this at all.

You know who I think, among your generation of movie stars, is probably a good lay—Jody Foster. That's right, her. That guy Hinckley was ready to kill for her. His only problem was he is a lousy shot. If he had practiced and improved his marksmanship, George Bush would probably be President right now. I read somewhere that Bush was supposed to have dinner with Hinckley's parents that same evening or shortly thereafter. But everyone decided it would be in bad taste if he went ahead with the dinner party anyway. It is important, if you are a politician, not to be caught doing something in bad taste.

Say, did you read the piece in *Esquire* by Jody Foster where she admitted that the first thing that flashed through her brain when she heard the news about Hinckley and all was: *Why me? Why not Brooke Shields?* Or something like that.

You didn't know Hinckley, too, did you?

Anyway, Brooke, Princeton and all that. God, it was wonderful in our days. And I hope it still is. We had more fun than you can imagine. For one thing, we were pretty much drunk the whole four years. I had a slight buzz on the whole time. Or so it seems. It probably wasn't true. I mean, nobody took academics very seriously, but you still had to study once in a while. I know I must have done some studying. Otherwise I wouldn't have graduated, would I? Still, I have no clear memory or recollection of studying anything. I can't remember what I majored in. Maybe I didn't actually graduate. Maybe I should look into that. I do know I was in my senior year, getting ready to write my senior thesis before I found out for sure which building was the Library. I never did learn about how to use the card catalogue. I just wandered around (it was an open-stack library in those days—why should a WASP steal a *book*?) and took things out of the stacks that interested me. I remember the Locked Library. That's where they kept all the dirty books and all the books with pictures of naked women in them. It was tough to get to see anything in the Locked Library. You had to go and see a lady who looked like everyone's grandmother and explain it to her. She would then make a disapproving face and give you a lot of shit and then go get it, about as fast as Steppin Fetchit on a slow day, if you persisted. It was worth it, though. I mean, that was your choice if you wanted to see a picture of a naked woman. I mean, that was even before *Playboy* came along. That's how old I am. If you had to see a naked woman, you could go to the Locked Library. (once in a great while you could see a little bit of titty in some foreign Art Movie at the Garden Theater, but not often). Or you could get on the train and go up to Newark and the Empire Theater and see a real naked woman on the stage there. (It was safe too, coming and going in those days. There were still some white people left in Newark.) I already mentioned Winnie Garrett. And there were plenty of others, too. But I would be deeply remiss if I didn't pause to salute the happy memory of Georgia Southern. She was something else, old Georgia! She could undress and get bareass faster than anybody I've ever seen on stage or off. She would come out dancing and tear off her clothes before you could say Rumpelstiltskin. Thus she would be naked longer than any of the others. Which we all deeply appreciated. Me and my roommates.

Who are your roommates, Brooke?

I had three. There was old Shag. He was really a fine guy, funny as can be. He flunked out senior year and managed (last I heard) to get the shit shot out of him in World War II. A lot of Princeton guys got the shit shot out of them in World War II and Korea and even Vietnam later on. You can probably find their WASP names on little memorials hidden here and there around campus. WASP snobbery didn't pay off much in wartime. The WASPS would fill up the Infantry, Artillery and Armor and leave the support units to the . . . rainbow coalition. It is very hard to get killed in the Quartermaster Corps, Brooke. So a lot more of Them survived. And now their children and grandchildren, sons and daughters alike, go to places like Princeton and study people like Nietzsche, Marx, and Freud, great thinkers whom, I assure you, girl, we never thought of, let alone studied. Shit, we were still reading Walter Pater. About as deep as we got in psychology was translating the good parts of Kraft-Ebbing.

Besides poor old Shag, there was The Fra and Big Lou. The Fra had been a wonderful wrestler in prep school. But once he got to Princeton he discovered booze. And after that he only wrestled girls in New York hotels. You would have liked The Fra, Brooke. He wasn't too bright, but he was good looking and could wrestle. Girls liked him a lot. Junior year he brought one back from New York and tried to fuck her in the dorm and got caught and expelled. They would expel you in those days if you sneaked a girl into the dorm after 7:00 p.m.

The Fra got wasted in the War, too. But I don't think it was in combat.

174

Somebody's husband walked in on him at the wrong time.

Big Lou didn't. He was 4-F. Which was funny, because he was the jock of the crowd. He played football when that was still something respectable to do. He got clobbered, both knees, playing football and thus was too banged up to serve in World War II. That was before the face mask came in. Big Lou blocked a kick in the Colgate game and that fixed his nose up just fine and dandy. And it took all his teeth. Every damn one of them. Imagine that! Twenty years old and not a real tooth in his head!

Anyway, Big Lou got into banking, what else? And everything was cool until about ten or twelve years ago he got caught in some kind of a suburban development scheme or scam, something involving the government's money, and had to take early retirement. (Thank God there are still enough WASPS and old-time Princetonians in the Judiciary to keep most of us out of jail. Usually gentlemanly arrangements can be made.) Hanky-panky or not, Big Lou is a very prominent alumnus and a leader of our Class. Which is why I seldom go to Reunions. There he is, drunk out of his mind, lost his false teeth somewhere, and still trying to be the life of the party. He is very conservative. He doesn't approve of all the changes at Princeton. When they had the big all-faith, ecumenical service at the Chapel a year or so ago and covered up the Cross so it wouldn't offend the Muslims and Jews and Pagans and Atheists or others in the Student Body, Lou was very upset. He even wrote letters to the *Alumni Weekly*. Funny thing is, Big Lou wasn't very religious in the old days. He would sit up in the balcony and read the *Times* during chapel. (We had *required* chapel in those days, Brooke.) He would get religious as can be just before a football game. He would pray a lot and lip-read from *The Book of Common Prayer* in the locker room. It made the other guys nervous, but Lou was too big and mean for them to mess with. So they tried to ignore him. After the Colgate thing, where he lost his teeth and his face changed considerably, he figured he had better pray before every game or else something even worse (maybe damage to the *family jewels?*) would happen to him. But once the game was over he forgot about it until next Saturday morning.

Besides drinking and playing sports and screwing around (the latter as much as we *could*, which wasn't much), what else did we do at Princeton? Well, we went to the movies a lot. And we sang. People were always singing in those days. We sat on the steps of Nassau Hall, on fine spring evenings, and sang songs, *Princeton* songs. Can you believe that?

How I wish we were all young again! I wish I was young enough to go back to Princeton. We would meet, Brooke, and become good friends. I'll never forget you in *Blue Lagoon*. I'll never forget your ass in that movie. It was wonderful. The memory of it—and you, too, because, of course, you were attached to it—doesn't have the Winnie Garrett Effect on me. (She was kind of like your ass all over, if you know what I mean.) But it's a warm, good feeling. And I know it's an image that will mean more and more to me as the years to by.

I just want to thank you for sharing your ass with all of us in *Blue Lagoon*.

And I want to wish you the best of luck in all your endeavors at Princeton.

175

I see where some old *alums* have written snotty letters about you. Let them scoff as may. I, for one, am proud of my old school for admitting you. Don't be troubled by all that intellectual stuff. It doesn't mean any more now than it did then. Student poets may be the (pardon) tailbacks of this New Age. But they still have the same basic thing in mind. You can count on it.

Stay well and don't study too hard. If it is any consolation, remember there's a nice old guy somewhere who thinks the world of you and wishes you well and is a lot better shot than Hinckley.

    All the best X X X
    Worthington Snood

P.S. If you mother does happen on this letter, I wish her well, also.
    W. S.

Dear Mrs. DeLorean,

One supposes, and not entirely without good reason and sound precedent, that simple candor has its place—and not a purely negligible one, all things considered—even in such an ephemeral document as this friendly letter to you.

(Oh, fuck it! That's not my style or my voice. I just wanted to sound good, educated and all, you know? But it won't work. I couldn't fool you or anyone else for long. Let me start over. Okay?)

Look here. As far as I am concerned, *he* is nothing more than a Scuzz and a Sleazeball, a veritable Scumbag, the original Rotten Apple (full of worms) In Person. Just imagine you are out walking in the woods. Not that you probably ever have been out there all alone by yourself in the woods for any good or bad reason; not that you probably ever will be prissing and sashaying around in the forest showing off your nice round ass and the nice tight fit of your designer jeans to appreciative chipmunks and woodpeckers; but, anyway, at least you can kind of imagine what walking in the woods would be like for somebody who would do something like that; maybe you can even actually imagine yourself doing it too; sort of poetic, when you think about it, an imaginary woods with real fashion models moping around in it. Okay . . . So imagine you are out there walking in the woods one day. You turn over an old rotten log. And out from under crawls something very snotlike and pale. If it had a face (and a facelift) and could talk pretty good English, well, that will give you some idea of just how I view the inward and spiritual truth of the outward and visible apparation; namely and to wit, your husband, the celebrated and inimitable John Z. DeLorean.

As far as I am concerned he is nothing but Cow Flap.

Now, I realize that one way and another he may eventually beat the rap on the cocaine caper. (As I write, even now, he is on trial. And you are by his side, looking good, babe!) Juries and Judges are getting dumber every day. Lawyers, on the other hand, are getting smarter and more expensive than ever. But guilty or innocent won't really change anything fundamental. By which I mean to say that a man is what he is and is likewise the sum of all his deeds, good and ill, no matter what the Courts may choose to say or not say and no matter how many many times you and your sweet-faced family may appear on the cover of *People* magazine. Say, be honest with me. Are those *really* your kids? Or did you just rent some good looking child actors from Central Casting to pose for the photographs? Excuse my cynicism and skepticism, but it has been done before, you know. And frankly they look quite different each time. Enough to arouse anyone's natural suspicions.

Anyway. To continue.

A man is what he is and so is always the sum total of all his thoughts and dreams and deeds no matter what press agents and lawyers may say and do to enhance his public image. And this selfsame rule applies to all of us, regardless of race, creed, color, gender, age, county of national origin, or ideological persuasion. Even me. I admit I have got some things, a few anyway, to be ashamed of and to feel sorry for. But I have also got a couple of things to be proud of. That's how it is in real life, you know.

All things considered, however, and as far as I am concerned, he is Doggie Doo.

What I can't for the life of me figure out is, except for his facelift and fancy haircut and his significant weight loss, what the fuck John Z. DeLorean has to be proud of? Maybe you can tell me. Unless it is a big secret. Like maybe he is secretly hung like a Percheron draught horse. Or something. But you can't just tell something like that to the whole world. If it is true that he has a (pardon the expression) "big secret," then I do have to admire your tact and discretion. Actually I also admire your dark, Italian-type good looks and your really swell bod. Insofar as I have seen the latter. I mean, lately you can't exactly run around doing string bikini numbers in public while your image is also supposed to be that of a lovely and loving housewife and mother, keeping a fairly straight face and a reasonably serious expression on it while you are hanging out in the best places. Listen, I think you are wonderful, as you probably have guessed. If I, myself, woke up, like in a Francis Kafka story, and found myself turned into John Z. DeLorean, I would probably lie, steal, and cheat as much as anyone. In fact I reckon I would do almost anything I had to do in order to be able to afford you and to be able to look forward to the pleasant prospect of coming home after a hard day of chicanery and double dealing and—after calming down with a couple of cans of lite beer and maybe watching a show or two on the tube—fucking your brains out. We would fuck like deranged rabbits all night long. Of course, that is my own particular hangup. When it comes to pretty women—and you sure are one of those, no one dast deny that, I am an incurable romantic. I have heard that most Italians are incurably romantic also and that they like to fuck as much as they like to eat and drink. Is that so? Of course, here I am just assuming that you are primarily of an Italian ethnic background. I could be wrong?

Am I wrong?

But please forgive me. I do not want to get personal in this letter. Nor

177

do I wish in any way whatsoever to offend you. And if I have managed, in spite of myself and all my good intentions, to offend you in any way, shape or form, I hereby apologise and take it all back.

You may wonder why it is that I am writing to you instead of directly to Captain Douchebag, himself. I mean, he is the one who is in the deep shit, right? He is the one who is currently standing one trial and will probably have to stand some others, too, before he shakes off this mortal coil. It is, after all, he alone who gives us folks out in the cheap seats a true Aristotelian and cathartic belly laugh. We can laugh our collective ass off at his fall from greatness. Up and down it goes, the old Wheel of Fortune and all that jazz. Some people get a case of the herpes. Well, he's got the hurbis. (If you know what I mean.) And the latter is, finally, a whole lot funnier than the former. At least from my limited point of view.

In any case, it certainly doesn't have a whole hell of a lot to do with you and those cute kids in the photographs. Like England, the old U.K. as they call it, may be out a few millions of pounds. A large number of Northern Irishmen may be out of work again. Some of the smart money boys over here, together with the usual boring quota of widows and orphans and the like, may have dropped a few bucks, betting on the future as it was envisioned by John Z. DeLorean. (Rule of thumb: don't ever bet on anybody whose middle initial is Z.) But, by and large it is a pretty banal story. If it weren't for you, Cristina, the whole thing would be on a level of ho-hum interest about the equivalent of a mini-series on "The Adventures of Billie Sol Estes." Now, I know that some people see it as a symbolic story—the flip side of the American Dream, the dark side of America The Beautiful. And there might even be something to all that. I have just read three hardcover books all about your husband. That's a whole lot of hardcover books about one Horseturd, wouldn't you agree? I have purchased—and at the full retail price, not patient and willing enough to wait for them to appear on the remainder tables, *DeLorean: Stainless Steel Illusion,* by John Lamm (Santa Ana, CA: Newport Press, 1983. 160 pp. $17.95); *Dream Maker: The Rise and Fall of John Z. DeLorean,* by Ivan Fallon and James Srodes (New York: Putnam's, 1983. 455 pp. $16.95); and *Grand Delusions: The Cosmic Career of John DeLorean* (New York: Viking Press, 1983. 336 pp. $15.95) by Helen Levin. And thus, unless my addition is all wrong and not counting expenses like buying copies of *People* which have had stories about you all, I have, it seems, already invested a minimum of $50.85 in basic research materials concerning that Creep, that Personification of Poopoo. At the very least you will have to concede that I have put some good money where my bad mouth is. Seriously, however, and speaking of bad-mouthing, I may not be exactly complimentary when I refer to him, from time to time, in colloquial terms as various kinds and forms of Animal Excrement. But, believe me, all purely stylistic considerations aside, I have not even come close to saying the terrible things about him that these three published books do. Admittedly, they are smoother, at once more suave and polite. They do not, for example, at any time refer to him as Shitbird or as Birdshit either. But, nevertheless, they are extremely derogatory in their discussion of his many scams, cons, and hustles. They are always quoting him as saying things that, in the context of how things are turning out, are more than a little bit ironic. Personally, I especially like the one that is cited on the jacket of Levin's book, where your boy, old Mousedropping, is quoted as saying: "As hard as I've struggled, I'm one man who can say that my dream has come true."

Ha-ha! And Double-Ha!

Speaking of irony (if we must), I really do like the ad for Cutty Sark Scotch which was published in a whole lot of magazines a little while back, you know the one with a photo of the DeLorean Sports Car and the wonderfully inspiring headline: ONE OUT OF EVERY 100 NEW BUSINESSES SUCCEEDS. HERE'S TO THOSE WHO TAKE THE ODDS. A real collector's item! (If you are into collecting irony.) It goes on to say: "John DeLorean anticipates the needs and wants of car buyers. He does no less for the scotch drinkers he invites home. That's why he selects and serves the impeccably smooth Cutty Sark." Tell me the truth, my impeccably smooth Cristina, did he used to invite a whole lot of scotch drinkers home? Did they all get sloshed and crosseyed on Cutty Sark? Did they fall down? Did they barf in your piano and your potted plants?

What kind of booze does he plan to drink if he ends up drawing some hard time in the slammer? Sterno?

Anyway.

The three books are all different from each other. And yet each one has a multitude of insulting things to say about old Ca-ca. There are also various and sundry very ironic photographs. Like pictures of the two of you together, smiling and looking sincere as you toast the world (& the flesh & the Devil?) with glasses of champagne on the occasion of the ground-breaking for the famous DeLorean factory in Northern Ireland on October 2, 1978. Probably the best photographs are to be found in *Stainless Steel Illusion*, although the most extensive pictorial coverage is in *Dream Maker*. There is a fine photo of Mr. Chickenshit, himself, dancing with an earlier wife of his, Kelly Harmon, the great Tom Harmon's daughter. If you don't mind my saying so, she was quite a good looker too. Say, did you ever see Tom Harmon play football? No, I would guess not. Even if you are a few years older than you look or will ever admit to, you are still much too young ever to have seen the great Tommy Harmon run the ball for the good old U. of M. Suffice it to say, that son of a bitch could really get up and haul ass with a football in his hands. But be that as it may have been, however, my special favorite ironic photograph in *Dream Maker* is the one with him, Roachfeces, sitting, barefooted and with no shirt on (oh I wish it was just you being shirtless!), sitting on a big rock and holding his son, Zachary. Down in the lower right hand corner is printed (without attribution): "It's life's illusions I recall . . ." And if that ain't irony enough for you, why there is the actual caption of the photograph in the book. "Never shy about promoting himself or his new laidback lifestyle, DeLorean had this still photograph from a Chevrolet promotion film, featuring him and infant son Zachary, printed into a color poster as a holiday gift to friends and the Chevrolet dealer network." *A holiday gift*, eh? What holiday,

I wonder. Guy Fawkes Day? Bulgarian Independence Day? No matter, you can bet your sweet ass those posters are worth some good money these days. If any of them have somehow or other managed to survive the ruins and ravages of time.

But I see I have been wandering away from the main point of this letter. It was never my intention or purpose to get into the subject of Shit-for-Brains, your husband. Nobody's perfect. Except Jesus. Even measured against Thomas Jefferson or Abraham Lincoln or famous secular historical people like that, DeLorean doesn't look so hot. But, on the other hand, compared to, say, Al Capone or Atilla the Hun or Adolph Eichmann, he comes off somewhat better. That's how it is. Context and comparison are everything, as they say. And what the fuck! Even if, all glitz and glitter aside, both of you demonstrate a taste that is . . . well, just a wee bit tacky, why one has to consider and bear in mind the truth that you all (separately and equally) have come quite a long way from essentially humble and disadvantageous backgrounds. If the DeLoreans aren't in *The Social Register* yet, please don't be downhearted. It is possible that your great-grandchildren might make it.

But none of this, none of the above, is the main reason I am writing you. I tend to get distracted a lot of the time. That is probably because I got to be a speed freak in the 1960's back when that was considered a respectable alternative lifestyle. And I must admit that my habit got me through that turbulent decade fairly quickly and quietly. To be sure. But it has left my brain a little mushy, if you know what I mean. My memory (like Melody's in *The Random House Handbook*) is somewhat smoky. It has also left me looking somewhat older than I actually am. So, in that sense at least, I can genuinely sympathize with you and with Fartface, working ceaselessly to try to look younger than you are. I would, too, if I could, except that it's too late. The only good and positive thing about my condition is that now I can take advantage of all the various senior citizen special rates with no hassle and no questions asked whenever I feel like it. Which is a lot of the time. Because a lot of the time *I actually feel like a senior citizen*. I suppose that in a relative sense I really am one. All that speed back in the 60's really fucked me up good. Sometimes I wonder if I couldn't sue somebody about all that. Like the government for not stopping me.

Anyway you two will know how it feels someday. Some day you, too, will be senior citizens. Heck, if your expensive lawyer doesn't work a deal with the jury or with that Judge Robert Takasugi or *somebody*, old Bupkisshead, old Dingleberry, may be a real senior citizen before he gets out of the "big house" on parole. We'll see.

The original occasion of this letter was that I have just read the article, "DeLorean's Days Of Reckoning," in *People* magazine for April 16, 1984, pp. 97-106. In there, among a great many other fascinating details, it says that you all were both baptized as born-again Christians in your own swimming pool last summer by somebody who calls himself the Rev. Robert Gustafson. Said Reverend judges old Ratshit to be "sincere." "If he's faking it," Gustafson is quoted as saying, "it's the best con job I've ever seen." (Wonder how many good con jobs the Reverend has actually seen?) Well, why not? Why not the best? As a former president, whose name temporarily escapes my speed-ravaged memory, always used to say. (Who was that guy, anyway? I wonder if other people have so quickly forgotten him also.)

By the way, speaking of your conversion, I want to congratulate both of you for one thing. A stroke of genius! I quote again from the text of *People*: "At a baptism ceremony attended by 200 other Christians—many of them handicapped—DeLorean was dipped in the pool behind his Bedminster mansion. On that hot July day Cristina donned a flowing white robe to be christened along with her husband—not her first baptism, but certainly her most dramatic." (Dramatic! Boy, you can say that again! In the accompanying drawing on p. 99, that there white robe looks like a wet T-shirt and you can clearly see both your titties and your nipples. Is that drawing really accurate? Well, it is sure sexy whether it is accurate or not. In any case, you appear to have very nice boobies, if you don't mind my saying so. Of course, we, your adoring public and circle jackoff fan club, shouldn't be surprised at that. I doubt if Possumdropping would have given you a second look, let alone married you if you didn't have good tits.) But the really brilliant part is disposed of in one simple phrase—"*many of them handicapped.*" Was that his idea or yours? I bet it was yours. Whoever thought of it deserves an Oscar or a Grammy or a Medal of Freedom or something. A prize anyway. Some recognition. For unmitigated, unadulterated and utterly shameless (pardon the yiddish expression) *chutzpah*. Where did you *find* all those handicapped Christians? Once you located enough of them, how did you get them to come? You probably couldn't offer them booze and dope and broads to come over to your place and hang out. What kind of an inducement works well on handicapped Christians? What kinds and varieties of handicaps were involved? Where there any things which were really ugly and disgusting? I am inclined to believe that some of the more repulsive handicaps might prove counterproductive. Were there any handicapped little children among them? On the whole crippled kids tend to have an impact upon the beholder exceeding that of your average screwed-up handicapped adult.

In a sense I am kind of handicapped, myself. You see, I chopped one foot pretty bad with an ax (on purpose) while I was splitting wood so I wouldn't have to interrupt my alternative lifestyle and go to Vietnam and get hurt there. It worked too. And I laughed my ass off when all my buddies, who were too chicken to maim themselves and just too dumb to act psycho or to pretend convincingly to be queer and get away with it, got drafted and shipped out to Nam while I remained home more or less safe and sound (except for the godamn fucking limp and the occasional aches and pains from that one fucked-up foot). But I'm here to tell you, Cristina, I didn't laugh so very much when they all came back pretty much the same as they went in, all in one piece and all of them with various G.I. veterans' benefits that I am not now eligible for. I don't know if you know anything much about basic statistics, Cristina, above and beyond your own sweet vital statistics. I don't see why you would give a fist-flying fuck about statistics at all; though

I bet you that old Roachleavings knows his numbers and his odds, always, at any given moment. But, anyway, I can tell you what neither the Peaceniks nor Jane Fonda nor Daniel Ellsberg nor Daniel Ellsberg's Psychiatrist nor anyone else ever made clear at the time. I can tell you that, statistically, your chances were a whole lot better in a line Infantry outfit in Nam than they ever are on any given day on any given Interstate Highway. Actually, believe it or not, your odds would be better in actual combat situations, in a fire fight, than they would be on the Los Angeles Freeway during rush hour. And that is no bull. So, anyhow and anyway, completely ignorant of the statistics, I stayed home, happy on speed and downers, and made my living as the drummer for a rock-and-roll band you will never have heard of. Until, in time, the speed messed up my mind so bad that I couldn't keep the beat any more. After that I just kind of drifted and had a whole string of your average shitty jobs (and a couple of average shitty wives, too, if the truth must be known) before I finally hit the absolute bottom. I probably would be dead and gone by now if I hadn't become a born-again Christian, myself. And I did so quite a while before that became respectable and meaningful enough to pay off promptly and directly. We, all of us Fundamentalist neo-Christians owe an awful lot to prominent people like Chuck Colson and Eldridge Cleaver and Jimmy Carter. For they have proved that Faith can pay off, and handsomely, too, as long as you keep on talking about it. Is it true, by the way, like it says in *People* that Chuck Colson, himself, actually counseled your husband, old Pooper Scooper? Speaking of whom—hey, he is a good deal older than you, isn't he?

Where was I? Oh, yes, my big conversion. Well, at first all it led to was some good homecooked meals and a few easy scores with Christian broads who wanted to welcome me back to the Faith as joyously as possible. A lot of people have the wrong idea about Fundamentalist Christian girls. It is perfectly true they don't drink or smoke or cuss, and often they won't dance. But they are usually clean and neatly dressed. And they just love to fuck. It is true, also, that they are not, as a rule, either adventurous or innovative in their love-making techniques. But they are very good at what they will do, if you know what I mean. And they really seem to enjoy every minute of it. Which is a definite plus. It has been my experience that Jewish girls will get into all kinds of crazy, cockamaimie positions of the kind you only see in books on the subject. And they will do all kinds of basically disgusting things. You cannot gross them out. But, on the other hand, they piss and moan, complain and *kvetch* a lot. Very few Jewish girls seem to really enjoy it, regardless of the position. I hope you are not Jewish as well as Italian, Cristina. But if you are, I apologize for bringing up the subject. Fair enough?

Eventually my reconfirmed Faith and the good contacts I made led me into the line of work I am presently and quite successfully engaged in. In essence I am a Bible salesman. I sell Holy Bibles—big, beautiful, expensive ones, bound in the best soft leather, the acid-free pages tipped with real gold. And with the words of Jesus printed in bright red. These Bibles cost a whole lot, but people still want them in the worst way. And never mind the cost. Actually, as I guess someone like yourself could well imagine, our main customers are poor and downtrodden folk, the kind who want the best and most effective Holy Bibles that money can buy. We offer an amazing (and amazingly complex) and various series of E-Z Payment Plans. And these people are perfectly willing to pay us off, at fairly high interest rates, over time. Now, even as worldly-wise and sophisticated as you may be, Cristina, you might be surprised to learn that the very same kind of people who will regularly fail to make payments on their cars, their T.V. sets, their appliances, etc., will nevertheless 99.9% of the time always promptly and fully make payments on their Holy Bibles. Like nobody, not even me at my most down and mean and desperate and dirty, is going to come sneaking around and try and repossess a Holy Bible. The beauty of it is that we don't have to. Because they don't want to take a chance on God. They do not wish to bet that there is no Hell that they can and will be sent to for defaulting on their Holy Bible deals. They would rather do without eating than to miss a payment. Worse come to worse, they will cheerfully knock over a gas station or a liquor store or a supermarket rather than fall into dishonor. I mean, they bought the Holy Bible in the first place all in high hopes that maybe it might bring them a little bit of good luck for a change.

What I mean, Cristina, is that sellers of Holy Bibles can't hardly lose as long as they go after the right customers, the appropriate clientele. At first I had to learn all alone and the hard way. I was turned away from many a fine suburban doorway. Sometimes they would even set the dogs on me. Even with my hobble and my limp (left over from my days as a Peacenik), I could outrun most suburban dogs except for your Dobermans and the Rhodesian Ridgebacks. Those latter are some kind of ferocious beast and looked (to me) likely to solve most of our racial problems if they had imported enough of them. But I guess they had to quit bringing them in. I never heard of a Zimbabweian Ridgeback, did you? I reckon the Natives ate them all up when they took over.

Where was I? Oh yeah, learning to avoid Suburbia, U.S.A. I soon learned to go where poor folks live and hang around, the poor of all shades and colors. I don't mean to be a bleeding heart or sentimental about it, but I tell you, ma'm, they would treat a Bible salesman as good or better than they would treat a preacher. They would share whatever they had with you. And they would buy the most expensive, top-of-the-line Holy Bibles we had. Sometimes you could (if you were feeling a little mischievous) sell one each to every member of a large family, on the strength of the irrefutable philosophical argument that if a communal Bible is good and good for you, then an individual Holy Bible is just that much better.

So, all in all, it has proved to be a pretty lucrative enterprise for me. And I thank the Good Lord for that! Nowdays I am more of an executive type. I am very seldom in the trenches. Mostly I sit around the office doing paper work while my young salesmen, women too, *salespersons* these days, get out there and sell Holy Bibles and bring home the bacon. I attribute a lot of my success to the fact that neither as a salesman nor as a chief executive officer have I ever *mixed* my products. I sell Holy Bibles and Holy Bibles only. I do not traffic in magazines or record or cassette subscriptions. I refuse to sell encyclopedias. I offer no burial insurance. And I do not, under any circumstances, peddle mail order goods. They can trust me completely and my people, too. We sell the best of the Holy Bibles and that is all.

Now, Cristina, there was a time, and I'm willing to admit it now, when I was so broke I engaged in one additional activity. One which paid off and paid off well, too. I wouldn't do it now. Because I don't have to and it is beneath my executive dignity. But if I *had to* do it again, I just might. And I pass it on to you because it is entirely possible that you and old Rhinocerous-Poo may be up against it when you have paid off all the lawyers and creditors, etc.

What I did, Cristina, was sell autographed pictures of Jesus Christ. I would go out and get this big stack of color prints of a very WASP-looking Jesus. Strictly the blue-eyed blond model. Then I signed them all in the same flourishing, yet clear and masculine signature—"Yours truly, Jesus Christ." Or sometimes, "Best wishes from Jesus Christ." Now, I would never make any extravagant claims concerning these items. None at all. (Because, among other things, I could be busted for fraud if I did so.) What I would do is go some place where Fundamentalist Christians hang out. I would limp in there, looking as poor as the poorest of them, and set up shop, so to speak. I explained how I got all these pictures and was planning some kind of fraud or scam with them. But that there was a huge clap of thunder and a bolt of genuine lightning that knocked me cuckoo and into a deep trance. And while I was in that deep trance—Praise the Lord!—my hand took up my Bic Ballpoint Pen and proceeded to autograph every single one of these pictures with a signature strange to me and different from any I had ever used, even when I was still unreformed and would commit all kinds of forgery and fraud. I read aloud from the testimonial of a bona fide (if self-appointed, actually a wino from Santa Monica) handwriting expert. Who attested and affirmed to the fact that he had never seen a handwriting like that in his whole life. And if it wasn't the actual handwriting and personal autograph of Jesus, well, it was a powerful facsimile of the same.

With no more claim or sales pitch than that I would sell a couple of hundred of them, all I had with me, in just a few minutes, for, say, $2.50 apiece. They cost maybe a quarter each, so there was an adequate profit margin in the business. And it cheered up a lot of people to have those autographed pictures. It was worth taking a chance that they were real.

If worst comes to worst, you guys could do worse than that. I'm happy to share the idea with you. Even though I would guess that in some more secular circles you could do better with autographed pictures of yourself.

Do I feel bad about possibly saddling a lot of poor folks with even more debt and trouble than they have already got by selling them my Holy Bibles? Not even a little bit. Look, didn't even Jesus, Himself, predict that the poor will always be with us, even until the end of the world? Everybody knows that Jesus did a lot of good things while He was around. He actually performed some miracles. He healed sick people, both chronic and acute cases. And He freely shared a lot of His wit and wisdom with the general public. But He was not crazy. He didn't try to organize no Poverty Programs. He didn't declare a War on Poverty. Lyndon B. Johnson tried to go Jesus one better, and look how he failed! So, it's logical, if the two of them, between them, couldn't fix it, then how in the hell am I supposed to?

But I will not continue in this vein. For I am sure that, at one time and another, old Kittylitter, John Z. Himself, must have presented the same basic and overwhelming argument in reply to any number of smartass suggestions that he should try to use some of his (hard-earned or ill-gotten, who cares and what's the difference?) profits to help the poor and to alleviate human suffering. Never mind all that. Just like him, old Merde-for-Brains, I figure I am doing the people a favor. I am actually selling them hope. Hope is hard to come by, especially when you are down and out. Faith is good and so is Charity; but without Hope life is too frigging tedious for words. As long as they can at least hope and pray that things may get a little better, they can hang in there (albeit by their thumbs) and keep on trucking.

What kind of a pricetag can you put on Hope?

But I am not writing to you to sell you Hope. (I know you all have high hopes already, with every good reason.) And I am not even seeking to sell you all a couple of our high class Holy Bibles. Indeed, I ain't fixing to try and sell you *anything*. What I have in mind is, believe it or not, to give you something for nothing. Or next to nothing, if you insist on being crudely and brutally candid. It's just that in *Stainless Steel Illusion* there is this photograph (p. 15): "After posting $10 million bail, DeLorean leaves Federal prison on Terminal Island with Cristina, toting a Bible in his hand." Very nice picture. Deeply moving. Except you don't look so hot, Cristina, all kind of slumped over. But he looks okay, considering. I like that word—"toting." Kind of witty when you think about it. And actually that was a good while before his conversion in the swimming pool. Maybe toting that Bible gave him a dim sense of his religious vocation. By osmosis.

What I would like to propose is as follows. I will give you all, free of charge and no strings attached, a couple of big, wonderful, family-size Holy Bibles with the words HOLY BIBLE emphatically embossed on them in real gold. You can carry these with you on public occasions, especially going to and from various courthouses during the many trials that lie ahead of you. I am aware that Sheepshit probably isn't much of a reader by any standards. But I think he would be well-advised to read at least some of his Holy Bible. Especially the red parts. It might prove to be a solace and a spiritual comfort to him on bad days to realize that even a complete and utter Asshole (like he seems to me to be) is not beyond the love and care of Jesus Christ. Actually, if the preachers haven't been lying to us for the past two thousand years (and there's got to be at least a chance that they are telling the truth) nobody is beyond the power and love of Jesus.

Not me.

Not you.

Not even Hamsterdroppings.

True believers will tell you that the same rule applies to *everyone*. That Hitler and Stalin and Idi Amin may have earned themselves terrible reputations for their wicked deeds (and probably their wicked thoughts, too), but that it is not beyond the power of Jesus to love them, too, if He feels like it. We can judge people like that (and we do, too, don't we?), but we don't have the power to forgive them. They can't even forgive themselves. But Jesus can. He can forgive anybody, high or low, no matter how guilty or innocent they happen to be. It does not matter. He can forgive Charles Manson and Richard M. Nixon. He can forgive Jack Abbott and Norman Mailer. He can even forgive me for writing this letter. And I sure hope He will. But the main things is that if He can do all that, then forgiving your husband, old Canaryturd, is no particular problem for Him, either. That ought to be cheerful news.

And if I am, as I sometimes suspect in my dreams and dream visions, of no more solid shadow and substance than a character briefly in a book, if, therefore, I, with all my aches and pains, my joys and sorrows, my smiling and gnashing of teeth, am no more than a minor character invented by the feverish, speed-haunted, idle and mischievous imagination of an utterly unreliable narrator, himself, or maybe even herself these days when women are proving they can be as dirty-minded and foulmouthed as the men who have oppressed them since the first time Adam laid a guilt trip on poor Eve, if I have been invented by the narrator in a minor fiction by a minor author, just as in a very real sense you, Cristina, are not the real Cristina DeLorean but *de facto* an invention of my idle and mischievous imagination, why then, dear hearts, I ask the forgiveness of Jesus for all of us in this crazy daisy chain, but most especially on behalf of the unknown author of us all, who is most sorely and surely in need of redemption, and I do earnestly and heartily ask You, Smiling Mighty Jesus—which is what Black Folks in the old pre-literate days sometimes called that terrible disease, spinal meningitis, I pray You to forgive us our folly and wickedness and to look down with love upon us one and all. Amen . . .

I ought to add the reminder that, of course, He is completely unimpressed by your good looks and good health and good luck and all your material possessions. We aren't. We are deeply impressed and sometimes probably even jealous. But you have to figure that none of that means anything to Him. As far as we can tell, He never owned anything much except the clothes on his back (probably a robe kind of like the one you were re-baptized in, only I doubt His was a see-through model). And the Roman soldiers ended up owning that, anyway. What I mean is you can't pull the wool over Jesus's eyes.

My Holy Bibles will surely help you through the many tough days and nights ahead. And if they ever do finally nail you all, and you run out of delays and appeals, and you have to pay back all your multitudinous creditors, etc., why then, you, too, are going to be poor, members in good standing of the underclass, poor as Job's turkey. And you will need your Holy Bibles

even more then than now. Besides which none of your creditors will try and take your Holy Bibles away from you.

As I said I don't want any money for them. I don't even want gratitude, really. However, Cristina, if it makes you feel better, if you feel like giving me something in return, why a signed photograph (preferably in a two-piece bathing suit or maybe your underwear; or even, best of all, a nude and buck naked one, if you have any of those laying around) would be deeply appreciated. I think one of you would be enough. I really don't fancy a signed photo of old Hippopatamuspatty.

All the best to you. The truth is you are much too good looking to have to put up with all of this shit. It isn't fair. And as for Captain Bullshit? Well, I am convinced that he will find a way to beat this thing and continue his career as a Twentieth Century American Culture Hero. Maybe he can claim he was crazy like Hinckley did. I wouldn't try to bring Jody Foster into it, however. People are sick and tired of her being blamed for everything bad that happens. I would guess she may be tired of it too. But even if he loses big and ends up in the Clink, don't you worry. There are plenty of guys who will be very glad and proud to help you out during your hour of need.

Among which I beg to remain faithfully—

Yours truly,

Elmore ("Scooter") Fudge

P.S. I see by the Sunday paper that you have a brand new book out, one called *Cristina Ferrare Style: How to Have It in Every Part of Your Life* (Simon & Schuster, $16.95), which the newspaper reporter describes as "a glimpse into the life of John DeLorean and family, complete with money-saving entertaining tips and a look at the family's bathroom." The news story (*Detroit Free Press,* June 10, 1984, 1G, 6G, if you don't trust me) also has this fascinating sentence: "Ferrare calls herself a foodaholic and admits she goes up and down in weight so regularly that she keeps dressmaker models of herself thin and thick." For some reason that is exciting to think about—two versions of you! Anyway I guess I will have to buy the book for my DeLorean Collection. But I hope you don't mind if I wait until it is remaindered. I just don't have the money for it right now.

As long as I have your attention, I would like to add one thing I forgot to put in my letter. I just want you to know that I like you much, much more than I do Mary Cunningham. She is so full of what I always accuse your husband, old Dungbeetle, of being replete with that I can hardly believe it. I hope you keep your looks a lot longer than she does and keep on being notorious long after she is nothing but a bad memory of our age.

Scooter

An Additional Note Apparently By John Towne

God, things move along fast nowadays. Especially if you happen to live on the fast track. I'm on the slow track, by and large; and, more to the freaking point, I am a very slow typist—about as slow as that poor fella who wrote the letter to Hugh Hefner, if truth must be known. Anyhoo, by the time I finished typing up this letter to the inimitable Cristina (on behalf of Scooter, of course; it is he and not I who is writing to her, bless her soul and her extraordinary body, too, not I, not I, not I . . .), by the time I got it typed up, much had changed: (a) Old Ape Barf, though clearly guilty as guilty can be, nevertheless got off, managed to extricate his bony ass from the sling, thanks to a very smart lawyer and a very dumb judge and jury. He's free until the next litigation comes along. Then this lovely couple surprised the whole world by separating and (I think) getting a divorce. I'll never forget my shock and dismay when I picked up *The Washington Post* for Wednesday, September 19, 1984 (p. B1) and read: "DELOREANS SEPARATE/Pressures Too Much Lawyer Says." It made me sad. It probably would have made Scooter sad, too. I mean, what's the point of being rich and famous and beautiful and officially, legally innocent of what you are obviously stone guilty of unless you can be happy, too? It just isn't fair. And what about their lovely children? They weren't even mentioned in the *Post* piece. Maybe they forgot and left them somewhere. Who knows? But, to tell you the truth, both Scooter and I were even more surprised to read (in *The Roanoke Times & World-News* as it happens) about how Cristina had some topless photographs of herself published in a Brazilian magazine (What Brazilian magazine? Does it have a name? Does anybody out there know how to order a copy? Do any of you out there have a copy you'd like to sell? Please contact Elmore Fudge c/o the publisher of this book, whoever that may be . . .) But then, in *The Roanoke Times And World-News* for Friday, September 28, 1984 (p. C-11), the story took a, (pardon the expression & heh-heh to you,) bizzare twist: "Cristina Ferrare, estranged wife of John DeLorean, said Thursday the topless photographs of her published in a Brazilian magazine were not new and had appeared in a *Harper's Bazaar* story on a spa seven years ago." Just in time! I was about to go to my travel agent and mortgage my future to fly to Brazil when I discover that you could have seen her inimitable bare boobies right here in the old US&A. How the hell did I miss that issue of *Harper's Bazaar*? If anybody out there has a copy and would like to unload it, please contact me (John Towne) c/o the aforesaid publisher. Fudge can have the Brazilian version. I'll take plain vanilla American, thank you very much. Fudge, the dumby, will have to invest in a Portugese dictionary to find out what these Latins are saying about her and her tits. Meantime, I sure hope they are saying nicer things about Cristina and her boobs than her manager is quoted as saying:

"The layout is not a nude layout," said her manager, Arthur Gregory. "She was 27-years old and she was so skinny then that she had no breasts. I remember saying to her and John (DeLorean), 'She looks like a boy'."

I'll tell you one thing, Cristina. I wouldn't ever say anything like that. That is *terrible* Public Relations. Look, Cristina, are you really happy with your manager, this so-called (can't prove it by me) Arthur Gregory? If not, I want you to know that there's someone out here (and I don't mean Scooter Fudge, either) who admires you and (sight unseen so far) your breasts without reservation or qualification and who would love to help you turn your career into more fun and profit for the both of us. Contact John Towne c/o whoever is dumb enough to publish this book. And if you happen to have any good T & A Photos that did not yet make it into print either in *Brazil* or *Harper's Bazaar*, send along a couple of samples. You can count on me to be careful and not to do anything that isn't in good taste.

      J.T.

My Dearest Darling Cheryl Tiegs,

    Listen, I know full well, and nobody need (notice the subjunctive form of the verb there, babe!) remind me of it, either, that you are a fucken Superstar, a famous and beautiful and full-time celebrity person; while it must be equally apparent to you (already) that I am no more or less than just another typical and unknown American teenager, ravaged, damn near ruined by acne and puberty and pure frustration and all the rest of it. As far as anyone can tell, you and I have nothing at all in common unless you want to get all mushy and sentimental and claim that, everything else aside, we are both examples of poor, suffering, doomed humankind, both sharing, as our birthright, at least a good chance, unequal as that may be, to leave this world a little worse place than we found it. Anyway, it would be a safe bet to say that our separate and very unequal paths will never-ever actually cross . . . not in this sad and sane old world at least. However, in all good faith and good will, Ms. Tiegs, let me sincerely urge you, please ma'm, not to make such a bet with anybody. For if you do, you will surely lose your ass on it. As it happens our paths and lives are absolutely preordained to cross whenever I feel like it and get around to it. Make no mistake about that! Whenever I am good and ready we will sure enough meet. And very shortly after that meeting, again whenever I am good and ready to, I will proceed to fuck your brains out.

    Do I have your undivided attention yet? I hope so. For your sake.

    Look, I could be crude and gross and just send you a card and say: "Get ready, Cheryl Tiegs." But I won't. At least not yet. Instead, please permit me to explain myself and to take this opportunity so that we can get a little bit better acquainted before I come bombing into your life, your *real* life, like, say, Warren Beatty or Atilla The Hun.

    Adolescence, especially late adolescence, is really something else to put up with. If you can still remember how it was. No offense intended, but even if you are only about as old as you officially admit to, you are still about twice as old as I am. You are just about the same age as my mother, I would guess. By the time she was my age, I was already born and yowling for her attention. I was one, the first actually, of several thoroughly obnoxious children in the family. Mom has had a pretty rough life, all in all. And she has developed and cultivated plenty of bad habits, too: smoking and drinking, eating fried foods and junk food, flatly refusing to take any form of physical exercise beyond sex. So she looks like anything else you can think of except a successful model and a famous and beautiful celebrity. In fact, the truth is that on a bad day (and there are plenty of those around) she looks about old enough to be your mother. That is apparently what a hard life and a whole lot of bad habits can do to a person over the years, appearance-wise at least. Not that she ever had a real chance to be as lucky or good looking as you are even on the best and finest day she ever saw. She may have been a little bit pretty once upon a time, but not enough for anybody to bother to take notice. She was never seriously good-looking, if you know what I mean. Just common and ordinary. Just like all the rest of us.

But you needn't waste any of your time feeling sorry for her. She doesn't waste much time or energy feeling sorry for herself. And so she probably would not be particularly grateful if she were (there we go again; I *love* the fucken subjunctive!) to find out that you were feeling sorry for her. It is her view and considered opinion that. . . . At least it was the last time we tried to have a serious and sober discussion concerning the whole matter; namely on last Saturday morning when she tried (unsuccessfully as usual) to persuade me to take down all of my Cheryl Tiegs posters and photographs and magazine covers, etc. off the walls and ceiling of my crummy room. She was hoping, I think, to negotiate maybe a full or partial change of photographs to ones, you know, featuring new and different (and younger) women to replace you. You, whom she persists in referring to, to others as well as myself, as my (pardon the expression, Cheryl) "jackoff queen and wet dream obsession."

"Variety is the spice of life. And it is a lot more exciting, too," she asserted. "If you were actually, really and truly diddling that dumb, tacky broad, you would be sick and tired of her twat and her conversation both in a week or ten days at the outside."

I vehemently denied that crazy prediction. I likewise denied her old argument that with more than the average to lose to the ruthless depredations of Time and the wild whims and reverses of Fortune, you are the more to be pitied than you are to be admired and envied. That argument is just too fucken metaphysical for me. Mom has a weakness, a tendency to retreat into the realm of metaphysics whenever she starts losing an argument with me. Or, also, if she has been drinking Mount Gay Rum and grapefruit juice. Which is as often as she can afford to.

I would like very much to pause here briefly and to explain to you Mom's damn-near-irrefutable philosophical arguments about how, all things considered, it is probably better to be an old broad, overweight and about half-smashed on rum and grapefruit juice, clad mostly in a man's ratty, cast-off bathrobe and a pair of wornout, laceless Nike running shoes about twice the size of her own actual feet, just goofing off, watching the Soaps and the Game Shows while waiting around for the big event of her day, which happens to be the McNeil-Lehrer Show (that guy Lehrer really truns her on), than it is or would be to be Cheryl Tiegs, in person, sitting around in her swell peignoir counting her money and her wrinkles and her former and future lovers and husbands. But I won't do it. This letter would have to go on too long, and you might not see the point of it. Besides which, even though you and I are ordained to share some profoundly intimate times and experiences together, I'm not sure that you will ever actually meet my mother and get to know her. It is not as if I wouldn't be proud to introduce you to her. And chances are that she would be very polite to you, if only so as to prove that any apprehensions I might have had on that score were altogether misguided. For she does dearly love to surprise people. But, honestly, I do not believe that she could ever really understand or deal with our relationship. Or that she will ever be able to understand how or why you are going to feel about me. Moreover, even if I were able to overcome her stance of rational skepticism and to convince her of the essentially magical, supernatural basis of our relationship (by which I mean yours and mine, Cheryl honey), she might still be against it on the predictable grounds that I might have much more wisely chosen from among the many eligible, expensive, and eligible pussies available in modern America.

Lately she has spent a lot of time trying to drum up my interest in Vicki Lamotta, for instance.

"If you are so horny for the old timers," she has said and will say again, "why not go after Vicki? For she is probably much better equipped to deal with the problem of your insatiable teenage lust and all your puerile fantasies than the afore-and-too-much-mentioned Ms. Tiegs, whose own experience seems to have been limited to only a few guys, and some pretty creepy ones to boot, like that Peter Beard she was married to who gets himself turned on by conservation and crocodiles and stuff like that . . . !"

Here I better stop and explain how my mother borrowed my copy (my copy that, by the way, I bought and paid for with my own money, money I earned the old-fashioned way by delivering papers and not, as she claims, by selling her Valium in the schoolyard) of that wonderful book, *Hype*, by Steven M.L. Aronson. She borrowed it without asking and she read the whole exciting and inflammatory chapter entitled "Cheryl Tiegs: Cheesecake Served As Apple Pie," pp. 19-58. She read that chapter first and then the rest of the book, all of it, the whole fucken thing! Which may be more than anyone else alive has ever done. Except, maybe, the author, himself. But, anyway, regardless of whether or not she was setting some kind of a record, she actually did read the whole thing from cover to cover, even including the "Epilogue," which is subtitled "A Lesson In Moral Style From Mrs. Trilling." From which, somehow, she got the idea that maybe Mrs. Trilling would be more my speed and a better prospect for a longterm relationship since she (Mrs. T.) and I are both kind of intellectuals. I just let that one pass. I have long since given up trying to explain to my mother how the only reason that I have been classified, in the neighborhood, as an intellectual is that I am such a clumsy *klutz* at sports.

(*All sports but one, my dear Cheryl.* Heh-heh.)

Speaking of the book, *Hype*, and of its gifted and probably intelligent author, I actually got a chance to see him in person on Memorial Day Weekend of 1983, out in (of all places) The Hamptons. It was a big, huge brunch party and a whole hell of a lot of beautiful people were there, too. You weren't one of them, alas. I wasn't one of them either, exactly. I was just working for the caterer (never mind *how*; I got *relatives* on that part of Long Island), passing around shrimp and shit like that. You know. Well, anyway, while I was passing a plate of shrimp or whatever around, I saw this guy Aronson. I recognized him from the book jacket. He was out on the lawn, overlooking the sea, talking to two people I didn't recognize from anywhere at the time. Later I got a chance to ask and I found out. The good-looking lady was Gloria Jones, the widow of James Jones who wrote *From Here To Eternity* and other stuff. The other one, the guy who was with Mrs. Jones, didn't look like he belonged at the brunch at all unless it was to pass shrimp like me or something. Maybe mow the lawn. Anyway he turned out to be a writer named Garnett or Gary (probably short for Garibaldi) or whatever, just your run of the mill, typical unknown American writer. Who cares? Anyway I was kind of hanging around the area, hoping to get a chance to talk to Mr. Aronson and maybe ask him some important questions about Cheryl Tiegs. And this writer was talking, telling a story. So I stood there and listened to it. Why not? The three of them kept scarfing my shrimp the whole time and nobody seemed to notice me enough to say beat it or butt out, kid.

This fellow Aronson for some reason (who knows?) mentioned the name of Francine DuPlessix Gray. . . .

(Which is, in my opinion, a swell name and fun to pronounce and get your mouth around. Kind of like saying Giscard D'Estaing, you know. And besides enjoying saying her name once in a while, like in the shower, I also have to admit that I really enjoyed the very exciting description of a—pardon the expression, Cheryl—blow job which was in one of her novels. A lot of that novel I didn't understand. But I understood about blow jobs, intellectually at least. And, all in all, I thought she did a memorable job dealing with the subject.)

Anyway, see, Aronson mentions her name. And I pick up my ears and start to listen carefully. And then this poor unknown American writer, this prole-looking fellow in all the wrong clothes—they were nice enough clothes and clean, too, but they were the wrong clothes to be wearing in The Hamptons in 1983; Aronson, of course, had on all the right clothes—told his story.

—Ah, Francine DuPlessix Gray, he said, sort of savoring her name just as I do.—Let me tell you my Francine DuPlessix Gray story.

—Last summer I was out at Bloomington, Indiana, at the Indiana Writers Conference. Now, that is a pretty big show; it lasts a week and has a large staff. All kinds of people are there teaching classes and workshops and seminars on this and that. A lot of the stuff is going on at the same time. So it would be fairly easy to work there for the whole week and not actually manage to meet everybody else on the staff. And—what else do you need to know?— The whole thing takes place in the Indiana Union. Which is a great big huge building with classrooms and lecture halls and movie theaters and cafeterias and bowling alleys and bookstores—everything. And the top floors are a hotel for visitors. That's where they put us to live.

—Well, the first day of the Conference I got downstairs to where my classroom was about ten minutes early. I had a little time to kill, then. And so I noticed this big push broom leaning up against the wall. I picked it up and started fooling around, sweeping the hall. . . .

—Just about that time I heard this woman's voice saying, "My man? Excuse me, my man?"

—I looked around. And there, lo and behold, stood Francine DuPlessix Gray, in person, and all dressed up with what seemed like lots of jewelry and scarves and stuff. And she was holding a big bunch of packages in her arms.

—"Yassum?" I said.

—"My good man, would you please help me carry these packages to my room?"

—I thought, what the hell. Why not? I'll be back here in plenty of time for my class.

—"Yassum," I said.

—So I took her packages and we went up the elevator to her floor and then to her room. She unlocked the door and I went in and put the packages on the telephone table and the bed. Then I started to leave. She opened her purse and gave me two quarters.

—"Thank you," she said.

—"I'm sorry, ma'm, I said, "But we are not allowed to take tips."

—"Never mind," she said. "Let it be our little secret. Have a beer or something."

—"Well, thank you very much," I said.

—And then I hurried off to meet my first class.

—It all seemed pretty funny at the time. Except it occurred to me that Ms. Gray might get really pissed off if she found out that I wasn't a janitor and that the whole thing was some kind of joke. I didn't want to embarrass her in any way. And above all, I didn't want that woman to get pissed off at me personally and put my name on some Establishment Deep Shit List. I have enough trouble with the Establishment already, and I am still anonymous.

—So after that I kept a dust cloth with me at all times. And whenever I would see her coming, I whipped out my cloth and started dusting and wiping things.

—"How do, Ma'm," I would say cheerfully.

—"Hello," she would reply.

—Well, everything went along just fine and dandy until the very last evening of the Conference. Then, at the last minute, somebody or other got sick and they asked me to fill in, in very short notice, and give the final farewell reading. That's something I do a lot of. Story of my life. Filling in, at the last minute, for other people. No sweat. No problem.

—Everything was cool until I actually got up there at the podium and looked down at the audience. There, right smack in the big middle, about four or five rows back, there sat Ms. Francine DuPlessix Gray. She did not look amused. Not even a little bit. But she didn't take it the way I was afraid she would.

—Suddenly I had a kind of mystical vision. I could see right directly above her sternly amazed face and shining head a large balloon like the ones you see in comic strips. And I swear to you I could actually, for just a moment, read the words she was thinking to herself.

—Here is what I read: "This Conference is so fucked up they are letting the janitor give the farewell address." That's all. . . .

I don't know if anyone else laughed, but I did, unfortunately, and that caused me to drop a bunch of boiled shrimp and toothpicks on the ground.

Well, so much for *Hype* and The Hamptons and Aronson and all that. Except to say that I, personally, don't think that Aronson was completely fair with you and your fabulous career in the eternal cosmic scheme of things?

Time to get back to us. To you and me. If you don't mind. Not that it would do you a whole lot of good if you did mind. It's all out of your hands at this point. Doesn't matter what you do. But if I were you, I would go ahead and read the rest of this letter. Because there are some things you need to know about here.

As I sit here writing to you, Ms. Tiegs, I am reminded of my old man. When I was just a little kid and he had to spank me for something or other, he would send me upstairs to my room. He would let me go up there and think about it for a while. Then I would hear him coming, clumping up the stairs.

"You better give your soul to God!" He would yell. "Because your ass is all mine now."

He had been a Sergeant in the Army, and he still used a lot of quaint military expressions like that.

You will see the relevance of that idea as we go along. Patience, please. I shall try to be brief, however. I have gone on long enough without coming to the point. The time has come to fish or cut bait.

Fishing. . . .That's exactly what I was doing. I was over there in Fuller Park, sitting on the bank with a cane pole, fishing for anything that might be alive and swimming in the polluted Huron River. These names and bits of local color indicate, to all those in the know, that I was in Ann Arbor, Michigan. Which, in fact, is where I happen to live. And which, at certain times of the year, namely the spring and summer months, is a very fine place to hang out. As you, yourself, may come to realize and agree if I decide to take you there.

Anyway. There I was fishing away and not having much luck. But frankly, Ms. Tiegs, that didn't bother me a whole lot. People fish for a variety of all kinds of reasons beside the catching of fish. I go fishing because I am lazy and like to sit on the bank of the Huron River with tall green trees behind me and the river flowing by and the wonderful ducks—and the ducklings, too, this time of year—out there messing around and making their reedy quacking noises. I can just lean back and look up at the pale clouds running across the blue sky. And I can fantasize. One of my favorites was how I was somehow (never mind how) the sole and only male survivor of a plane crash. Together with approximately one dozen hale and hearty and horny stewardesses—I think they call them flight attendants nowdays, but I prefer stewardess; and it's *my fantasy*, isn't it—I am stranded on an uninhabited little tropical desert island. One with plenty of food and fresh water and a swell sandy beach. And we all get along fine and have ourselves a purely wonderful time, day after day and night after night, until we all get rescued, whenever I feel like it, many years later.

So there I was, deep in my South Pacific dream, when I felt something pulling and tugging against my fishing line. I yanked and pulled it up. But it wasn't a fish. Just an old wine bottle with a cork stuck in the top of it. I was about to throw it against some rocks to see it shatter and to listen to the very satisfying sound of breaking glass, when I suddenly heard this voice, a woman's voice with an odd, foreign kind of accent, strange but pleasantly hoarse, kind of "whiskey-voiced" like my mother, calling: "Help me! Please help me, young man. Help me and you'll be glad you did. . . ."

I looked all around, but there wasn't a woman in sight anywhere. I started to think it might be some kind of a dumb joke. *Candid Camera* or something like that. Then I happened to hold the bottle up against the sunlight. And there she was, sure enough, a little bitty, teeny-tiny woman in some kind of a belly dancer's costume waving her arms to get my attention and telling me that all kinds of good things would happen to me and for me if I would only uncork the bottle and set her free.

Now, I'll tell you the truth, Cheryl, I really thought for certain that if it wasn't *Candid Camera*, then I was probably in real trouble, mental trouble, don't you know? Like maybe I would have to completely quit smoking dope and take other unpleasant austerity measures. Which would make my crummy adolescent life more miserable than ever.

Somehow it was as if she could read my mind.

"Trust me. Trust me," she said. "What have you got to lose?"

"What should I do, lady?" I whispered, in case anyone was secretly watching or there were microphones hidden somewhere near.

"Pull the cork, kiddo, and let me out."

"What happens if I don't?"

"Bad shit," she said. "Plenty bad. Don't even think about it."

"And good things will accrue if I should let you out of the bottle?"

"You better believe it. Didn't I say so?"

"Well, I don't know. . . ."

"Look, kid, I can read your banal little mind like a bad book. I know exactly what you want and I can give it to you."

"You're a good looking woman," I said, "But you are too little for me."

"Let me out of the fucken bottle and we'll see about that."

And so I thought to myself, *what the fuck, why not?* I mean, suppose I tried to keep the bottle with her in it for a souvenir and tried to sneak it home and keep it in my room? Sooner or later Mom would be bound to find it. Probably during one of her shakedown searches. And then she would lay a guilt trip on me for keeping a little teeny-weeny woman all corked up in a bottle just for my own private and perverse, chauvinistic amusement. Lately Mom is a little bit into feminism and sisterhood. So she would probably take it away from me and then try to make a deal down at her favorite bar to use it for show and tell. For a price. . . . Who knows? Anyway, it was almost bound to create a very bad scene when Mom found out that I had a captive broad in a wine bottle.

I decided to negotiate and see what, if anything, I could get out of it. I don't want to bore you with all the longwinded and sordid details. Except to say this. It was a tough deal, the roughest negotiation session I have ever been through or can imagine coming my way. Like at the beginning I couldn't figure what there was to negotiate. I had the bottle and she was in it and couldn't get out until I uncorked it. The only question I could figure was if she really and truly wanted out. And if so, how much. Of course I was overlooking the absolute key thing. She had magic on her side. I mean, even if she had gotten herself somehow stuffed and corked in an old wine bottle, she still had magical powers and could deliver some interesting things if we worked a deal, (And maybe, who knows?, some bad shit if we didn't.) But what I couldn't have known or guessed was how smart and tough she was. I guess that negotiating with the Russians is a rough ride. Those guys don't give away anything. And I reckon a session with, say, the Teamsters or the U.A.W. could give you one hell of a headache. But I can't believe that any of these, or all of them at once, could hold a candle to the difficulty of working a deal with a smart lady genie in a wine bottle. What can I say? Try to imagine trying to discuss human rights with Pol Pot. Imagine trying to work out some basic affirmative action goals and guidelines with Idi Amin or the Emperor Bokassa.

Well, what we finally came up with is as follows. She taught me two basic magic spells, one to turn a woman on, the other to turn her off when I'm ready. The trick, the limitation, is that it is only good for three times in my lifetime. She figures that three *guaranteed* scores with any three women of my choice is enough for one lifetime. The rest of the time I'll be completely on my own. Maybe I'll make out and maybe I won't. But for at least three different times (if I want) I'll have magic on my side and I cannot lose. Or so she said.

What happens, Cheryl, is this. When I cast the first spell, the woman in question, whoever she may be, will instantly go wild with love and lust and animal desire for little old me. She will be absolutely, totally, completely under my control and will do whatever I want to do and tell her to, gladly, without hesitation or reservation. And (here's the beauty part) this situation will continue for as long as I want. It will go on indefinitely, full blast, until I decide to end the spell by the appropriate, secret ritual and words.

You might wonder, as I did, why I would need that . . . well, escape hatch. I mean, suppose I actually found a real satisfactory woman, an authentic winner like you, Cheryl, then why would I want to end such a perfect relationship?

197

She offered a number of explanations for that aspect of our arrangement. Some were philosophical and some were pragmatic and some were a little of both. But what it all boiled down to was that nobody who ever lived (or ever will) could possibly handle an unlimited potential for guaranteed scoring. True, the faggots in San Francisco have come pretty close and without benefit of magic, either; but what do they have to show for it? AIDS, that's what they got, along with herpes and clap and syph and hepatitis and all the other afflictions which bedevil an incurable contemporary romantic. No, Cheryl, she argued, on the basis of her considerable knowledge and experience over the centuries, that neither men nor women are equipped physically, mentally, emotionally, or spiritually (no, she didn't mention *morally*, or morals at all, for that matter) to fuck around as much as they think they would like to. The only place (said she) you can do that in Real Life with both impunity and success is deep in your own private imagination. Which is exactly where that kind of stuff belongs. Just as pornograpny belongs in the home and not out on the public streets. She allowed as how some people may be able to handle and deal with a whole gnarled string, a veritable tangled web of tempestuous and fully activated sexual relationships, there are many others who can't hack it even for one kind of average one. Moreover, among men and women both (though please remember we are, in fact, speaking of men), there are an enormous number, many of whom are brighter, better looking and more gifted than I shall ever be, who by dint of bad luck, the breaks, don't get a chance, not even one little chance to test themselves against the full-scale and focused love and lust of an attractive and dedicated partner.

Three is a lot more than you deserve, she told me. And three times as many as you could ever get on your own.

Besides, she continued. . . .

More than three would be pushing my statistical luck. With only three of these total magical scores scheduled for my lifetime, I will be more thoughtful and less careless and impulsive. Less likely to come up with a case of AIDS or Genital Herpes or Chlamydia or Venereal Warts or any other among the long list of little goodies whereby Mother Nature lets us know how she feels about sexual revolutions and promiscuity and perversion.

Besides, she added. You will never be completely happy with the kinds of love and pleasure (unlimited) earned by your magic spell. Sooner or later, like every other chauvinist asshole since Adam ran around the Garden in his hairy birthday suit, you will want to be loved and desired for yourself alone. Which is not likely to happen even once in a lifetime.

However (she asserted) you have a chance to learn something very special during your three magic experiences. Once you have cast the spell, it will work for you, to precisely the same degree of effectiveness, no matter what you do or don't do. Indeed, you will be completely loved and desired quite aside from anything you may do or leave undone and entirely without reference to your appearance, your attitudes, your abilities, your character, etc. That is to say, charm (or the total absence of charm, which seems a more relevant possibility in your case) will get you nowhere. It's all magic. Therefore, young fella, in a strictly logical sense, there is no *seduction* involved. Enchantment (in the sense of a magic spell) yes. Seduction no.

Now, as you will find out soon enough from personal experience, most guys can't stand that situation. They like to believe that they can *win* a woman's love through charm and seduction. They like to imagine, if they are ever so fortunate as to gain, however briefly, the love of a half-decent woman, that somehow they *earned* it. By words and deeds and skills. And, of course, that is what causes the rapid demise of so many otherwise possibly adequate relationships: that, like politicians, men are deeply and supremely self-contemptuous. Therefore, the urgency of escaping self-contempt through becoming worthy of love in the eyes of another. But also therein lies the inevitability of disappointment. Just as all politicians develop a deep contempt for anyone crazy enough to vote for them, so the seducer has to conclude that the woman who falls in love with him is not only a fool, but also, by definition, unworthy of everthing except a share of his self-contempt which he will cheerfully pass along as if it were a little dose of clap.

"You understand what I'm telling you, boy?"

"No, ma'm. Not exactly."

"I didn't think so. What do you understand?"

"That if I uncork that wine bottle and set you free, you will teach me a magic spell that will allow me to fuck the brains out of any three women I want to in the whole wide world."

"Well, that's over-simplifying, but it's about right in substance if not in style."

Pause. . . .

"Well?"

"Well, I just don't know yet. I mean, I'm enjoying the conversation (I'm learning all kinds of stuff). And the situation is interesting, too."

"You want conversation? Talk to your Mama. Or maybe one of your Love Slaves . . . of course, chances are a thousand to one that anybody you pick for an Enchanted Partner won't be what we would call a graceful talker."

"That's what I mean. If I let you out of the bottle, this may be my last chance for any serious discussion with a member of the opposite sex."

"Let me tell you something, kiddo. Any time you run out of things to talk about with a woman, just start a discussion of your relationship. They all love to discuss their relationships. And that's the last inside scoop you'll get from me."

I could see that the genie lady was beginning to get pissed off as well as bored. So I made the deal with her. Hoping she would keep her word. And I let her out of the bottle. What a rush! After the puff of smoke she was invisible. But she whispered in my ear and taught me the two magic spells. No big deal. Even I could remember the words and the routine.

But all of the above is prologue, Cheryl. The reason I am writing to you is to report that the thing really works! Just exactly like she said it would. I admit I was skeptical. I figured she had done a number on me, taking advantage of my youth and inexperience and general condition of perpetual horniness. After I thought about it I began to picture her out there somewhere in the wild blue yonder laughing her genie ass off at the dumb kid she tricked into letting her out of the bottle.

Well, there was only one way to find out. I had to run a test. I had to waste one of my three times just to see if it would work. Now that may not seem too logical to you. But you don't understand, really. From the beginning my principal goal in this matter has been you. The other two I conceived of, from the outset, as practice, training and experience, getting ready for you. At least that's how it was in the beginning. Also I wasn't planning, originally, to tell you anything about all this or to give you any advance warning. I figured it would be more fun to cast the spell and all completely by surprise. But now that I know a little more about all this I am here to tell you this is powerful stuff, Cheryl. No fooling. I am now aware that it would be very unfair to take complete command of you, body, mind, and soul, without at least some advance warning.

I gave a good deal of thought to my first trial run. Who should I try it on? Well, there were all kinds of excellent prospects. There is a really sexy divorcee in the nieghborhood, a friend of my mom's; but she has always considered me an asshole and isn't shy about saying so, either, in just those words. I mean, just that word. She would be an excellent choice for the test because of her obvious and outspoken contempt for me. If it worked with her, it would work with anybody. And it had another potential satisfaction also, in that I could get even for all the times she made me feel shitty, by subjecting her to many humiliating and degrading practices. Only I still didn't have enough sex experience to know one humiliating and degrading practice from the other. Oh, I still had a lot to learn! Then there were a couple or three really good looking and popular girls at school, the kind that have all the hotshot athletes and the rich and goodlooking guys buzzing around them like half-crazed honey bees. The kind who go swishing down the hall at school, shaking their round, firm, wonderful butts, and their nice boobies bouncing and all. And somebody like me, myself in particular, they either don't actually see at all (I might as well be Ralph Ellison in that book he wrote that they make us all read so we will be more thoughtful and sensitive when Black kids mug us and beat up on us and charge us money to let us go to the bathroom, etc.) or they do see me and with one withering glance convey the news that what I look like to them is a fresh pile of dog do-do . . . . Oh, Cheryl, you can understand the temptation, I am sure. If the spell really worked, there I would be strutting up and down the halls at school with one of those incredible chickieboos all over me, mad with desire, love and lust. Boy, that would show everybody a thing or two. Sweet revenge.

Only there were potential problems also. The main one being that I wouldn't really be learning a whole hell of a lot from any of these girls. I mean, they may not be (technically) virgins. But according to all the best authorities, whose books I could get ahold of in the Ann Arbor Public Library and at Borders Bookstore, women that age, at least American women of that age and basic background, are still quite a long way away from being classified as fully competent in performance and enjoyment of the sex act. (I guess the same thing holds true for most all American women, really. At least if you believe Ann Landers—and why would she lie to us?—that something like 90% of all American women of all ages would much rather hug and cuddle than to seriously get down and dirty. Of course, I can tell, just by looking at my posters and magazine covers—boy, I love you, smiling on the cover of *Time* for August 30, 1984 and holding a copy of the Sears catalogue with your smiling picture also on the front of it, wow!—that you are not among the dumb, slothful, lazy, insensitive and indifferent 90%. At least I sure hope not! If you are, Lord help you. . . .) Anyway, why waste my magic powers on some girl of my own age and background. To whom I would probably have to teach everything anyway. It would satisfy my adolescent vanity, to be sure. And it might even make me a better person, at least if, as everybody says, feeling good about yourself is the key to being a better person. (I have some trouble with that idea, Cheryl. Like—if what makes me feel good about myself at the same time makes some other person, or persons, feel bad about himself/herself/themselves, then, in order to feel better about myself am I not likely to end up making this world a little worse and unhappier than I found it? Seriously, on the basis of my own admittedly limited personal experience, I would have to say that most of the primary things that can serve to make me feel good about myself involve making other perople feel lousy about themselves. It is no fun at all to be superior unless other people feel inferior to you. How do you feel, Cheryl? Does it enhance your self esteem to walk around and see how ugly and ordinary most people are? Does it make you a better person to realize that at any given moment of the day or night some common ordinary guy is probably getting an erection looking at one of your posters or pictures and imagining getting it on with you? I'll tell you this much, it has made me a better person just to realize that I can get it on with you whenever I feel like it and for as long as I want to.)

Anyhow, as you can see, weighing and sifting all the complex practical and ethical considerations, I arrived at the conclusion that I wouldn't screw around with the teenage queens of Huron High.

For a while I didn't know what to do with myself and my new-found powers. I just pondered and pondered and wrinkled my brow. I hardly paid any attention to what was going on around me, so deep was I in thought and perplexity. Then my very abstraction from reality served to come to my rescue. Purely by accident one day, while headed disconsolately and reluctantly for my Physical Education class, I took a wrong turn or two (I was just looking at my feet, anyway) and wandered into a locker and shower room where the Women's Field Hockey Team was getting dressed or undressed. I don't know. All I know is the minute I walked in the room I was awakened from my pensive mood by ear-piercing screams. And I looked up, and there they all were bareass or in scanty attire yelling and screaming at me. I was stunned. I didn't know what to do first. Unfortunately I laughed. Boy, that was a huge mistake, Cheryl! Never laugh at a room full of nekked women, especially field hockey players. They came after me with fire and castration in their eyes.

I ran for it, dodging in and out of rows of lockers, running right through the shower room and so forth. Until I got trapped in this office. Where, lo and behold, there was the Coach, a nice healthy looking broad, freckled and wholesome, sitting at her desk doing paperwork. She jumped up and grabbed me where it hurt the most. And I went right down on my knees.

"You filthy creep!" She said. "You have sexually harrassed females for the last time in your life. What I am going to do with you, pig, is turn you over to the field hockey team for a little while and then I'm going to take you or what's left of you, to the Principal's Office where you will be officially expelled from this institution. What do you have to say about that, you disgusting turd?"

The field hockey girls, crowded around the office door, cheered wildly. She was squeezing my jewels so hard that I could hardly breathe let alone answer her. The only thing I could think of was . . . the Spell. I mumbled it to myself.

Cheryl, you are going to have trouble believing this. Well, so did I, even while it was happening. But it did happen and instantaneously. The minute I said the magic words she eased off her ferocious grip (she didn't quite *let go*, if you know what I mean) and her whole demeanor towards me changed. Her eyes kind of bugged and brightened and sweat popped out on her brow and she was all of a sudden smiling and smiling and licking her lips.

"Okay, girls," she said quietly and calmly. "That's it. Show is over. Back to the locker room. I'll take care of this matter from now on."

They groaned, but she pushed them all out and shut the door and locked it. Mumbling something about the Constitution and due process as she did so.

About a minute and a half later we were on the floor having at it, flopping about like a couple of fish in a creel.

Well, Cheryl, I don't want to go into all the details, sordid and/or otherwise, except to say that it was, in my judgment, a lucky liason, a wise choice on my part. We maintained our close relationship (if you can call three or four times a day, seven days a week, as an average, fairly close) throughout the semester right up until graduation day. (The last score I did it in my cap and gown just for a lark.) After which there didn't seem to be much point in it. I had gained all the knowledge and experience I needed from this healthy, wholesome, eager, athletic and adequately experienced lady. And I figured I was ready for you or anybody else. Besides I was wasting away. My clothes were drooping and hanging on me. Mom was starting to ask all kinds of suspicious questions. And some of the kids, especially on the field hockey team, were beginning to put two and two together and to smirk and wink at me in the hall. And to tell you the truth, Cheryl, I was starting to like her. We were getting to be friends. There is nothing like a little too much friendship and respect to ruin the basic animal spontaneity of sex. Of course, I will want to be your friend, too, I guess. But at least I have learned from my experience with Coach Nina, that's her name, how to keep friendship at a low level and in its place. I learned a lot of things from her actually. Since

202

she is basically a fine athlete and also academic in orientation, Coach Nina made every effort to improve her personal best performance level and to increase my pleasure as well. She made me watch that crazy little fucker, Dr. Ruth, on T.V. and videocassette. She got out all the books from *The Joy of Sex* through *Dr. Dollar's Aerobic Kama Sutra*. And before the semester was done we tried out everything those guys had ever heard of. And then some! I'll tell you, Cheryl, there are a lot of interesting things I can teach you when the time comes. You may be surprised at my assertion that there are some things that even you don't know about. But there are. And you will be grateful for the knowledge. On the other hand, I am also in the (pardon the expression) position to spare you a certain amount of grief and woe. Now that I have done it all (or almost all; I keep an open mind on these things; there may be some sage or guru in Nepal or Sri Lanka or Santa Monica who can add a new twist or wrinkle to my repetoire), I'll be the first to admit that a lot of the things in those books are too complicated and uncomfortable for anybody except a contortionist. And some of the others require training and a good warmup to work right without pulling muscles and injuring joints, etc. But don't you worry your pretty head about it. I know what works best in every case.

The other good news is this. That once the second spell is cast and the fun and games are over, there is no bitterness or bad feeling. I thought probably she would forget the whole thing. Or maybe hate me or something. Not so. It turned out to be real simple.

"I don't know what got into me," Coach Nina told me on graduation day. "But it sure was fun while it lasted, wasn't it?"

"Yes ma'm," I replied. "I enjoyed every minute of it."

And that, Cheryl, was that.

And now we arrive at the main reason I am writing to you. As already indicated, I am saving you for my last spell. Best for the last. (I was the kind of kid who saved and saved my dessert until all the others had eaten theirs. So I could really enjoy it.) But that leaves me one to go before I get around to you. I thought maybe you would like to have some input in this matter. I mean, I will be coming into your life directly after the conclusion of my next enchantment. And it occurs to me you have a legitimate right to at least indicate your own preferences, likes and dislikes. Or even if it's all the same to you who I screw around with, maybe you have got some good suggestions.

For instance, sometimes lately I have considered doing a season with Christie Brinkley. Because she really is something. And let's face it: she is prettier and sexier and livelier and above all younger than you. But you have the first claim on my attention. I barely know her at all except for the 1985 *Christie Brinkley Calendar* and *Playboy* magazine for November of 1984 where she is on the cover, though well-covered—"Christie Brinkley Dresses Up." And a couple of spots on MTV where she appears with Billy Joel. Cuckolding Billy Joel might be fun, but I better be very careful. Besides if she is half as good as she looks, then maybe I will get waylaid and may never get around to you.

You can see it's a perilous dilemma.

What about the possibility of some really young and fresh and flat-tummied, amazing quiff? Say maybe Paulina Porizkova of *Sports Illustrated* or Tracy Scoggins or Chris Alderson of *Inside Sports*?

What about Jodi Foster? People go around shooting other people in her behalf. So there must be more there than meets the eye.

I liked Sigourney Weaver a lot in *The Year of Living Dangerously*. Do you know anything about her? Is she available?

It's too bad Ingrid Bergman is dead and gone. For she would be a definite possibility as far as I'm concerned. At any age or stage.

Linda Ronstadt gets to me all right, but in her case it's more a matter of her voice than her looks. Same with Juice Newton. I think I can do without Carly Simon.

Oh, there are so many, many celebrities to consider and conjure with that I hardly know where to begin and end. As you can plainly see.

Maybe I should stick with celebrities, but try other fields of fame.

For instance, poetry. In our poetry textbook at Huron High there were several of what seemed to me (you can't tell everything from a picture, a simple, pardon, headshot) interesting candidates: Carolyn Forché , Elizabeth Spires, Dara Wier, and Louise Glück.

I like the last one best. That umlaut in her name is really a turn on.

Or maybe some people in other fields.

Gloria Steinem? Admittedly she is almost a candidate for admission to a nursing home, but I have always loved her a little and we might actually be good for each other. In any case she sure could (heh-heh-heh) raise my consciousness. In the same sense Jane Fonda might be fun.

Phyllis George looks pretty nice on the T.V. as do Leslie Stahl and Judy Woodruff. But I am a little bit leery of messing around with Media types.

If anyone wants to know, both Liz Taylor and Joan Rivers are definitely out of the question. Surely someone lusts after them, but that someone isn't I.

Decisions, decisions!

Maybe that is the fly in the ointment of my magic spell.

Well, I guess it really is too much to expect you to help me out on this. Unless you have strong negative feelings about any of these people.

Do you have any feelings about Bo Derek? Linda Evans? Ann Margret? Diane Keaton? Mary Lee Settle? Ann Beattie? Francine DuPlessix Gray?

God almighty, there are just so many of them out there! I'm so glad I thought of you first.

Well, I guess it's time to close now. I sure hope that you don't misinterpret this document as some kind of a crackpot letter from a lunatic. That would be a Big Mistake. I am very, very serious, as you will find out soon enough. Meantime please take good care of yourself. Eat right, take your vitamins, get plenty of exercise and sleep. Cultivate your self-esteem. And don't worry about getting old and all. I'm going to give you plenty of memories to take with you.

All the best, Cheryl.

Be Seeing you—
Vernon ("Sugar Boy") Whitehead

P.S. I would enclose a photo, but it wouldn't tell you much. Not the whole story at least. I am not particularly impressive. Especially in a photograph and with my clothes on. It is only fair, however, to inform you that I am more than adequately equipped for any relationship. I don't know about the men in your life I have read about in the magazines—Stan Dragotti, Peter Beard, and now (they say) someone named Anthony Peck—but I will bet ten to one that none of them can . . . well, *measure up* to me. I'm not bragging, believe me. It's just a fact. The Black boys at school were in awe of me. As Coach Nina put it (simply and directly) "Boy, you are the best hung white man I've ever seen." Of course, I never asked her how many she might have seen. Even I recognize there are tactful limits to idle curiousity.

V.W.

Part Ten

A Very Personal and Private Letter

Still, if the portico sports were to ask me where I get off
dissenting all the time from what the rest of the world
takes as revealed truth, I might offer a sop
in reply, citing the fable of the fox and the sickly lion
where the fox declines the malingering fat cat's invitation:
"Those footprints scare me. A mob rushed in, but who came out?"
                    (Horace—"Epistulae I,1", translated by David Slavitt)

Dear Reader,

This is the author, himself, speaking.

You have got to admit that I have pretty much stayed out of this whole thing so far. Not much more for me, at the beginning and now at the end, than you usually get from the Captain of a jetliner as you zoom along in sweaty and cramped discomfort (unless you go First Class which I certainly plan to do someday, especially if somebody else is picking up the tab for it) a few miles above this weary world. I would as lief stay out of it completely, if you want to know the truth. I have so little in common with John Towne and Lee Holmes, or any of their friends and enemies, real and imaginary characters, that I would hate for anyone to get the wrong impression and tar me with same brush by association. Tarred and feathered by association. Very unfair. I am not so worried about you all, the readers, who by and large tend to be able to discern the difference between, say, your arse and third base, the distinction between, for example, human excrement and Shinola or peanut butter. It is critics, especially (if you'll pardon the expression) *literary critics*, who have a lot of trouble trying to separate appearance from reality. I don't want to get into that right now, because this book is almost over and done with (thank the Lord!); and I don't want to waste space on no theoretical arguments or provocative words and deconstructive gestures. Just let me say here and now, reader (or readers), that I've got a lot more respect for you than I do for them. I think they are really and truly full of it. And I don't mean shinola or peanut butter, either. Not that they are not smart. At least in my book they are. Last year in Ann Arbor I went to hear the great and famous critic, Harold Bloom (and may he rest in peace if he has died since then and I somehow unfortunately missed his obituary), lecture on "The Sorrows of Fat City." I understood maybe the first five minutes of it. Then my mind wandered briefly. And when it and I came back we found that Bloom was long gone. He took off like a bigass bird, and we (my mind and I) never caught up again or had a clue what he was saying. My colleague, Russell Fraser, claimed he understood the whole thing from beginning to end. But Russ gets carried away sometimes and, you know, even exaggerates a little.

Anyway, gentle reader, fuck the critics, that's what I say! If they will just leave me alone, like they always have until now, ignoring me consistently for the first 30 years of my so-called career, why, I will be glad to ignore them also. Fair enough? I will even resist the temptation to make fun of Helen Vendler. Call that my middleaged contribution to the civility of literary discourse in our time. A first step on the long march towards detente.

But, actually, I digress. All I wanted to tell you was that I know I can count on *you*, reader, not to make the mistake of identifying *me*, the author, with any of the characters in this book. (Or any other books, either, mine or anybody else's for that matter). I am the author. And I am in charge. They are nothing but characters. As such, they are of course entitled to a certain amount of freedom. They can do pretty much what they please (and then suffer the consequences for their actions) and can believe, think, and feel what they please (or who they please, as the case may be), without giving the author a bad name. As far as their various unacceptable and misanthropic opinions. . . . Well, you can be sure that I find them just as offensive as you do. I am basically mainstream (pardon). I remain grateful that I am a once-born Democrat, an Episcopalian, and a Southerner, first, last, and always. I like being in *The Social Register* (look me up there sometime) and various editions of *Who's Who* (ditto); and I wish I were respectable enough to be allowed into some of the better literary clubs like, for instance, the National Institute of Arts and Letters. Yet, on the other hand, I console myself with the knowledge that many of them (though they will deny it as categorically as Peter denies any personal acquaintance with Our Lord and Savior) would like to find a way to get into *The Social Register*. And they can't. And they won't. For one reason and another.

Anyway, reader, we're all in this together. And I respect you. And I sure hope you respect me or anyway know me (by now) well enough to know that, despite Towne and Holmes and all the rest, I have no desire to offend anyone at all.

Now then.

Where was I?

Oh, yes.

This is your author speaking.

I want to ask you. . . .

No, I want to *warn* you. DO NOT READ THE FINAL LETTER. Do not read my letter to Christie Brinkley. It is for her edification, not yours. It is a personal letter, to tell the truth. And I would rather you didn't read it. It is a personal letter from me, the author, to her, the . . . well, Muse; that's it. The Muse. It's none of your business or concern. It's more than you have a right to expect for whatever you paid (probably too much if you paid *anything*) for this book. When you finish this brief author's note, I ask you (and please note that I am asking you politely) to stop reading. The rest is private, between me and her.

I can anticipate your doubts and arguments. You are wondering why, if I don't want people reading my mail, I would put it in a published book rather than a sealed, stamped, addressed envelope.

That's not a dumb question, either.

210

What you have to understand, reader, is this is the only way I have half a chance to reach her. I mean, I don't even have her permanent address. And even if I did, how could I be sure (considering the present state of our Affirmative Action Postal Service) that it would ever get to her? Lots of things don't get to the right address, even in spite of correct zip codes designed to help Postal Persons who don't read English or, even if they do, only know the names and general locations of a few big inner cities and some of the more liberal states. No, this letter is much too important to entrust to the U.S. Postal Service.

And even if they didn't manage to lose it or send it by mistake to Sri Lanka or Bangladesh, even if somehow, and more or less in one piece, it actually got there (there being wherever Christie Brinkley hangs her string bikini and calls home), how do I know that some secretary or some flunky or somebody wouldn't read it instead of Christie? How do I know that Billy Joel wouldn't read it (if Billy Joel is still her husband)? How do I know (heh-heh) that Billy Joel can read? Or if he can read, that he is a truly sensitive reader? Does he know irony from Iron City Beer? Probably not. Anyway, I can't take a chance on it either way.

No. The point I want to make is this. If you think about it from all angles, I am sure you will agree with me that the best possible way, under these difficult circumstances, for me to make (ho-ho) contact with Christie Brinkley is to print the letter at the end of this book. To ask readers (if any), very politely, not to read it. Nevertheless to hope that somebody will point it out to her. Or that maybe she will accidentally run across it somewhere. I might be better off putting it in a bottle and tossing it into the York River in front of my house, while the tide is running out. The odds might be better that she would get it; for I have every reason to believe that Ms. Christie spends more time on beaches than in bookstores. But, call it a hunch, I feel like this is better than writing a letter & stuffing it in an old wine bottle & dropping said bottle in the water. [Dumb? I'll tell you! Since writing the above I have heard a reliable rumor that Christie and Billy actually came to York Harbor on their honeymoon and anchored their yacht and spent a July 1985 night there. Wow! I *could* have sent this in a bottle had I but known.]

Of course, there is another real and present danger. She might, say, hear about my letter to her, or, as I say, run across it while riffling pages in a bookstore or at a remainder table or something. Anyway, say Christie finds this letter and actually reads it. The danger is that she might want to read, if only out of idle curiosity, the rest of the book. And then what? Maybe she wouldn't think it was funny worth a hoot. Maybe irony would be as lost on her as it would be on Billy Joel. I can't be sure.

What I have in mind is this. A fair exchange. You, reader, promise not to read my letter to her. And I'll do everything in my power to persuade *her* not to read the rest of the book. Which was (more or less) addressed to you.

God, modern life is so complicated! So *complex*, as Liberals are always saying when they don't want to deal with a problem.

I don't want to be forced into the position of having to choose between you and Christie Brinkley. You know. Just as I don't want to force you to choose between me and John Towne.

Sure, I like her. Who wouldn't? But I like you, too. Sight unseen. Reader, you don't have to put on a scanty bathing suit and run on the sands of the beach or splash in the water to get my attention. You have my full attention now, just as, I hope, I have yours . . . or some of it, anyway.

Let me put it this way.

I have done the best I could for you. I hope you enjoyed at least some of it.

Now. Go in peace. Have a nice life. And please don't read my personal letter to Christie.

All best wishes to you.
> Sincerely,
> The Author

Plus
A Few Final Remarks to the Great American Reading Public
by Lee Holmes
> Assistant Professor Emeritus,
> Nameless College

Folks, I have sure enough done the best that I could with all this stuff against the odds and in the face of circumstances that (sometimes anyway) would have given St. Francis of Assisi or St. Cuthbert of Lindisfarne a migrane headache. I could tell you some tales of woe about my last twenty years spent in penal servitude at Nameless. Deans have died, Presidents have come and gone, old buildings have crumbled and new ones have gone up. And many a bottle of booze has been my nourishment. Life goes on. Sort of. . . .

But, anyway, I am at last almost done with this thankless task.

There were a few more letters, of recent vintage and probably by Towne, himself, that I wanted to add here for the sake of a well-rounded narrative and for verisimilitude. But my publisher (so-called) denied me that privilege. My latest editor, a chap named (improbably; but when it comes to names, what is probable in this age?) G. Gordon Glitz . . . Have we come that far already? Has so much time passed as I struggled over these papers that the *children* named after prominent figures in the Watergate Scandal have grown up and come to positions of power and authority like the kinfolk and children of *New Yorker* writers???

Anyway, this young lad, G. Gordon Glitz who was assigned to my literary project ("put on your case," is how he phrases it), has argued strenuously against my proposed inclusion of some additional letters.

"Listen, you old fart," he wrote me. "Forget that stuff and cut the crap. This manuscript, worthless as it is, is long overdue. We aren't going to fool around and wait any more. Get off your old duff and get it in the mail or else get ready to get sued. Get it? Rounded? Narrators don't have to be rounded. I don't even like rounded. The only kind of rounded I really like is a nice ass in tight designer jeans. As for that other thing, *verisimilitude.* What the fuck is that?"

Well, folks, we negotiated briefly in that sort of tone and mode. And in the end, acting out of *"noblesse fucking oblige,"* Glitz has permitted me that rare privilege of a few final words here and a brief description of some of the letters I had to leave out in this last part.

I shall be brief. I have to.

Among the various poison pen letters from these times are the following which I really had intended to use before Glitz laid the guilt trip on me.

(1.) A letter from a big bosomed and religious woman, author of *Get Bigger Boobs By Means Of Prayer And Meditation,* addressed to the industrious American author Joyce Carol Oates. Offers her a free copy of book, though warns that you can't keep on typing while praying and meditating.

(2.) A letter (curiously enough signed G. Gordon Glitz) offering former President Nixon a contract for a non-fiction book to be titled *A Little Treasury of Great American Burglaries.*

(3.) A letter addressed to "John Belushi in Heaven," inquiring about aspects of angelic experience. Asking if angels get high and, if so, how they do it. Inquiring if angel wings are aerodynamically sound and strong enough to keep even Belushi airborne for long. Wondering if he is required to play a harp like all the others.

(4.) Letter to Sen. Alan Cranston politely informing him that he has just been named the Strom Thurmond of the Old Left. Asking if his "consistent, not to say regularly reflexive support of the State of Israel in all matters and all things" has served to help him achieve any real financial security for his golden years.

(5.) A letter to Susan Stamberg complimenting her on the success of "All Things Considered" and on her wonderful voice. Which, the author maintains, never fails to give him a huge erection. No other radio voice has the same effect. And since he is impotent most of the rest of the time, as a result of early exposure to militant feminism, he and his fiancée, can only have sex during the broadcast of "All Things Considered." Whenever La Stamberg is not on the program or on vacation, it is extremely frustrating for him. He wonders if a tape recording might not be the answer. Encloses a blank 90-minute Memorex cassette asking her, in the name of science and the scientific method, to record some key passages from the anthology *Great Pornography of the Civilized Western World* for him. Of course, *anything* she says works fine. But he wonders if maybe the sound of her voice reading porn might even heighten his experience in the same way as, say, amyl nitrate does.

(6.) A letter to Gloria Steinem congratulating her on her 50th birthday. Written by a former Playboy Club Bunny who remembers Bunny Gloria from *her* days in the N.Y.C. Hutch. Years have been less kind to the author of the letter than to Gloria. She confesses to being "a beat up old broad." But argues that she probably had more fun getting that way than Bunny Gloria has had maintaining herself in near mint condition.

(7.) Brisk business letter from an Avon Lady evidently replying to a query letter from Betty Friedan. Allows that there probably isn't anything that either Avon or anybody else can do for Ms. Friedan. Advises wearing a decorative, colorful, and interesting paper bag over her head.

(8.) Letter to Noam Chomsky on correct spelling and meaning of the word *chutzpah*.

(9.) Letter to critic Leslie Fiedler asking if he knows whatever happened to fellow critics John Aldridge and Ihab Hassan. Also inquiries if Fiedler may happen to know of any good treatment for premature ejaculation.

(10.) A letter to a publisher named Stuart Wright asking if he is brave enough or dumb enough to publish a collection of poison pen letters to celebrities to be called *Poison Pen*.*

In my opinion it would have been a much better book if these letters could have been included. But Glitz was, to put it mildly, adamant. And so you'll have to *imagine* them. Try to imagine them as really swell examples of the form, full of vulgar vigor and crude humor and satirical comments about many a sacred cow.

As for me, try to imagine how I feel as I finish this MS. and head for the P.O. to mail it off to Glitz.

Greatly relieved.

Sure, I'm a little sad and pissed off too. Especially since I will never make back the crummy advance which was spent almost 20 years ago. No, I fear it won't bring me bucks. And I know it won't bring me fame and glory or any of that. But it gives me a warm feeling to think that somewhere out there John Towne has a big surprise coming to him.

Get ready, John, you have a lot of explaining and apologizing to do.

Sooner or later that's what it all comes down to—explaining and apologizing and hoping to get away with it.

I hope you get away with it, Reader, whatever it may be.

> Yours truly,
> Lee Holmes

P.S. If any of you are former students of mine at Nameless, I wouldn't mind hearing from you from time to time. Even a postcard can make my day these days.

> L.H.

P.P.S.

In fairness and for the sake of accuracy (if one twin was named Accuracy, what would the other one be named: Media? "S.R." for Sliderule? how about Advocacy?), I need to mention that I have received from an anonymous source, in a plain brown envelope, two items which, on the basis of internal evidence and a pretty good guess, I would say have come to me, directly or indirectly

---

*The Devil made me do it. S.W.

from Towne himself. Indicating nothing, I suppose, except that he was, at least until very recently, alive (who knows whether he was or is well? who cares? could someone with his running-dog-fascistic-racist-sexist-envy-and-greed-ridden-inner-and-outer life be described by anyone, except maybe Dr. Joseph Mengle, as "well"?) and unchanged and up to the same old japes and pasquils. The first of these has some importance; for it helps us to date Towne's recent activities. It is a clipping from *The Washington Post* for Tuesday, July 30, 1985. Attached to the clipping is a typed comment—"More good stuff for the AMERICA THE BEAUTIFUL? file." (I ask you, reader, who else could that be, but John Towne? Unless, of course, other people, perfect strangers, have taken up the same subversive game.) The clipping—"DEATH FILMS, for RENT or SALE/ Grisly Movies of Real Killings Prove Popular at Video Stores"—speaks for itself and tells us nothing new. Except as Towne has put it elsewhere, "that old Wog is right—America *is* the Great Satan." Those of us who honor and revere the sanctity of the First Amendment—and, by golly, there are some of us who do, too, besides newspaper owners and TV anchorpersons, believe that it is altogether fitting and proper that all people should be able to rent or buy and watch or not watch such things as those described in the article: autopsies, open heart surgery, slaughtering of animals, remains of Auschwitz victims, people jumping to death from buildings and being electrocuted, seals being bashed to bloody death with clubs. (This latter particularly offends me; for I like seals much better than people.)

Where was I?

O yes, the envelope. Also in it was (again internal evidence that it's got to be from Towne or a clone of him) another list of American poets being teased and gently satirized. I here offer the list as I received it. Without comment. I can't comment, anyway, since I never heard of most of these people and don't have time to (pardon the expression) expose myself to their "sullen art or craft," as the Poet put it. I'm sure they're all wonderful and deserve all the grants, awards, and prizes they seem to get with their breakfast cereal. I'm not bitter. I'm not sour. Just because the NEA wouldn't fund this study of Towne and his permanent place in American Lit, doesn't mean I can't rejoice in the good fortune of others. Right? Anyway, here are Towne's additions to his original list. Some appear to be duplications. That is, some people appear on the earlier list also. So what? It probably just means he thinks about some of these poets more than others.

L.H.

MORE POETS

Philip Booth is the L.L. Bean of American Poetry.
James Seay is the Hathaway man of American Poetry.
Hayden Carruth is the Mr. Whipple of American Poetry.
Richard Howard is the Judy Garland of American Poetry.
Stanley Kunitz is the Yoda of American Poetry.

Karl Shapiro is the Nehi Grape of American Poetry.
John Stone is the Dr. Pepper of American Poetry.
Peter Davison is the Sominex of American Poetry.
Erica Jong is the Dolly Parton of American Poetry.
Miller Williams is the Tom T. Hall of American Poetry.
Ellen Gilchrist is the Minnie Pearl of American Poetry.
William Matthews is the Wyatt Earp of American Poetry.
Dara Wier is the Dale Evans of American Poetry.
Lucille Clifton is the Lucille Ball of American Poetry.
Nikki Giovanni is the Gina Lolabrigida of American Poetry.
Margaret Gibson is the Ali McGraw of American Poetry.
Czeslos Milosz is the Lawrence Welk of American Poetry.
Marion Montgomery is the Ronald McDonald of American Poetry.
John Updike is the Fred Astaire of American Poetry.
Harold Bloom is the Elmer Fudd of American Poetry.
John Updike is the Bugs Bunny of American Poetry.
Heather McHugh is the Fay Wray of American Poetry.
Louise Glück is the Lassie of American Poetry.
Bin Ramke is the Ben Kingsley of American Poetry.
Allen Ginsberg is the Gunga Din of American Poetry.
Gregory Corso is the Bonnie and Clyde of American Poetry.
David St. John is the Cheech and Chong of American Poetry.
Cid Corman is the Sid Caesar of American Poetry.
A.R. Ammons is the Don Knotts of American Poetry.
Reg Gibbon is the J.R. of American Poetry.
Heather Ross Miller is the King Kong of American Poetry.
Mona Van Duyn is the Mamie Van Doren of American Poetry.
Alicia Ostriker is the Betty Friedan of American Poetry.
Maya Angelou is the Sapphire of American Poetry.
Anthony Hecht is the Adolphe Menjou of American Poetry.
Leslie Silko is the Pocahontas of American Poetry.
William Jay Smith is the Sitting Bull of American Poetry.
Gregory Orr is the Raging Bull of American Poetry.
James Applewhite is the Bull Durham of American Poetry.
James Dickey is the Bull Connor of American Poetry.
William and R.P. Dickey are the wrong Dickey of American Poetry.
James Dickey is the Mr. T of American Poetry.
X.J. Kennedy is the wrong Kennedy of American Poetry.
Stanley Moss is the wrong Moss of American Poetry.
Harvey Shapiro is the wrong Shapiro of American Poetry.
Lawrence Lieberman is the wrong Lieberman of American Poetry.
Daniel Hoffman is the Daniel G. Hoffman of American Poetry.
Adrienne Rich is the Adrienne Cecile Rich of American Poetry.
James Hall is the Jim Hall of American Poetry.
Jim Harrison is the Rex Harrison of American Poetry.
Wendell Berry is the Nabih Berri of American Poetry.

Garrett Hongo is the Yo Yo Ma of American Poetry.
Gerald Costanzo is the Daniel Halpern of American Poetry.
William Heyen is the W.D. Snodgrass of American Poetry.
W.D. Snodgrass is the Rudolph Hess of American Poetry.
Imamu Amiri Baraka is the Buckwheat of American Poetry.
Richard Eberhart is the Spanky of American Poetry.
Donald Hall is the Wonder Boy of American Poetry.
Robert Pack is the Wonder Bread of American Poetry.
Deborah Nystrom is the Banana Daquiri of American Poetry.
Cynthia McDonald is the Andrea Dworkin of American Poetry.
Michael Ryan is the Top Banana of American Poetry.
Michael Pettit is the Roy Rogers of American Poetry.
Gary Soto is the Edsel of American Poetry.
Ellen Bryant Voight is the Lady Bird of American Poetry.
Denise Levertov is the Rosa Luxembourg of American Poetry.
Theodore Weiss is the Menachem Begin of American Poetry.
Mary Kinzie is the Maud Gonne of American Poetry.
Tess Gallagher is the Bernadette Devlin of American Poetry.
Marie Bullock is the Lady Gregory of American Poetry.
Leslie Ullman is the Joan Benoit of American Poetry.
Cathy Hankla is the Jill Krementz of American Poetry.
Margaret Atwood is the Moosehead of American Poetry.
Carolyn Forché is the Christie Brinkley of American Poetry.
Stephen Sandy is the Charles Atlas of American Poetry.
James Atlas is the Tom Thumb of American Poetry.

Dear Christie Brinkley,
 Well, now.
 Here we are.
 Alone together at last.
 Sort of. . . .
 Truth is, I've been planning and trying to write you this letter for almost
a year now. Trying to find and to seize the time to do it. And to do it some
justice, too. Trying to get my act together so that this letter would really
say something. Something (pardon the expression) cogent and maybe even
coherent. I had hoped to be able to put not only the story of my life and
all that, but also my philosophy of life and art. I mean, it was my hope to
get it all (somehow) into one at least memorable letter to you.
 But, what with moving from one job in Ann Arbor, Michigan to a new
one in Charlottesville, Virginia, and all the chaos and confusion that go along
with a move like that, I never did find the time. Or, to be honest, when it
seemed as if I might have the time, I would discover that I wasn't really in
the right mood for it. Or I would be in an okay mood, but just too pooped
to write anything or anyone. Or I had to spend what free time I had meeting
deadlines or honoring utterly inconsequential commitments of one kind or
another.
 Does it sound like a busy and productive life? Don't be fooled. Busy, it
sure enough may be. But productive? That is something else. To put it as
simply and directly as possible, Christie, when you are at last over fifty years
old and are a serious candidate for the Tomb of the Unknown American
Writer, you have got to keep your feet moving. You have to keep hustling
and cranking it out. You do not have the considerable benefit of a comfortable
reputation (like a whoopee cushion?) to sit down on. You can't sit down on
your reputation and just take it easy.
 There are brief moments of secret pride in all this, to be sure. Once in
a while it is possible to hold up your head and even to strut a little when
you manage to do something which is at least half decent in the face of and
in spite of all the shrugging indifference and yawning discouragement. Some-
times a perfectly vulgar pride allows one to surmise that not everyone among
one's famous peers and/or betters could have persisted and endured. But that
pride softens and shrinks from its arrogant tumescence thanks to the irre-
pressible knowledge, the unsuppressable awareness that you are, ever and
always, with each beginning, back at Square One again; that you have to
compete against the entire field always; that you must prove yourself each
and every time, over and over and over again. . . .
 And it finally does get tedious, believe me. It can wear you down if you
let it.
 But that's not your problem, Christie. And most of the time it's not mine,
either. Because the whole thing is that most of the time I don't have time
to even think about it. I'm too busy most of the time to piss and moan.
 Another thing. Coming back to Charlottesville and to The University of
Virginia, after an absence of some twenty years, is a very strange experience.

I taught here in the early 1960's. Taught here for five years, had Tenure, owned a house. And a very nice house it was. My children went to elementary school, Venable School, here. But, for one reason and another and mostly so that I could get some writing of my own done, I had to pack up and move on. Either that or sell out. So we moved on. And on. And on. My replacement at U. Va. was Peter Taylor. He was (in my humble opinion) just exactly right for the place. After he retired, they searched and searched for his replacement. (I even helped them try to find somebody.) And, as I understand it, a lot of Big Shots, at least in the context of our teeny-tiny literary world, came and went, looked over the place and the job and were looked over themselves. Frankly, I don't know who all was considered; and I hesitate to ask. I do know that John Hawkes and John Barth (and neither of *them* is a candidate for Tomb of the Unknown American Writer) had a shot at it, could have had it if they wanted to.

Look, Christie, I don't want to bore you to death with all this stuff about my life and hard/odd times. Let's just say that, all right, somehow the job finally fell to me and I took it like a flash. Because the pay is (in my terms) pretty good. And the perks aren't bad, all things considered; and besides it is an endowed chair. Like everybody else in this academic racket, I guess I got caught up in the spirit of the thing in spite of myself and my best intentions. I actually wanted to be a chaired professor, you know? So now I am the Henry Hoyns Professor of Creative Writing. They even gave me an actual chair, one of those black ones with the university seal in gold on it and a little brass plaque on the back of it. Very classy. . . .

Listen, Christie, just to simplify things a little, to introduce myself to you efficiently and without rambling on and on for pages, I here enclose a document, Document in Evidence Number One. Namely my official academic *vita*. You can skip it if you want to, refer to it if you feel like it. Or whatever. To me it's a pretty depressing little document, but it will at least give you some idea of the back roads and byways I have travelled on.

George P. Garrett
Department of English
University of Virginia
Charlottesville, VA 22903

Hoyns Professor of
Creative Writing

BIOGRAPHICAL INFORMATION

Born
11 June 1929 in Orlando, Florida.

Marital Status
Married to Susan P. Jackson, 14 June 1952; three children.

Education
—Graduated from Sewanee Military Academy, 1946; from the Hill School, 1947.
—B.A. Princeton University (Phi Beta Kappa, Magna Cum Laude), 1952.
—M.A. Princeton University (English), 1958.

Military
Served in Active Reserves, U.S. Army (Field Artillery), 1950-1956. Includes two years' service overseas. Honorable discharge.

Previous teaching positions (fulltime)
—Wesleyan University, 1957-1960, Assistant Professor of English.
—(Alley Theater, Houston, Texas: Ford Foundation Grant, 1960-1961).
—Rice University, 1961-1962, Visiting Lecturer.
—University of Virginia, 1962-1967, Associate Professor of English.
—Princeton University, 1964-1965, Resident Fellow in Creative Writing.
—Hollins College, 1967-1971, Professor of English and Director of Graduate Program in English.
—University of South Carolina, 1971-1974, Professor of English and Writer in Residence.
—(Guggenheim Fellowship, 1974-1975).
—Florida International University, 1974 (final quarter of 1973-74 academic year), Visiting Professor of English.
—Princeton University, 1974-77, Senior Fellow of the Council of the Humanities.
—Columbia University, School of the Arts, 1977 (second semester of 1976-77 academic year), adjunct Professor of Writing.
—University of Michigan, 1979 (winter term of 1978-79 academic year), Visiting Writer.
—Bennington College, 1979 (fall semester of 1979-80 academic year), Professor of English.
—University of Charleston, 1982 (spring semester of 1981-82 academic year), Writer-in-Residence.
—Virginia Military Institute, 1982 (fall semester of 1982-83 academic year), Eminent Scholar and Conquest Professor of English.
—University of Michigan, 1983-1984, Professor of English and Senior Creative Writer.
—University of Virginia, 1984—, Hoyns Professor of Creative Writing.

Courses taught (undergraduate and graduate)
American Literature, Southern Literature, Modern Novel, Contemporary Literature, Contemporary Poetry, Film Studies, Reading Poetry, Creative Writing.

Fellowships and Grants
Sewanee Review Fellowship in Poetry, 1958; Rome Prize of the American Academy of Arts and Letters, 1959; Ford Foundation Grant in Drama, 1961;

Sabbatical Fellowship of the National Endowment for the Arts, 1966; Guggenheim Fellowship, 1974; Award in Literature from the National Academy and Institute of the Arts, 1985.

Editorial positions
Editor, University of North Carolina Press, Contemporary Poetry Series, 1962-1968.

Editorial Advisor, L.S.U. Press (short story series), 1966-1969.

Poetry Editor, *The Transatlantic Review*, 1958-1971.

Contributing Editor, *Contempora*, 1969-1973.

Contributing Editor, *The Hollins Critic*, 1965-1976; Co-editor 1967-1971.

Assistant Editor, *The Film Journal*, 1970-1973.

Co-editor, *Poultry: A Magazine of Voice*, 1980—.

Consultantships and Readerships
Have served as cousultant for the Ford Foundation, the National Endowment for the Arts, National Endowment for the Humanities, Maine Council of the Arts, Doubleday & Co.

Have served as a reader for the following presses: University of Texas Press, Princeton University Press, L.S.U. Press, University of Alabama Press, University of Georgia Press, University of Illinois Press, University of Pittsburgh Press, University of Missouri Press.

Organizations
President of Associated Writing Programs, 1971-1974.

Membership in:
Modern Language Association, College English Association, National Council of Teachers of English, Friends of the Folger Library, Florida Historical Society, Authors Guild, Writers Guild of America (East).

Fellow of the American Academy in Rome, 1958.

Trustee of Pen/Faulkner Award.

Writers' Conferences
Suffield Writers Conference, Southwest Writers Conference, University of Utah Writers Conference, Hollins Conference in Creative Writing and Cinema, University of North Dakota Conference of Southern Writers, Eastern

Washington State Writers Workshop, Hollins Literary Festival, Boatwright Literary Festival (Richmond), Archive Literary Festival (Duke), Rollins Writers Conference, Bennington Workshops, Stonecoast Conference (Portland, Me.), Green Mountain Conference (Vermont), Cumberland Writers' Conference, and others . . .

Lectures and Readings
Have given lectures, readings and participated in panel discussions at more than 200 colleges and universities; also at a large number of museums, libraries, clubs, organizational meetings, high schools and preparatory schools, Poetry in the Schools Program.

Miscellaneous
Have been employed as a writer by C.B.S. Television and as a screenwriter by Samuel Goldwyn, Jr. at Goldwyn Studios.

A fairly complete checklist of published writings by George Garrett—"George Garrett: A Bibliographical Chronicle, 1947-1980," by Stuart Wright—is available in *Bulletin of Bibliography*, Vol. 38, No. 1 (January-March, 1981), pp. 6-19, 25. Following is a selected list

CHECKLIST OF PUBLISHED WRITINGS (books only)
I. BOOKS

The Reverend Ghost (in POETS OF TODAY IV, ed. John Hall Wheelock), New York: Scribner's, 1957.

King of The Mountain (short stories), New York: Scribner's, 1958.

The Sleeping Gypsy and Other Poems, Austin: University of Texas Press, 1959.

The Finished Man (novel), New York: Scribner's, 1959.

Abraham's Knife and Other Poems, Chapel Hill: University of North Carolina Press, 1961.

In the Briar Patch (short stories), Austin: University of Texas Press, 1961.

Which Ones Are The Enemy? (novel), Boston: Little Brown, 1961.

Sir Slob And The Princess: A Play for Children, New York: Samuel French, 1962.

Cold Ground Was My Bed Last Night (short stories), Columbia: University of Missouri Press, 1964.

Do, Lord, Remember Me (novel), New York: Doubleday, 1965.

For A Bitter Season: New and Selected Poems, Columbia: University of Missouri Press, 1967.

A Wreath for Garibaldi and Other Stories, London: Rupert Hart-Davis, 1969.

Death of The Fox (novel), New York: Doubleday, 1971.

The Magic Striptease (short stories), New York: Doubleday, 1973.

Welcome to The Medicine Show (poems), Winston-Salem: Palaemon Press, 1978.

Luck's Shining Child (poems), Winston-Salem: Palaemon Press, 1981.

Enchanted Ground (play), York, Maine: Old Gaol Museum, 1982.

The Succession: A Novel of Elizabeth & James, New York: Doubleday, 1983.

The Collected Poems of George Garrett, Fayetteville: University of Arkansas Press, 1984.

James Jones (Biography), San Diego: Harcourt Brace, 1984.

An Evening Performance: New and Selected Short Stories, New York: Doubleday, 1985.

II. BOOKS EDITED BY

New Writing From Virginia, Charlottesville: New Writing Associates, 1963.

The Girl in The Black Raincoat, New York: Duell, Sloan and Pearce, 1966.

Man and the Movies (with W. R. Robinson), Baton Rouge: L.S.U. Press, 1967.

New Writing in South Carolina (with William Peden), Columbia: University of South Carolina Press, 1971.

Film Scripts One and Film Scripts Two (with Jane Gelfman and O.B. Hardison, Jr.), New York: Appleton-Century-Crofts, 1971.

The Sounder Few: Selected Essays From The Hollins Critic (with R.H.W. Dillard and John Rees Moore), Athens: University of Georgia Press, 1971.

Film Scripts Three and Film Scripts Four (with Jane Gelfman and O.B. Hardison, Jr.), New York: Appleton-Century-Crofts, 1972.

Craft So Hard to Learn: Conversations with Poets and Novelists About the Teaching of Writing (with John Graham), New York: William Morrow, 1973.

The Writer's Voice: Conversation with Contemporary Writers (with John Graham), New York: William Morrow, 1973.

Intro 5 (with Walton Beacham), Charlottesville: University Press of Virginia, 1974.

Botteghe Oscure Reader (with Katherine Garrison Biddle), Middletown: Wesleyan University Press, 1974.

Intro 6: Life as We Know It, New York: Doubleday, 1974.

Intro 7: All of Us and None of You (with James Whitehead and Miller Williams), New York: Doubleday, 1975.

Intro 8: The Liar's Craft (with Stephen Kendrick), New York: Doubleday, 1977.

Intro 9: Close to Home (with Michael Mewshaw), Austin, Texas: Hendel & Reinke, 1978.

Sorry about the interruption, Christie. I just thought maybe it would be a little easier for both of us, you know? Only, of course, that whole thing doesn't really tell you anything, does it? Not even in its own very limited terms.

For a real obvious example, it doesn't even mention yet (because I haven't figured out a way to do so without looking more ridiculous than I do already) that I finally earned my Ph.D. from Princeton. If you look, you'll see I was a graduate student there more than thirty years ago. As a grad student I took all the courses I had to take and passed all the exams I had to pass, even the language exams (French, German, Latin and Old English.) (Drank a few beers and had some good times, too.)

But, in the end, I never turned in my dissertation. Well, they fooled me. Thirty years later, this year, 1985, some emeritus professors got together and decided that my two historical novels, *Death of the Fox* and *The Succession* could qualify as a dissertation. No kidding! And they invited me to come up and on Friday, May 3, 1985, to have a Final Public Oral Examination.

Here (Document in Evidence Number Two) is the official announcement:

FINAL PUBLIC ORAL EXAMINATION
George Garrett
Friday, May 3, 3:00
Frelinghuysen Roam, Firestone Library 2nd Floor

George Garrett (B.A. Princeton '52, M.A. Princeton '58) is at present Hoyns Professor at the University of Virginia. He has taught in the

English departments or creative writing programs at Princeton, Columbia, Bennington, and the University of Michigan. Professor Garrett is the author of several novels, volumes of poetry, and short stories. Two of his major novels, *Death of the Fox* and *The Succession*, treat historical themes (the life of Raleigh, the death of Elizabeth I) with an extraordinary scholarly as well as novelistic imagination. At the suggestion of several of his former professors in this graduate program, George Garrett has submitted those two novels in partial completion of the requirements for the Ph.D. Professors Carlos Baker and Michael Goldman have approved the work and prepared the necessary readers' reports. (Professors Fleming and Danson concur.)

Professor Garrett will complete the requirements for the degree at the Final Public Oral Examination. Along with his novels he has sent an article, "Dreaming with Adam: Notes on Imaginary History" (from *New Directions in Literary History*, ed. Ralph Cohen) and two recent lectures delivered at (respectively) the Renaissance Conference in Charleson, S.C. (March 15) and the North Carolina Historial Museum (March 12). The article and lectures deal with the idea of historical fiction and with the uses of scholarship in Professor Garrett's own work. He suggests that people who attend the Final Public Oral Examination might like to read one or another of these pieces, if they have not time to read or re-read the novels. They are available from Marilyn Walden.

As with *all* Final Public Oral Examinations, everyone is welcome to attend. The Department picnic for undergraduates happens to follow immediately.
LD/ibm pc

So, anyway, Christie, I got into my (wonderful) old car, a green and rusty and battered and utterly dependable 1978 Ford Fairmont, its hatchback and rear bumper riddled with parking stickers and permits from a dozen institutions of higher learning, I got in the car and drove on up to Princeton. Took my exam and managed to pass it. Then went out and had me a swell martini and a fine dinner (lamb and pasta and superb asparagus) with John McPhee and his wife Yolanda. John showed up for the exam. We were undergraduates at Princeton together. He is definitely not a candidate for the Tomb of the Unknown American Writer.

Anyway, it was all fine and dandy. And now I have got me a Ph.D. I can't fucken believe it, you know? It is very ironic, too.

I don't know if you are into all the different kinds and forms of irony, Christie. If not, don't feel too bad. You have to have a taste for it like for escargots, and even then it is greatly overated. Irony doesn't offer much deep inner satisfaction, if you know what I mean. Irony is all foreplay. But the irony of this is, see?, that the proximate cause of my original resignation from

Virginia in 1967 was that I had just been awarded the first and last and, in fact, only grant I ever received from the sometimes beneficient National Endowment for the Arts. It would give me a whole year off, and I was just desperate to get that time off and to do some of my own writing. Well, They said, Yes, I could have the time off—after all the Government was paying for it, anyway; it wasn't costing Them anything. But They (in this case Fredson Bowers, the Chairman of English and Edgar Shannon, the President of the University) wanted me to promise that I would use the free time not to write some dumb novel or something, but instead, to finish my dissertation and to get my Ph.D. I couldn't honestly promise to do that, Christie. So, I quit.

The big irony is that the book I was working on and trying to finish at the time (it would take five more years instead of just one) was *Death of the Fox*. Which turned out to be my dissertation after all.

Get it?

That's irony for you, Christie. A twenty year joke on somebody. Probably on me. . . .

One thing more. A list of names: Louis Landa, Carlos Baker, Maurice Kelly, Dick Ludwig, Sam Howell, Larry Danson, Bob Howarth, Jerry Finch, Michael Goldman. . . . These are some of the people who showed up at the Final Oral. And some of them even asked questions. This book here, I mean *Poison Pen*, is supposed to have an index, someday, according to Stuart Wright, the so-called publisher. So I want to be sure they get in it if it is really here.

Also Johnny McPhee. Who was already mentioned.

Tom Roche wasn't there. Nor Walt Litz. But I know why they couldn't make it. Mike Keeley was in Greece. I don't know where Joyce Carol Oates may have been. But I really didn't expect to see her, anyway.

Where was I?

Oh yes, I was trying to get this letter underway with an apology for not writing sooner and trying to explain this crazy, busy year in a new/old place.

Sorry about that digression. Ever since I got mixed up with John Towne, I just can't stay on the literary straight and narrow. You don't know him, of course, or anything about him. He's all involved in the rest of this book. The other part that you aren't supposed to read.

Anyway, take it from me (and not him), it is very strange to come back, even trailing some modest little clouds of glory, to a place where you once lived and meant to live. And then they threw you out. Probably that has never happened to you. Nobody has even given you the old heave-ho, Christie. At least not yet. Maybe when you're old and gray and flabby and wrinkled. Who knows? Of course, you may end up being incredibly beautiful and desirable, just like you are now, for all the rest of your life. It's possible. But I kind of doubt it. Don't you? But pay no attention to me. I tend to be pessimistic about a lot of things in real life.. Even when I would prefer to take a more optimistic view. It is really and truly possible, though just barely, that nothing of or on you will ever sag or wrinkle or get rough instead of smooth and that all your internal organs, which are probably—I hope so—just as nice as your externals, will continue to function smoothly and painlessly and effi-

227

ciently. It is possible that nothing bad will ever have to happen to you. It's possible and let's just leave it that way, okay? Besides, like a whole lot of other people obviously, I have myself a wonderful collection of Christie Brinkley materials: calendars for the last 3 years, old magazine covers (including *Playboy!*) and magazine stories and even your very own book. I have one huge and colorful and very revealing poster which was presented to me by my students (led by Kim Kafka and Alyson Hagy) at my last class at Michigan. (How did they know I cared?) Anyway, the thing is, even if you do gradually sag and wrinkle and get old and gray, even if you do develop some dread disease or maybe just some unpleasant and boring chronic conditions, even if bad things do begin to happen to you and change your appearance and your lifestyle significantly, I'll still be able to see you as you once were. And you'll still have memories of how it was to be young and beautiful. So neither one of us will have a legitimate cause for very much complaint.

So, anyway, I have newly returned to an old place. And it's a place that has not outwardly changed very much. Because it can't. Oh, there are three times as many students as there used to be; and it's (thank the Lord!) coeducational now; and there are three times as many people; and the traffic is now incredible; and parking is an horrendous problem (if I parked where the University allows me to, I would be farther away from the University that the house that I live in); and real estate is inflated beyond the means of most of us (the house I once owned and sold at a loss years ago is now beyond any possibility of my buying again); but, because Mr. Jefferson's central part of the University—the Rotunda, the Lawn, the Ranges, etc.—was all built by him and is so maintained, the essential core of the place is just exactly as it was. As is my neighborhood less than a mile from the Grounds. The trees are twenty years older and taller. The hedges are higher. The shade is greener and deeper. But there are only two new houses in the whole area. Many of the same people still live where they did. In short, it's pretty much the same.

Thus, the impact of the experience of returning is mixed.

My wife put it this way: "Coming back to Charlottesville is like living in a strange place where you know what's around every corner."

Exactly. As in a dream. . . .

You would like my wife (I think). She is a wonderful woman and good looking, too. However, I'm not so sure that she fully understands the meaning of our special relationship. Yours and mine, I mean. But that's my problem.

Anyway, as I was saying, it has taken a good long time for me to get down to the serious business (and the pleasure) of writing this letter to you. Not all that much happened to me. I moved here. The year went by. Last week, or was it the week before?, I had my last class. And I still haven't managed to unpack everything.

A lot happened to you, though. For one thing you went and got married to Billy Joel. I read all about it in *People* magazine (April 8, 1985; cover and "A Dreamboat Wedding: Downtown rocker Billy Joel and uptown model Christie Brinkley go for a cruise and return as man and wife," pp. 54–56, 59, 62). It sounds like it was a swell wedding in every way. And I hope you all live

228

happily ever after. I really do. Actually, I have to confess I like Billy Joel pretty well. His music and all, I mean. I know that my own kids think he's not worth listening to, but they take Pop music seriously. And several of my students have called him an asshole, not meaning any harm or even insult, just indicating that they tend to prefer other kinds of sounds. But I see no particular reason to be narrow-minded about these things. Let us all strive to be open to all kinds of experience. Even the music of Billy Joel. I said I liked it pretty well and I do. I used to play Billy Joel tapes when I had to make trips in my old car. Which was pretty often. I liked to sing along with them.

Another thing. When I am teaching young writers, I try to help them get ready for some of the many bad things that are bound to happen to them. Like, for instance, bad reviews. Of course, the Silent Treatment, which is what most of us get in return for all our labors, is far worse than any bad review. Except sometimes. I don't mind telling you, Christie, that I have every hope and expectation, indeed I am *depending on* the Silent Treatment as far as this here book, *Poison Pen*, the one your letter is attached to, is concerned. I'm not sure that I can expect much sympathetic critical understanding on this one. With my luck, the rotten bastards will probably choose to *read* this book and review it! And wouldn't that be a laugh at my expense? Oh, well. . . .

So, anyway, I do my best to prepare my students for the inevitable shitstorm of bad reviews they will have to face if they write anything with any merit or originality in it. Sometimes I read them the reviews William Faulkner earned, book after book, over the years. "There now," I tell them. "Nothing that bad is likely ever to happen to you." And once in a while I actually read them a review of your husband and his work, by Robert Palmer in *The New York Times*. I have the clipping, but I have lost the date of it. It is headlined "Pop: 5 Nights of Billy Joel at the Garden," and it has a photo of your husband, looking bug-eyed and surly, credited to one David Gahr. Maybe Billy saw it when it first appeared. If he did, I reckon he will still remember it. If he didn't see it, you should look it up in the *Times Index* and make a copy of it. You never know when your husband may need a little basic lesson in basic humility. This will be a quick one. Basic humilitation is more like it. Palmer really socks it to him. "He has won a huge following by making emptiness seem substantial and Holiday Inn lounge shlock sound special." After using a number of fairly strong qualifiers, such as "utterly repellant," "obnoxious," and making a number of insidious comparisons ("rock-and-roll and Mr. Joel have about as much in common as a Beethoven symphony and a sneeze"), he concludes that "this listener can't stand him, not on the radio and expecially not in person. He's the sort of popular artist who makes elitism seem not just defensible but necessary." Wow! My students always laugh their asses off, never dreaming that anything that bad can possibly fall down on top of their heads. Not unless elephants learn how to fly.

So what? You say. And I agree. So what, indeed? Billy J. probably laughed all the way to the Bank and back. And that was even before he had Christie Brinkley for a friend. Now he can go around laughing all the time. Right?

So you went and got married. And Cristina Ferrare DeLorean got a divorce and then got herself a new husband by the name of Anthony Thomopoulous. And, according to *Time* (April 29, 1985), the amazing Mary Cunningham is now pregnant. And Brooke Shields (no flies on her) has gone and written a book called *On Your Own* in which, according to *USA Today*, (April 18, 1985, p. 1D), she claims to be a (pardon) virgin. Do you believe that? And all kinds of other wild and wooly things happened in the teeny-tiny, ho-hum space of one little old academic year. During the brief period while I was *not* writing this letter to you, the folks on the celebrity fast lane went round and around the track at a dizzy and glittering speed. It makes my head swim. Just to think of it all. And, also, here comes the future, ready or not. In your case, Christie, I would say the future (or maybe she is the present already) is named Paulina Porizkova, a real exotic cutie on the cover (and richly displayed on the inside pages) of *Sports Illustrated* for February 11, 1985. A lot of people thought it would be Kim Alexis on that cover this year, but she didn't make the cut and that's that. Too bad, Kim. They had a lot of excellent pictures of you in that issue, looking ever-so sexy in all kinds of little bitty ole bathing suits. But in the end the cover went to our lady Paulina. I guess because she looks just a little more . . . well, *refined*, Kim, than you do. There is something extra sexy about a good looking and very refined woman doing the bikini exposure number. It may be the same principle that causes San Francisco Topless Bars to advertise, in bold neon, "TOPLESS COLLEGE GIRLS. XXX!" The fact that college girls can be, evidently, assumed to be more intelligent and refined than their uneducated sisters makes their bare boobies sexier. If you don't understand that, you don't understand Men. American Men, anyway.

Never mind depth psychology. Point is that Paulina Porizkova is coming on strong. She is featured in *GQ* for May, 1985 ("Paulina at the Beach: The Etiquette of Topless," pp. 195-205), showing plenty of bare and handsome booby and even her bare ass on page 203. If this keeps up, pretty soon I'll be one of the very few who still remembers you. Me and Billy Joel.

No, I doubt that. Only kidding around. Paulina has a good way to go before she can give you any serious competition. And nothing lasts forever (except herpes, heh-heh), not celebrity and certainly not physical beauty. To bet on these things, to bet your life and then win, even for the briefest time, is truly an act of (pardon) existential daring. All the more so since, win or lose, you are still doomed to lose it all finally. That is something you share with all the rest of us, Christie. You, too, are plugged into the great network of everlasting equality. For we are all born to lose. At least to lose all those things. Along with other things that seem to matter most to most people. And the *equity* of the System is that the more you have got, the more you have got to lose. See? So in a serious, almost scriptural way, it is sort of sad about you people with everything the world has to offer—health, wealth, fame and beauty, happiness, plenty of good things to eat and drink, a comfortable place to get out of the weather (a warm place to take a shit), good clothes and pleasant memories. It is easier for us with so much less to shed and lose when we leave this world behind us, as the song goes. We shouldn't grind our teeth in envy of you. We should pity you. And love you much more than we do. You should have even more honor and admiration than you get.

You want to know something truly wierd about fame and celebrity, Christie? You won't believe this—it's hard to believe—but it really happened. Richard Dillard's wife, the poet and story writer Cathy Hankla, taught a course here last semester, undergraduate creative writing. And one day in her class they were all talking about music and groups and MTV and the usual stuff. And one student turned to her for advice and authority: "Is it true, Miz Hankla," he asked, "that Paul McCartney was in a group before *Wings*?"

Times passes. Figure it out. That level of ignorance is just barely possible at about the sophomore level these days. If it is honest ignorance—and, in this case, no reason to believe otherwise, then what about all the other famous people in the world? What about guys like Billy Joel?

Instead of *Poison Pen* I could just as well have called it *The Big Book of Big Losers*. Or, maybe, *A Losers' Guide to the Galaxy*.

Speaking of this book. Even if you haven't bothered to look back and skimmed through any of the earlier pages, you still may somehow have acquired the general impression that it is, all of it, in large outline and in small details, in absolutely the worst of taste. Maybe so. If so, however, I ask you to blame John Towne for it, not me. It is he who insists upon the cultivation of unacceptable ideas. It is he who is willing to arrive at unthinkable conclusions. It is he, a mere character, a pure figment, who does not know his place. I know mine. And, in terms of the intellectual and spiritual trends of the times, these times, my place is strictly in the back of the bus.

I don't want to argue with anybody. But I would like to say a few words here about . . . bad taste. Look, Christie, there is a whole literary tradition of bad taste, long before tasteless jokes ended up on the best seller lists, long before *Mad Magazine* and *The National Lampoon*, long before "Saturday Night Live" and "Monty Python" and "Not Necessarily the News" and all that crap. And more. And nobody seems to be wholly immune, in either Art or Real Life, from the thoroughly tasteless gesture. Even you, if *USA Today* for March 12, 1985 (p. 2D) is correct in its story "Christie Brinkley hopes to help clothe the needy." If the following is accurate, it shows you are willing to be as absolutely tasteless as anyone else:

> Brinkley, jumping on the benefit bandwagon for African famine victims, talked about her own effort—The Warm Project.
> "Bob Geldof (who organized the Band Aid benefit project in Europe), said to me that people aren't only starving, they're dying of exposure. As a model and designer, I'm in the clothing business and they need clothing."

Actually, it's a half decent idea. Those folks *do* need clothing. And all kinds of other basic things also. It's just somehow so . . . *grotesque* in the context of the paper. You will have to admit that it is a story that lends itself to a certain satirical appreciation. (If irony is foreplay, then satire is kind of like

231

clitoral orgasm. Not as earth-moving-and-shaking as the vaginal kind, but not so bad, either.) Never mind my idle metaphorical speculation. The point is that, in a certain context, even you can seem to be guilty of bad taste.

Back to bad taste in this particular book. Towne is in tune with all the bad taste of these tasteless times. He also has some thoughts on the subject. Among his papers, his former friend and present editor, Lee Holmes, found the following typescript. It is entitled "Notes For The Occasion Of My First Press Conference Upon Being Awarded the Pulitzer Prize." Please note, Christie, that this is some kind of crazy, cockamayme dreaming on Towne's part. He never won any kind of prize—not even the Pullet Surprise or the National Duck Award. And, Lord willing, he never will, either! What is the point in having a live Literary Establishment in the first place if guys like Towne (even in blackface or other disguises) can rise to the top? I ask you. The answer is that the Literary Establishment knows exactly to whom to give prizes and to whom not to, too. Towne will never get a prize so long as we continue to have a Literary Establishment worthy of the name.

Anyway, here's what the scumbag had to say:

I suppose I would honestly have to say that the greatest single influence upon all my writing has been magazines. All kinds of magazines. Not just the ones you will always find in the waiting rooms of doctors, dentists, lawyers, politicians, psychiatrists, agents, producers, editors, etc., all those people whose relative share of professional dignity and self-esteem is in direct ratio and proportion to the amount of time they can keep other people waiting to see them.

Of course, away off in a class by itself, unique and irresistable and not to be surpassed, is MAD magazine. MAD is the most important magazine published in America today even though it is devoted to a Lost Cause, the aim of exposing to ridicule and for health as much as possible of the fungus of phonus balonus which has infected every conceivable aspect of American life, society, and so-called culture.

MAD is doomed to failure. The subject is too big, too vast, too complex. Phonus balonus blooms and thrives everywhere. Like crab grass. Like Kudzu.

MAD is able only to hit the high points, to satirize only the more obvious examples and excesses.

I believe that the time has come—if indeed it is not too late already—for us to create *specialized* versions and editions of MAD. These should be created for specialized groups. They should be a force for sanity and order to counteract the "learned" publications of special groups which, though small in circulation, are not less blithely insidious than the primitive and obscene mass media.

I propose, as a beginning, the following essential titles as examples: "MAD THEOLOGY," "MAD LAW," "MAD SCIENCE," "MAD ECONOMICS," "MAD SOCIOLOGY," "MAD HISTORY," "MAD ART," "MAD LITERATURE," and so forth. Each allowing for any number of

Mad Subdivisions in due course. An optimist, I foresee the day when no library worth its salt will fail to display among its periodicals—"THE JOURNAL OF MAD ENGLISH AND GERMANIC PHILOLOGY." I look forward to reading important articles in "THE NEW ENGLAND JOURNAL OF MAD MEDICINE."

Turning from future hopes, however, I must say with pride that MAD has been a major influence upon all my thinking and my art.

Of course, in all fairness the Real Absurd, innocent and unselfconscious, is to be found among the multitudes of "straight" magazines and newspapers published in the U.S. I read them all eagerly. And thus I cannot hope to escape their pernicious influence upon my mental and spiritual health.

I am one of those unfortunate addicts—I confess it—who actually tries to *read* all the trash and crapola which is mechanically cranked out daily, weekly, monthly, and quarterly for the purpose of keeping the fires of city dumps burning and thus to maintain the present levels of pollution in the atmosphere and, in passing, to distract as many people as possible from encountering any of the truth or any of the real problems of contemporary life.

Perhaps in that sense American journalism does indeed perform a valuable social service. For if, even for a brief period, a large number of Americans stopped swallowing the . . . (let's call it Pablum so as not to be crude and vulgar) the unadulterated *Pablum* that is concocted to stifle their hunger for truth, and if they were permitted to enjoy the self-indulgence of allowing their encephalitic and atrophied brains the merest reflexive little twitch of thought, a vague, faint, dimly realized, atavistic tremor of vestigial skepticism, why, sirs, all hell would break loose!!

It would be worse (or better, depending on your point of view) than the Terror which followed the French Revolution.

If all the Leaders, all the Celebrated and the Celebrities in the U.S.A. in every field of endeavor were subjected to a Phonus Balonus Test or, in lieu of that, a simple Lie Detector Test, I am persuaded beyond the least shadow, thin as a single blade of grass, of doubt that there is not one among them who could pass. Not a ghost of a Chinaman's chance.

Can you name one, just one living American politician, for example, who could pass safely through even the most cursory and rudimentary examination of the integrity of his or her personal and/or public life? Don't be ridiculous. There is not one.

Gentlemen, you can see how serious all this is and could be.

If, for some utterly whimsical and unanticipated reason, *honesty* were to become a factor in American Life, it is obvious that the immediate result would be chaos and anarchy.

The People, instantly deprived of all their leaders in every known field of endeavor, would be a swirling mass of bleating, helpless sheep. And there would be no wolves left to profit from this condition.

Gentlemen of the Press, for the good of the People and for the good of the Nation, the present System must be maintained at all costs!!

Magazine editors, newspaper men, and publishers of America, I say to you that you are making a real contribution to the preservation of the American Way. Hold up your heads with pride. Always remember that it is easy to tell the truth, but it takes real courage, skill and daring to deal exclusively and continually in plausible lies and euphemisms. Take heart, though. In your arduous and often unsung (though never underpaid) labors you are not alone. Your rhetoric succeeds so well because it is exactly suited to the morality of your audience—a bunch of crooks.

Let us always remember that our great experiment in the creation of a Classless Society has come a long way. At the moment there are only two classes left—Successful Crooks and Unsuccessful Crooks.

Let us all thank God we can be numbered among the former. . . .

What a sour and misanthropic point of view, huh Christie?

But before you start feeling too superior, remember that Gloria Steinem used to work for *Mad* magazine. At least that's what I heard. I don't know if it was before or after she was a Playboy bunny. Somebody else told me that Gloria Steinem also once worked for the C.I.A. But I can't believe that. They say that about practically everybody.

Did Billy Joel ever work for the C.I.A.?

"Utterly repellant . . ." Gee, that's a pretty heavy thing to say about anybody, even if you are *The New York Times* and, thanks to your cronies on the Supreme Court, you can say whatever you want to about whomever you please with perfect impunity. I sure hope you don't find him "utterly repellant." That would be tough shit, as they say. To marry the little guy and get on the cover of *People* and everything and *then* (too late!) discover that the guy is "utterly repellant." It would be too embarrassing to admit it. Even to yourself, you know? Maybe Billy Joel *is* utterly repellant and you don't even know it yet. If so, then you'll never know. So you still have a chance to live happily ever after.

Don't mind me. I'm just jealous. But it's irrelevant. I'm too old for you anyway. Except in the timeless realm of Fantasy. About which the less said the better. At least at this preliminary stage of our "real" relationship.

Never mind about me, for the moment, however. Moments ago I was right in the big middle of trying to offer a few explanatory words about this book, *Poison Pen*, to which this letter is appended. Trying to offer some reasonable explanation as to why, in Towne's view at least, you are the authentic and appropriate Muse for it. In this matter, your (pardon) aptness (if it may be put that way), I am inclined to agree with him even though we are far, far apart on most other matters. For example, I contend that his letter to Hugh Hefner went much too far. It is almost Swiftian, in content if not in form and style, in its ridicule of the Playboy Philosophy as it may apply to the (pardon) human condition. Was that really necessary, even then, way back

234

in the exciting 1960's when Towne first wrote it and then it got published in some obscure little magazine? I ask you! Surely, at any rate, it is at best redundant, if not irrelevant, now that Hugh Hefner, himself, is considerably older and wiser. Or *should be* older and wiser. (How would I know?) Another thing that happened sometime during this selfsame academic year (1984-85) was that Mr. Hefner had a stroke. According to the papers, as I recall (to the best of my recollection, Counselor), the stress and the stroke were brought on by all the bad things written about Hefner in a book by Peter Bogdonavich concerning the late beautiful Playmate, Dorothy Stratton (sp?), who was later played by one of the swell Hemingway girls (Mariel, I think) in a Bob Fosse movie.

God, real life and pop culture do get complicated, don't they? Anyway, evidently Mr. Hefner had a mild stroke and then, more or less, recovered from it. Now, you and I know, Christie, that a stroke is not funny at all. Even when somebody like Hugh Hefner has one. Just as, in the same way, it isn't exactly hilarious that Larry Flynt has some kind of bowel problems and has to wear diapers. Even if you were one of these crazy fundamentalists who sincerely believe that we should reactivate a World War II crematorium or two to take care of types like Hefner and Flynt and Bob Whatshisname who runs *Penthouse*, (Guccione, that's it! A wop to remember!), even so you would have to admit that, except for our very worst personal enemies (and how can anyone feel *personal* about Public Figures?), very few people, outside of the major American medical schools, go around laughing at physical deformities and intense physical and psychological suffering. Right?

Nevertheless, Christie, and you are the living, breathing, shining, glorious proof thereof, we rejoice in physical beauty and achievement and we richly reward them both. You, yourself, seem to have made out all right, at least according to a piece in *Real Life* magazine ("Christie Brinkley: Beauty, Succe$$ and Tragedy," Vol. 7, No. 4, July 1983, pp. 34-41; some great and rousing string-bikini photos!), which claimed, way back then, that you were earning two million dollars a year (!!!) doing a number of different things, none of them, as far as I can tell, either unethical or illegal.

If we rejoice in physical beauty and achievement and celebrity and likewise richly reward these secular conditions, it is also the truth (and my sad duty to admit and report) that we take some pleasure in the inevitable end result of all these conditions—age, decay, death, and oblivion. We heap pure adulation, something about as close to worship as we modern secular humanists can come, upon certain of our celebrities. Then we turn right around and take great, if not equal pleasure in whatever misfortunes may fall upon them. I will never forget. I was in the barber shop in a small southern town getting a haircut when the news came down over the radio that Jayne Mansfield had been decapitated when the sportscar she was riding in drove right up under the back of a big truck. Everybody in the barber shop, including the barber who seldom, if ever, indulged in unseemly displays of emotion, broke up and busted out laughing. They laughed loud and long and even made cracks about other, perhaps more memorable and important parts of her celebrated anatomy.

I do not wish to defend their reaction, but I hasten to point out that these were good old boys, men of some character and decency. Their response puzzled me until I came to the conclusion that for them, as, indeed, for all of us, Celebrities and Public Figures are not *Real People*. Ergo: What happens to them, doesn't really happen to anyone. It is all just part of an on-going fable or fairy tale in which they (the Celebrities or Public Figures) are trapped or imprisoned. They are there by choice, of course, having accepted their essential unreality along with their first fame and first fat pay checks. People don't mean any harm, Christie. They just don't take Celebrities seriously. Or, to put it another way, they take them very seriously indeed (sometimes), but never in fact and flesh, only in fiction and fantasy. Truth is, many Celebrities don't even take each other seriously. How else to explain CBS TV's Phyllis George (see "A Prime-Time Rape Case," *Newsweek*, May 27, 1985, p. 30; and "Cathy and Gary in Medialand," *Time*, May 27, 1985, p. 66) asking Cathleen Crowell Webb and Gary Dotson (remember them?) to hug each other for the benefit and pleasure of the viewers. I haven't talked to Towne about that little episode. It altogether too perfectly confirms his wildest and most outlandish speculations. But I'm willing to bet that if he were to write a poison pen letter on the subject, he would cheerfully resurrect Jerry Wolf, the guy from Pacemaker Films who wrote a letter to Masters and Johnson, trying to cast all three of these late twentieth century media-creatures—Phyllis, Cathy, and Gary—in an X-rated movie. "Phyllis, you have got a great and admirable ass," Jerry Wolf would write, "and it is a real shame that you have to hide it (most of the time) on national T.V. Come and share it with your admiring adult public." It would be gross. Jerry Wolf has no sense of shame or decorum. He actually wrote to Solzhenitzin to see if he would agree to participation in an X-rated film about life in the Gulag. "It would probably have to be a Fag Film," he wrote. "But don't let that discourage you. Faggots have big bucks and plenty of influence in modern America these days. They are an important political constituency. Ask ole Walter Mondale. Of course, he didn't actually win any elections with their help. But at least he let us all know that he has no personal aesthetic or ethical hangup about blowjobs and buggery. Maybe he would even be willing to make a cameo appearance in our film. . . ." I have just read a whole big book on the subject, Christie. (Not Fags, but Celebrities of all kinds and forms of sexual preference.) It is called *Intimate Strangers: The Culture Of Celebrity*, by Richard Schickel (New York: Doubleday, 1985. 299 pp. $16.95). And whereas, on the whole, it isn't really as good or as interesting as it ought to be, still this fellow (he does, after all, work for *Time* magazine) gets in some good solid licks here and there. One of them, early on, is relevant to this letter, Christie, and, as well, to much of *Poison Pen*. A brief paragraph by Mr. S—:

> Most of us retain, in most of our private and professional dealings with people we don't actually know, a sense of their otherness, a decent wariness that protects both ourselves and the stranger from intrusion. But that shyness, if the term may be permitted, is not operative when

we are dealing with Celebrities. Thanks to television and the rest of the media we *know* them, or think we do. To a greater or lesser extent, we have internalized them, unconsciously made them a part of our consciousness, just as if they were, in fact, friends.

That seems fairly accurate to me, Christie. And if it didn't involve going back to the beginning and changing some things, I would probably use it as an epigraph for the whole book. It isn't all that badly written. And certainly it is a lot better than the very best of Towne's exploitative experiments with and abuses of the American vernacular. . . .

May I interrupt myself for a moment. Just to say a word or two, while it is on my mind and before I forget it, about Style? Especially Towne's style. By which I mean the basic anti-style of *Poison Pen*.

Now then.

I tend to agree with my old friend Wright Morris—hello out there, Wright and Jo!—that the poor old American vernacular is just about burnt up and burnt out for serious literary purposes. People, from Mark Twain on, have worked wonders with it. No denying that. But we need to move on to fresh woods and pastures new. Towne doesn't seem to think so, however. He still likes to screw around with the old American vernacular. He has fun with it, just cheerfully and carelessly writing along in the same way that a lot of cheerful and careless people talk along and even write letters and other documents. Towne gets his jollies by writing the way he does just as some good singers like to show off and showboat by doing a whole number slightly off key. He dearly loves the common language of common cliche. He likes it about as much as anybody you can think of off the top of your head. Even including the Great Donald Barthelme and his little brother Fred. But he is no kind of a Post Modernist or a Meta Fictionist, not Towne. He wouldn't know a real Post Modernist if one ran right over his toes on roller skates. He has nothing whatever in common with the great figures of American Literature in our age. John Barth and Thomas Pynchon mean not one thing to him. I seriously doubt if he has ever read word one by either one of them. There are others he may or may not have read. Who knows? The only evidence we really have is in the form of some unpleasant opinions he has expressed about some very distinguished literary culture heroes of our time. What can you expect from someone who has referred to John Hawkes (only as *author*, of course) as "an airhead"? About the much-honored and highly celebrated Robert Coover, Towne has written: "Robert Coover is a very short man." As if, even if it were true, that proved anything! So was Napoleon only a little bitty guy and look what he accomplished in spite of it! John Irving is fairly small also, but you won't catch Towne (or me either) making cracks about *him*. Why? "You gotta respect that kind of money and all that publicity," Towne says. "The rest is irrelevant dreck." As for myself, I may think Irving is an archetypal nerd, but I would never say so. Of the admirable meta-fictional stylist William Gass, all Towne will say in public is that "he is aptly named." I will not trouble you, Christie, with the various bad words of Towne on the subject of (as he puts it) "the Mickey Rooney of Post-Modernist Lit.— Norman Mailer." I will spare you, Christie. Mainly on account of I am afraid that Mr. Mailer might blame me personally. And then what? I shudder to think.

You get the idea, anyway. Towne doesn't know much about Literature. He thinks a Carlos Fuentes is a Cuban cigar.

I agree with everyone who condemns and criticizes his style. But I do not and cannot agree with those who think that I, myself, have not managed to escape from the deleterious influence of Towne's tin ear. No one in his/her right mind could read Towne's prose and mine and then proceed to confuse the two. I would ask you to make your own independent comparison and critical judgment, Christie. But I honestly don't think either one of us would gain anything much if you went back and looked at some of the other parts of this book. So, you can take my word for it. Towne and I are completely, utterly, absolutely unlike in our thoughts, words, deeds, and styles. Okay? Tell you the truth, I find Towne to be (pardon the expression) utterly repellant. Of course, you might feel differently. I don't know. Maybe you like utterly repellant.

Let's get back to this Richard Schickel and his book all about Celebrity. He has some interesting things to say on the subject. Some keen observations to make. He is worried (or at least he professes to be so) on account of the fact that people are running around killing Celebrities these days. As a sort of Celebrity, himself, he seems genuinely concerned that there is a high level of crazy hostility out there.

Now then. Let me be very clear about this. Personally, I don't approve of killing Celebrities either for fun or for profit. And I think I can safely say that I would never do such a thing myself or condone others who do so. Yet, from another point of view, Towne's for example, I can see that occasionally knocking off some Celebrities, just like blowing away a few Politicians from time to time, is probably a good and a healthy thing. In a Jeffersonian sense it helps the growth process of the Tree of Liberty. And in a practical sense, we need to remind them that we are still out here. We also need an appropriate symbolic gesture to point out to them that all their precious differences and distinctions from the rest of the great, sweaty, farting mass of common humanity are based upon a frail and vulnerable foundation. I think everyone will surely agree that it is absolutely essential, in a free country, that those who govern us, ruling and riding herd over us, should constantly have to be in at least some fear of us. So we go get a few of them from time to time. And they, in turn, get themselves a nice, firstclass, well-publicized funeral and usually some kind of an honored grave or shrine. It all works out for the best, I guess. As Alexander Pope said. Or something close to it.

What has happened, Christie, in my lifetime is that Politicians and Celebrities have become at last one and the same thing. From which, it could be argued, we now have the right not to take any Politician, living or dead, seriously. And, by the same token, we can now water the roots of the Trees of Liberty with the blood of Celebrities.

238

But enough of such morbid and misanthropic subjects.

What are we really dealing with here, Christie?

I have to answer any number of things and all at once.

One of them (clearly) is the complex wedding of fact and fiction. We see (as in an X-rated movie) how many ways they can couple, copulate, shudder in real or feigned ecstasy, and then, sooner or later, give birth to something else which has some of the traits and secrets of each. Of both. It is really a subject which concerns most writers (and some readers too) these days. Whether they know it or not. It is crucial to our experience during the last years of this dying century, this century of so much dying, so many untimely dead. If the truth (and nothing but the truth) will set us (finally!) free, then we have to try to find out what's true and what's false if we want to be free, don't we? (I have a suspicion, not a particularly original one, either, that most people desire anything else but Freedom, that most people fear and avoid Freedom, and its consequent responsibilities, the way people fear and seek to avoid the Pest, the Plague, and AIDS. But let's not get into that one.) To begin to separate the real from the apparent we have to try to know and understand the many subtle ways and means of the blending and mingling of fact and fiction which can become a truth. Just so, we must always seek to understand the precise measures of fact and fiction which add up to nothing less than a lie. It appears that this latter happens much more frequently and regularly than the former.

All of which leads us, Christie, my dear, directly towards an equally complex, if somewhat less cosmic corollary problem which we really cannot choose to ignore. By which I mean the problem of image (appearance) and reality. In some ways this is even more troublesome and knotty than the conflict between fact and fiction. For an image can be true and yet the "reality," concealed behind and within the image, may not be. . . .

You may not think this is pertinent to your life and your lifestyle, Christie. Yet, in just about every T.V. interview of yours that I have ever seen—and I have seen a bunch of them, early and late—you have always found a way to complain (I might even say *whine*, but that is a subjective judgment call; and far be it from me to criticize you for anything) that you are not, yourself, in real flesh and blood, exactly the same person as the girl on all the different magazine covers. You have usually managed to make the point that she is not the real you. Of course, they all say that. And, frankly nobody gives a shit, starting with the interviewer. You think Barbara Walters gives a fist flying fuck who or what the real Christie Brinkley is? Nobody except your family and kinfolks, your few true friends and maybe your husband, Billy Joel, is really interested in the real you. What everyone is interested in is that swell-looking woman in a skimpy, scanty bathing suit on the calendar, the one on the magazine cover. She is the one we all want to know, the one we do know, more or less, like it or not. She is all we care about or want to know.

Meanwhile, you want something else, I guess. Guess is all I can do. You are not dumb or innocent enough to want people to know and love the real

Christie Brinkley, the one with a past and a future, the one with aches and pains, bowel movements and periods, ideas and impulses and appetites, joys and frustrations. No, ma'm, even exposing the maximum allowable of your truly fabulous body on many a beautiful beach for the sake of high calendar art does not earn you the impossible privilege of rejecting the public image you have freely chosen to project. You are not entitled to be like everyone else. You know better than that. But, like many others who have successfully created some extraordinary image of themselves, you still seem to want the rest of the world at least to acknowledge that this is the case—that you are a creature who is brutally and ruthlessly self-divided between image and reality.

And clearly that fact (if fact truly it is) is of no interest whatever to anyone else in the whole wide world.

It may be that the World, cheerfully self-deluded, happily accepts your golden image, together with many other successfully created and enforced public images, as facts. It may well be, as I sometimes allow myself to think, that amid a wilderness of images, images hurled at us from all sides like the endlessly replicated and hopelessly distorted reflections of a Funhouse of Mirrors (remember T.S. Eliot's wilderness of mirrors?), we have lost our ability to distinguish between image and reality. Some people—I think *especially* Media People, the Press and suchlike—will argue that the distinction was arbitrary in the first place. They will argue that there is no other truth except the truth of the image. Thus, for example, the Tet Offensive of 1968, an overwhelming military victory over the Viet Cong by our side, was presented as a massive defeat by the Press, particularly the T.V. people (who may or may not have known better at the time); and thus it became a defeat, was perceived as a defeat by the American people in spite of all the facts and numbers to the contrary. I imagine that is what those who claim we were "betrayed" by our own Press are trying to say. But it was not our national policies or even the grunts on the line or the hopeful people at home who were betrayed by an elaborate structure of misinformation and disinformation. It was, rather, the *facts* that were not so much betrayed or even ignored but *transformed* into a false image which had the power and impact of truth. So it goes.

Christie, whenever I find myself thinking about this whole problem, I summon up, out of my own experience, perception, and memory the image of John F. Kennedy. Who was at that time (and thus forever after) a true hero for me. That perception was reality. Hasn't changed a whole lot with the passing of time and the disclosure of many more "facts" about him. But, nevertheless, there was at least one enormous deception in the presented and perceived image of J.F.K. He was, *in fact and without question*, the most physically unhealthy President we have had in this century. Sicker in fact than either F.D.R. and Woodrow Wilson who were (also in fact) quite healthy and vigorous until the end when their flesh finally failed them. Kennedy was a sick and frail man. We know this now. Yet his public image, carefully cultivated and presented, was one of great energy and (their word, remember?) "vigah." Energy and youth and vigor were communicated successfully. I remember energy and youth and vigor as if, in fact, they had been there. Which they were not. But which they now are. For the image has been indelibly super-imposed upon what was once "reality."

Take another, simpler example. I have read that J.F.K. was a fairly heavy cigarette smoker. (Well, so was I. O Lord, I smoked more than my share for too many years!) But I have never yet seen any photograph of him with a cigarette in his hand or between his lips. They say that he forbade photographs of himself smoking. So as not to set a bad example for others. And the Press (in his pocket as never before or since in America) scrupulously honored his wishes. But what they were really honoring was (in a self-reflexive, narcissistic way) the magic of pure imagery, the power of image over factual reality. Factual reality: J.F.K. was a smoker. Image: He was not.

What is the truth of the matter?

I'll tell you, Christie, that lately I have come to believe (against my better judgment and my hopes for the world and for humankind; hoping against hope, then; wishing it were not so) that what we still innocently call publicity is all the truth that we have left. That whatever publicity successfully proclaims becomes true. That whatever publicity ignores becomes . . . nothing. Nothing at all. Observing the American scene for a fairly full lifetime, and doing so with as much wonder and neutrality as I can muster, I have to conclude that they have finally stunned us into intellectual and emotional submission by and through a relentless barrage of . . . "information." I conclude that it has worked. That whatever they say is so. That truth is what they say it is, no more or less. And that anything and everything ignored and unsaid is not so. Not true.

Thus image is everything there is.

I therefore also am drawn to conclude that democratic government, at least in the sense that the Founding Fathers envisaged, is no longer possible. Democratic government depends upon full and free debate and discussion, upon the constant search for truth. That cannot take place in America any more. Or it *doesn't*, anyway. (Read Solzhenitzin's address at Harvard in 1968, the one that so enraged Mike Barnicle of the *Boston Globe* that he suggested we send Solzhenitzin back to Siberia.) When everything there is is image, then we are governed by the image makers. It is that simple.

My wife, Susan, (the one I said you would like if you ever got to know her; which you won't) says that my whole theory and argument is utter nonsense. Not only is it not true, she says, but also it is not true that I really believe that stuff. She thinks I am only kidding around. She also thinks I am prejudiced by my experience in the Literary World, where so many phonies and secondrate, derivative talents are so widely honored and celebrated, from the pages of the big papers and national magazines down to the cloistered dusty halls of Academe, while a great many at least interesting and often very original and gifted writers are completely ignored and forgotten.

She can understand how somebody looking only at the Literary World would begin to believe that Truth has vanished and Image is all.

She has added that she doesn't imagine that any of this is much of a problem for you.

"Frankly, my dear," she said. "I doubt if Christie Brinkley gives a shit."

She thinks I am wasting my time writing to you like this.

Am I wasting my time, Christie? I hope not.

I am sure that Susan imagines that she understands you, the real you, a lot better than I ever can or do. A gender thing.

Maybe she does.

Who knows?

Getting back to this book, *Poison Pen*, for a moment. Personally, I find it significant that John Towne never wrote you one of his poison pen letters and never, to the best of my knowledge, went out of his way to insult you or make fun of you. The only reference to you, by name, which I have found among his letters, notes, and papers is (as I intepret it) complimentary. "Christie Brinkley," he wrote, "is the incarnation and apotheosis of pure unadulterated sexual ecstasy." From which I take it that he likes you about as much as I do. Certainly we see eye to eye concerning that complex matter. Maybe he even *loves* you a little. Or, secretly, a lot. Surely something has got to be sacred to even a guy like Towne. Maybe you are the living essence of all that is sacred to him.

Why not?

I have to tell you, though, Christie, that he is a terrible person even if he does share my sincere awe and admiration for all your miscellaneous genetic gifts and your excellent general appearance.

It doesn't take much to prove what a crummy, lowdown, bad human being John Towne is. For instance, the most recent thing that I have seen by Towne is a query letter addressed to his literary agent, Sam. It is a proposal for Towne to do a non-fiction book, tentatively entitled, *Famous Modern Hit Men*. He proposes to deal with some of the better known assassins of our age, presenting a brief biographical and psychological profile of each together with some detailed discussion of their shooting habits and practices and their marksmanship abilities. In the case of a really crummy shots like Hinckley or Mehemet Ali Agca or Arthur Bremer, or complete klutzes like Squeaky Fromme, he will offer a serious critique, pointing out the things that they did which were wrong or anyway, counterproductive, not excluding the choice of weapon, the basic care and maintenance thereof, their favored grip and stance, etc.

In the case of others, the good shots or anyway more successful shooters— people like James Earl Ray, Sirhan Sirhan, Son of Sam, Mark David Chapman, Bernard Goetz, Bernard Charles Welch, Travis Bickle, Claudine Longet, etc., etc., etc., it just might be possible to get some personal interviews, oral history as it were, including some practical elements like good shooting tips and basic safety practices.

"Too bad Lee Harvey Oswald got blown away by Jack Ruby and then Ruby passed on to his reward by some means or other," Towne writes Sam. "I would seriously like to know how Oswald managed to operate that cheap, beat-up, old bolt action, Italian, piece-of-shit rifle so effectively and so fast. It was amazing!

"What was the name of that old broad (I forget already) who shot the

Scarsdale Diet doctor (whose name also has already escaped the confines of my consciousness)? You see, Sam, I am losing it fast. I can't even remember the names of these prominent public figures of our time. Maybe a mild case of Alzheimer's? Was it Shana Alexander? No, she wrote the book about it, as I recall. It was Jean Harris. Or something like that. Anyway, whoever it was, she ought to be in our book, too. I am sure you and the publisher can think of some others. Who was the little chickie who put some holes into the carcass of Andy Warhol? Who shot Allard Lowenstein? That sort of thing.

"And you can bet good New York City money, plenty of it, that there will be some other new ones on the front pages even before the book is in print.

"I have a special idea for an interesting little epilogue. If we can get the publisher to cough up the money—and I expect it would take Big Bucks, Sam. Maybe I could get an interview with Mailer and do a little walkout buck-and-wing on the subject of the use and abuse of knives. He would be speaking out of personal experience (if all these things I read are true), not only his own, but also that of his friend, Jack Abbott. Maybe, as well as Mailer and Abbott, I could deal with the Jap who stabbed their Prime Minister a few years back. Remember? They had pictures of the whole thing. Maybe I could wrap it up with Yukio Mishima who tried to cut himself in half. That was a sad story. Maybe I could get Mailer to say something about Mishima. Wouldn't that be interesting!

"In the end, though, Sam, any way we do it, I sincerely believe we can sell this book. And I am not just talking about the morbidly curious majority, either (both moral and immoral). Or the guilt-ridden Liberals, who read and write most of the books written or read in the U.S. Sure, I will have plenty of good material here for all the Liberal Pussies who are in favor of gun control and the banning of handguns. (Just think, I will argue, all these public figures could have been more humanely killed with axes, baseball bats, and tire irons.) But at the same time I will be addressing the N.R.A. crowd, all those serious sportsmen and marksmen who are eager to improve their performance with both rifles and handguns. If the dumb publisher will only (for once!) promote it properly, Sam, you and I could make a pot of money while giving the people what they want and deserve. Right?"

Wrong, Towne!

We the people, including Christie Brinkley and me, the Author, myself, will never stand still and idly by, allowing your senseless projects to come to any (pardon the expression) fruition! Sure we have to live with the First Amendment and the Supreme Court. And, yes, we have had people like Thomas Jefferson running around urging everybody (if I may paraphrase that Founding Father) not to shy away from the exploration of any subject whatsoever, not even to fear error so long as reason is left free to combat it. But the Founding Fathers can never so much as have *imagined* the likes of you. People like you, Towne, are ringworms of the Body Politic. You come along and try your best to make sport and a mockery of all of our finest feelings and our best hopes, ideas, and ideals.

You ought to be ashamed of yourself.

Who do you think you are—Jonathan Swift or Lenny Bruce or Seymour Krim or somebody like that?

Towne, you have already proved beyond a shadow of a doubt that you are basically racist, sexist, and (pardon the expression) conservative if not an actual mindless reactionary. You have demonstrated your insensitivity and lack of compassion by making snide and negative wisecracks about important American social and political institutions like Affirmative Action. You have made many unpleasant remarks about Art and Artists, Poets and Poetry, Reagan and Nancy, Mondale and Ferraro. Is nothing sacred to you? What is so funny about Walker Percy? You probably think that Apartheid is a good idea whose time has come at last. I know for a fact that you do *not* love N.Y.C. And you scorn the very idea of a Nuclear Freeze. Except as the name of a deadly drink whose principal ingredient is grain alcohol. You have also actually said that you were until recently under the distinct impression that a Nuclear Freeze was something you could *order* at a Dairy Queen.

Towne, you are truly disgusting!

Will you please butt out of my important letter to Christie Brinkley?

I know that we are all living in the last book of the Bible. But that doesn't give you the right to ruin my day.

Thank you very much.

And bye-bye. . . .

My sincere apologies to you, Christie, for that unpleasant interruption. I can't promise anything, but I intend that it shall not happen again. Not if I can help it.

Let's talk about something else, shall we? Let's talk about *your* literary efforts.

I own my own copy of your swell book—*Christie Brinkley's Outdoor Beauty & Fitness Book* (New York: Simon and Schuster, 1983; 202 pp. $16.95). And I consider it is a bargain, worth the whole price just for the sake of all the good pictures of you in all kinds of bathing suits doing all kinds of exercises and stuff. The text is fairly interesting, too. There are a lot of good ideas and tips in there. Some of them don't really apply, though. Ones like: "Flat champagne poured over blond hair and then rinsed out will give wonderful highlights!" (p. 153). I am pretty much bald-headed. What hair I have got is gray. Besides, if I had any champagne handy, flat or otherwise, I would probably give in and drink it.

I also very much enjoy the sequence of color photos, set between pages 174 and 175, entitled "My Travel Scrapbook." I like (sometimes) to think about all the exotic places that you say you have been to. I'm talking about the Seychelles Islands; St. Bart's, West Indies; Carreyes, Mexico; Aruba; Puerto Vallarta, Mexico; St. Tropez, France; Concha di Marini, Italy; Senegal, Africa; Curacao, etc. (Try to avoid the rocky beach at York Harbor, Maine. You will freeze your little twat in that water. What it does to the male genitalia shouldn't happen, even temporarily, to anyone, including Theodore Robert Bundy. No relation, as far as I know, to the other Bundy who worked for the Kennedys.) Anyway it all looks okay to me. Your life and lifestyle, I mean.

And I must confess that I especially admire the fact that after all this unabashedly indulgent and narcissistic (if necessary) stuff about the care and preservation of the outer and inner Self, you still choose to end your book with "A Serious Note" (p. 201). May I quote from it? Actually, I don't need your permission and I don't need to ask; because it constitutes what they (lawyers and judges) call "fair use." But I thought I would be polite, anyway.

Here is the part I underlined in my copy of the book:

"The beach and the ocean are my favorite places. They give me so much pleasure! But anyone who enjoys them has a responsibility to preserve them. I'm an active member of both Greenpeace and the Cousteau Society. They both work to maintain and preserve the natural beauty of our oceans.

"Maybe you should think about joining, too!"

As one writer to another I would like to compliment you on your elegant and judicious use of the exclamation point.

As a male animal, albeit a rapidly aging one, I would like to assure you that I would join any group, society, or program you recommended.

However, I shudder to think what Towne would make out of your "Serious Note" is he ever happened to run across it. I have a pretty good idea how he acts at the beach, though. Not only does he do old-fashioned anti-social things like kick sand on little guys and splash old people. But also he will take a crap in the sand dunes, throw candy wrappers and beer cans all over the beach. And he will piss in the ocean if he gets a chance.

Still, your special example and your powers of persuasion are very impressive. I am willing to bet he would give up some of his bad habits and (like me) join Greenpeace and the Cousteau Society and anything else, even the Ku Klux Klan and CORE, if he thought he had a chance to make an impression on you. Towne is as full of self-esteem as, say, Leonard Bernstein or Carl Sagan. He thinks if he could just find a way to meet you in person he would probably make out like a bandit.

Imagine that, at his age, too!

Of course, like all imaginary characters in stories (the good, the bad, and the ugly alike), Towne is ageless. Which is why he hasn't changed enough so that you would notice in the more than twenty years he has been around. Meanwhile—it isn't fair!—I have, as Macbeth used to say, fallen into the sere and yellow leaf.

You know, Christie, I spent an awful lot of my life, my youth anyway, on the beaches of Florida. Where I grew up. I could tell you some things, too. About that time. About these times. But we are running out of time and space, you and I. And you, I reckon, must be about to run out of patience.

Where is all this leading? You wonder. I wish I could tell you for sure. Actually, I can tell you. It is leading exactly . . . nowhere. I wish it were leading somewhere. I wish it was I, and not that kid in the Cheryl Tiegs letter that Towne wrote, who found the genie in the bottle and was given three wishes. In which case I would put the magic spell on you. And I wouldn't have to write a letter trying to justify my interest.

Never mind. Never mind. Never mind.

I'll tell you one true story about those times in Florida. All right. . . ?

245

Way back then in the middle of the Depression, a lot of the Florida beaches, especially on the East Coast, still were not very much built up or developed. In those days, before we bought the old cottage in the dunes at New Smyrna Beach (then known as Coronado Beach), we used to go to Daytona. And, believe it or not, there were miles and miles, whole stretches of beach and dunes, which had no more than a few isolated cottages and fishing shacks.

Well, Christie, one summer we rented one for the whole summer long (my father, a lawyer, would come over on weekends when he could). A big, rambling airy beach house on the dunes with only a couple of nearby neighboring cottages. And then nothing in either direction for miles. Lonely and beautiful. Of course we were never lonely. There was a whole huge bunch of us, cousins and other kinfolk and friends, sharing beds and large rooms. And living our lives out, except for a post-prandial nap, in the sun on the beach and in the surf. And we fished and caught crabs and collected periwinkles for the clear green broth they made. We ran and swam (and no doubt fought) all day long. At night we would listen to the radio. Or maybe read stories out loud. Or make up our own stories and put on plays. That's the way people were in those days. As I remember. And sometimes if the breeze was coming off the ocean so there weren't any sandflies or mosquitoes, we would go for long walks on the dark beach, dizzy under the vast sky with its turning canopy of bright stars. Or maybe we would build a big campfire on the beach and roast weenies or marshmallows; sing silly songs or tell ghost stories or hear someone tell tales of the family.

And naturally we were waiting eagerly for the coming of the Fourth of July. When we would get to shoot off firecrackers and roman candles and even a rocket or two.

Now the only people who were near us, living in the house next door, were a group of young men. Yankee men. Very pale and quiet men. They slept and stayed inside a lot. And whenever they went down to the beach, they wore bathrobes and sandals. A Yankee habit we had never seen before. They didn't bother anyone. And they weren't at all unfriendly, either. They would nod or say hello. And I remember once or twice one of them came to the back door and knocked. Didn't come in, just borrowed something—some flour, a cup of sugar or something like that. And once they brought us a string of fish they had caught in the surf that day. Which gift delighted my mother but annoyed us boys. Because, naturally, we had to clean them.

Came the Fourth of July. Except for fooling around with a few firecrackers in the daytime, we all waited eagerly for the dark. Then down to the beach with our sparklers and roman candles. And the grownups set off the rockets far out over the ocean.

We were having a fine old time when, all of a sudden, out on the front porch of their house came all the young men next door. They stood in a row and, amid wild blooms of flame and more deafening and earth-shaking noise than I had ever heard before, for only a minute or two really, they fired off together some automatic weapons. Shooting at the sky.

246

"Hmmm," my father said when the noise had subsided and they had disappeared into the house. "Those were sub-machine guns."

"Maybe they're from the F.B.I.," my uncle, the war hero said. "It's possible."

"Well, one thing for sure," my father said. "They are a patriotic bunch, one and all, aren't they?"

"Never mind," Mother interrupted. "They were just having fun. And they are all gentlemen, even if they are Yankees. And that matters."

My mother seemed to think that being a gentleman mattered more than just about anything else. Except maybe being a member of our family. Sometimes I think she was right.

Anyway, Christie. A few days later the men next door were all gone. Their house was empty and it was pretty quiet. For a couple of weeks. Until the police, in many cars and trucks, in large numbers came and searched all through the house next door.

"You boys are too late," my father told them, laughing. "Whoever they are, they're long gone now."

The Chief, recognizing my father, took him aside and told him who those Yankees were. And Daddy told us later. It was John Dillinger's gang. Whether John, himself, was among them, nobody knew. And I'm not sure that is known to this day.

I like to remember that.

Of course, Christie, gangsters had a place in our lives, then. And even though we didn't approve of them and their behavior, we were fascinated by them. Ma Barker and some of her boys and gang died in a shootout in a house by a lake not more than a dozen miles or so from the house where I lived. The cops and the F.B.I. caught up with them, finally, and surrounded the house and called on Ma and the rest to surrender. The result of that was a fight. Which lasted for a while, until finally a white handkerchief on a broom-stick appeared waving in what had been a window. And the Government men stopped firing their rifles and shotguns and sub-machine guns and waited. Out the front door came a Colored maid in uniform (she had been hiding under the dining room table, it turned out).

"You all can come on in now," she called out politely. "They's all dead."

I have seen that house. There wasn't a part of it, anywhere, as big as a fifty cent piece that didn't have at least one bullet hole in it. The only thing I ever saw that was more shot full of holes than that house was the car that Bonnie and Clyde got killed in. I saw that at a carnival one time in Orlando. My mother didn't want me to see it. But I did, anyway. I saved my money and paid for a ticket and went in with some other boys I knew. It was in a kind of pit in the middle of a big tent. Like a sideshow attraction. We stood around, leaning against a little fence and looking at that car full of holes.

I'll tell you something else, Christie. My uncle, the war hero, was also a newspaper reporter for the old *New York Sun*. And after that he was a screenwriter in Hollywood. He wrote a lot of pictures, some of them pretty good; and he had several wives, all of them good-looking. (One was from Bali! Can you beat that?) But the point is that he wrote the gangster movie that John Dillinger came out of hiding to see. And the Lady in Red betrayed him. And the F.B.I. killed Dillinger coming out of the movie.

How's that for the way things come together? I bet Nabakov couldn't have thought of a better wrap-up.

Are we a violent nation, Christie? Bet your tan ass we are. But no use complaining. Towne would say it is the secret of our national charm. And he may just be right.

Christie, I really hate to have to end this letter. Especially since it will probably represent the *alpha* and the *omega* of our correspondence. And our (pardon it) relationship. There was so much I wanted to tell you. So many things I never quite got around to asking that I wanted to find out about you! And, you know, I didn't have to worry about the Reader or anything like that. Reader had been warned against trespassing in this section. As far as Reader is concerned the book ended before this letter even began.

But Towne, true to form, used up far too many pages of the book with all of his stuff. He didn't leave me much room. And my publisher—*his* publisher, too; and if *that* ain't irony I will kiss your sweet ass!—is definitely not Simon and Schuster. It's a fly-by-night outfit, as you may already have guessed. My publisher cannot afford to allow me unlimited space to devote to my letter to you. I have to keep moving, then. And I doubt very much that my publisher would allow me to tag on something as "A Serious Note" at the end.

Speaking of that. I didn't mean to make fun of your "Serious Note." Or, put it this way, I didn't intend to make serious fun of your ideas and your creative writing. It was a cheap shot, and I take it all back. You don't need my apology. You are doing just fine. But it needs to be said that in terms of content, of importance and value and weight of meaning, your brief "Serious Note" has more to offer than the work of many American so-called literary artists. I would name a few, but am already in bad with the Literary Establishment.

Anyway, it takes all kinds.

I am glad that you are the kind you are.

I am glad that you have so much youth and beauty and energy, and that you are willing to share a lot of it with the rest of us. I wish you would share more, but some people are never satisfied!

It's a funny way to have to write a letter, knowing that more than just a few days must pass, knowing that, in truth, months will go by before it can reach you, if it ever does. The way I figure is that it's liable to be at the very least almost a year from now (I am wrapping this up on Sunday, May 26, 1985, Memorial Day Weekend) before you will even have a chance to hear about this epistle to you or stumble onto or over it. This notion makes the present not less transient, but sure enough more precious. Just as it makes the future seem more strange, exotic and unlikely.

Of course, back in the old days, good and bad, a great many letters must have been written with the full knowledge that they would not arrive at the appropriate and intended destination for many months. It may have very often been something like the messages in *The Sirens of Titan*, by Kurt Vonnegut, Jr. (and, yes ma'm, I agree that one is a greatly over-rated talent and not one half of the world class sage and guru that many, including himself, seem to think he is; yet, Christie, I have always enjoyed his literary work, I can't help myself, even at its silliest and most aggressively puerile). The real life situation being something like this: "Dear Sir Walter Raleigh, We, your most humble and neglected colonists find ourselves to be surrounded by a band (and I don't mean the musical kind) of hostile Indians. Who seem to have gathered together for the purpose of doing us some grievous bodily harm. We can hold them off for a while, I reckon. But then what? Do you have any good ideas or suggestions? If you were to send help by the next available boat, that would be best. But if you can't for any reason, then, please, sir, at least let us have the benefit of your worldly wisdom as soon as possible. . . ."

The world will be a lot different by the time you get this letter, Christie. Maybe it will be better or even slightly improved here and there (tho' I doubt it). It couldn't be a whole lot worse. It being (Pentecost!) Sunday, I have this morning managed (as I usually do) to wade through *The Washington Post* and *The New York Times*. Of course, being a masochist (I guess), I always hit the book reviews—*The New York Times Book Review* and *The Washington Post Book World* first. And thus I am almost at once the victim of high blood pressure, a splitting headache and growling indigestion. The main thing in the *Post* is Jonathan Yardley unfairly jumping all over, *stomping* on my friend Ann Beattie's new novel *Love Always*. He's dead wrong, Ann; but a lot of good that will do. The other paper celebrates John (pardon) Irving and, in the person of one Benjamin Demott, demands that we should take both Irving and his work seriously. Can you believe that? All the rest of the section is equally bad, wrong-headed, fixed, and phony. The only respite we get is in the letters section where a bunch of Big Name Feminists, Heavies in the Movement, have (for reasons of their own) decided to gang up on Gail Godwin because she wrote a review and expressed some opinions they don't approve of and don't intend to let pass. They are a tough bunch, Christie, and like the rest of the Establishment, they pay only a pursed or puckered lip service to the battered old concept of free speech. Free speech is when *they* want to say something. Get it?

My wife has warned me that they will not tolerate many of the words and opinions in this book. And never mind the source or context. Since they can't get at Towne, who is only imaginary, they will get at me. Thus, of course, confirming my basic paranoia and making me feel better about myself. Oh well, I guess it's worth it.

Some day I plan to write a book about the American Literary Establishment and some of our most celebrated literary culture heroes. It will be called WHY GOOD THINGS HAPPEN TO BAD PEOPLE.

Anyway, I went from the routine horror of literary hanky panky to the . . . news.

Pretty busy out there. Plenty mischief and bad news.

Here are three headlines from today's *Washington Post*:

249

KUWATI RULER
ELUDES ATTACK
BY CAR-BOMBER

ETHNIC CONFLICT SPREADING IN SRI LANKA

Tamil Separist Guerrilas Tie Down Government Forces in Jaffna Peninusla

(Do you know where Jaffna Peninsula is, Christie? I sure don't. It probably isn't some place you would want to go on a modelling assignment.)

SHIITES NEAR TAKING
PALESTINIAN CAMPS

Refugees Report Executions

And here, dear lady, are a typical 3 from the *Times*. (Stories I couldn't even find in the *Post*.)

VIETNAMESE FORCE KILLS
5 THAI SOLDIERS

8 BOMBS ROCK CORSICA
4TH ATTACK THIS MONTH

MAJOR BLACKOUT IN CHILE
ATTRIBUTED TO TERRORISTS

(The good old *Times*. Only the *Times* uses words like "attributed" in headlines.)

In addition to the stories mentioned I find other pieces dealing with internal and external on-going armed conflicts in Afghanistan, Cambodia, Central America, Ethiopia, India, Iran and Iraq, the Phillipines and, Ulster. And that isn't even half of it.

It's a shitstorm out there, Christie.

America?

Well, you know. Same old stuff. On a slightly different level. There's a spy case, Navy stuff, made newsworthy because it's a father-son team operation. The Septuplets aren't all doing too well. The Claus Von Bulow case goes on and on. Never a dull moment there. And it looks like old William Sloan Coffin is trying to stir up a beehive and get himself in the papers once again. (It's been too long, Bill.) Funny story in today's *Times*—SEX ISSUE DIVIDES

RIVERSIDE CHURCH—about (as I understand it) an attempt by Coffin and some of his buddies to change the Bible and Christian doctrine to make sodomy (for the first time since the destruction of Sodom) a theologically acceptable sexual preference.

Oh what a lucky silly country! While all the rest of the world is having at each other with axes and clubs, bazookas and flame throwers, we can sit around and argue about things like this. Of course, it is only fair to point out that even as Coffin and company discuss these cosmic and comic matters, right down the street in all directions from his church honest-to-God N.Y.C. predators, disguised as human beings, more or less, are robbing, assaulting, maiming and even killing those whom we neither protect nor allow to protect themselves. In animal husbandry it is called culling the herd.

Good old New York!

Still, we are lucky. Happiness is still a possibility here in America even if it falls clearly under the terms of Swift's definition, namely "the state of being well-deceived". And you are proof of that, Christie. I bet that you and Billy Joel don't care about Cambodia or Cuba or any of those boring places. I wouldn't either, if I were lucky Billy. I mean at the time of this writing. By the time you read this everything may have (ho-hum) changed. Or it could get *even better*! Life is full of little surprises, don't you know?

Where was I?

Oh, yes. Comparing America with the rest of the bloody and godforsaken world.

Well, Christie, not everyone agrees with you and me. Not everyone really appreciates America. Here is John Masefield, the English poet (and a good one, too) on the subject of America during the First World War. While we were still neutral and making profits off of both sides. "It is a land all false teeth and spectacles, the most tragic hollowness I know, the elaborate shell of a coffin, without the humanity of a corpse inside." (Quoted from *Letters From the Front*, in a review in *The Washington Post Book World*, Vol. XV, No. 21, Sunday, May 26, 1985, p. 13.)

   . . . *the most tragic hollowness I know.*

You know, John Towne had some anti-American sentiments, or at least he affected some back in the 1960's and early 70's when it was paying off pretty well to knock everything American. At one point he even tried his hand at poetry, figuring if guys like Ginsberg and the rest of the Beats could trash the U.S. and get fame and money for doing it, maybe some of that would rub off on him. He gave it a shot. But he never made it in the poetry racket. Only one of his late 60's/early 70's trash poems survives. And I here offer it in evidence to show you why Towne was better advised to stick to prose:

ADIEU TO THE ICE CREAM KINGDOM

The Poet rises to address the multitudes where they have gathered
to enjoy a few miracles, a couple of remarkable cures, and a picnic lunch
of loaves & fishes & some Ripple.

Saying; Goodbye to the Ice Cream Kingdom.

Saying unto them. . . .

The Last Honest Man has vanished, disappeared like the ghosts of the wild herds of bison, gone with the whooping crane & the bald eagle. . . .

Now let the buzzard be your symbol, feeding richly on death & excrement; or the magpie, that assiduous collector of junk & trash; let the crazy catbird be your nightingale!

Let the diseased Dutch elm be your National Tree, stately & deeply blighted & spreading blight; let the rootless orchid, grown in hothouses, sucking its substance from thin air, extravagant, expensive & brief-lived, a beautiful fungus be the National Fungus Flower with which you celebrate your births, weddings, deaths & departures.

The Last Honest Man is long gone & the Last Man with any Balls too has bit the dust, forlorn & savage, quixotic, vainly assailing your wagontrain of Cadillacs and Toranados.

See how your famous melting pot bubbled & then poured forth its molten substance & scum; see what came forth from the common mold; look and behold; who is your New Man?

What else can he be, since all you began with were the two immemorial types of Man, the knaves & the fools; what else can your New Men be but knavish fools & foolish knaves?

You have nothing pure left, not even the simple purity of naked knavery nor the purity of high banana peel folly; your only known form of purity is that of the pure & simple hypocrite.

All hail to the hypocrite, then! Hail & farewell!

I ask to see a leader and you produce a—movie star!

Upon a screen swift images of a montage . . . A mindless, faceless set of fat lips, a mouth chews bubblegum . . . Mother & daughter buy deodorant, shopping in matching haircurlers . . . A politician parks in front of a fire hydrant . . . A fat man sports with a nude & equally fat woman in a blue plastic swimming pool . . . Captain Kangaroo . . . Cash registers vomiting . . . Harry Reasoner exchanging bad puns with Bennet Cerf . . .

Show me the face of your manhood, then. It need not be carved & whittled in hardwood like Lincoln's or Sherman's or Calhoun's or Webster's. I do not expect the natural marble of Jefferson, Jackson, Adams, or Monroe. It need not even be the noble bronze of Learned Hand.

Show me a gallery of faces upon whose lineaments are etched indissolubly the lines of your aspiration.

Bill Moyers? Barry Goldwater? Jack Valenti? Frank Sinatra? Murray the K?

Your women, then. Let there be one from among them to symbolize your deepest dreams of love & sex, the courage & patience of all your mothers.

Marilyn Monroe decorates a calendar & then dies young & childless. . . .

I would pause to weep here by the waters of this Babylon, but your waters stink of sewage & pollution & dead fish.

If a sane or brave man should speak out, who could hear his words over the cacophony of cash registers & computers, the chorus of 200 million voices crying a counterpoint of *me! me! my! mine!????*

Neither quite sane & never brave for very long, I fear I have fed too often on your cotton candy & frozen custard.

Oh irony of ironies, that in the only Kingdom of Ice Cream, they cheat & do not use real cream in making it!

I turn away then, neither in shame nor pity, feeling not even the nostalgia of & for Paestum, Palmyra, or Baalbek.

Where are your poets? You turn on two spotlights. I see Goofy Allen Ginsberg dressed in a *sari*, picking his nose. In the other stands sad Robert Lowell in front of a mirror, holding his celebrated locked razor.

Who will build your buildings, your monuments & tombs (there being no more cause for arches of triumph)? You present a mincing fop who cries *eleganza!* Elegance above all!

Who will make the music for your dancers, for labor, for marching, for love? You introduce a middleaged lunatic beating a rusty bedspring with a spatula.

Who will lead your soldiers, the last of your fading manhood, to bleed brave and lonely in far places for ambiguous causes? You offer an executive type in steel-rimmed glasses, his slick hair parted up the middle.

Who are your prophets, your sages & wisemen, those who advise you with caution, consistency, courage & wisdom? Is all you can give me an off-print of Walter Lippman?

Well, then, who keeps your history; who is the solemn custodian of the truth & secrets of your tribe? Why do you point to a picture of Arthur Schlesinger, Jr. as he leaps, fully-clothed into a Georgetown swimming pool?

Perhaps the servants of the people, the captains of the kings, perhaps they are men of probity, honor & discretion, worthy of admiration & emulation. See "Nick" Katzenbach do the Frug. See E. William Henry in His Batman costume.

Are your students, your young, in love with truth, humble before the ideal ardor and rigor and unapplauded eyestrain of the true scholar; do they seek to learn the discipline of the honest critic who would bite off his tongue rather than speak the injustice of half-truths?

Someone hands a microphone to Mario Savio. . . . Cotton, anyone?

The people, yes, the people, what of them? So long as they are strong, so long as they love justice and mercy, so long as they keep well the twin eternal flames of *pietas* and *caritas*, all things will be well. . . .

Saying unto you this & only this. . . .

Saying

So long, Ice Cream Kingdom. Farewell Frigidaires & Fords. Keep your

Ice-Blue Secret. And may your Micrin mouthwash ever be sweet enough to snuff out the taste of dust on your tongues.

I won't stop to explain who all those people were, Christie. They date the poem rather precisely. Here today and gone tomorrow. Like they say.

It's a lousy poem. But it will give you some idea of where Towne was coming from. Or, more accurately, where he wanted people to think he was coming from.

It was after Towne bombed out as both a modern and post-modern poet that he began collecting morbid and sordid clippings about our life and times. There are huge envelopes stuffed with them.

Some are just odd: WOMAN PLEADS NOT GUILTY/TO ASSAULT WITH MILK SHAKE: "A Rocheport woman charged last week with assaulting an off-duty police officer with a milkshake pleaded not guilty to the charge Friday in Boone County Circuit Court. . . ."

Some are fairly funny: DENTIST CHARGED IN RAPE ATTEMPT: "A 45-year-old Brooklyn dentist was charged yesterday with having tried to rape a female investigator while she was helpless under the influence of nitrous oxide in a treatment chair at his office Monday night. . . ."

Or this one, for example. ARRESTS: "Columbia police arrested a 16-year-old girl Wednesday on charges of sexually abusing a 35-year-old man. . . ."

Some are as morbid and disgusting as can be, as, for example, this excerpt from a long story, MAN CONVICTED OF KILLING 6 WOMEN:

> She testified that she had been "virtually mesmerized" by Clark and "overwhelmed by his sense of dominance and charm."
>
> Together, she said, they cruised the Sunset Strip, looking for prostitutes for Clark . . . .
>
> She recalled telling him, "If you're going to go around killing people, killing hookers, you might as well make it as gruesome as possible and do some weird thing like cut off their head (to) make it look like some psychotic did it."
>
> Bundy said she was surprised when Clark took her "facetious" remarks seriously.
>
> "When he first brought (the head) home (after leaving the body at a location in Burbank), he was laughing," she told police after her arrest. "He thought it was funny as hell, that it was a great trick to play on a police department—make them think they've got a freako out there."
>
> Bundy said that she was a first "moderately repulsed" by the head, but later learned to have "a lot of fun with it . . . ."

Towne's clippings collection is fairly evenly divided with clippings from the 60's, 70's, and the 1980's. He has, for example, quite a complete collection, an entire file, as it were, on the Bernard Goetz, "Subway Vigilante" case. He appears to be especially pleased with a statement by Barry Allen (one of the four "youths" who were shot by Goetz). He has marked it with a handwritten note—"Worth doing in needlepoint." The quotation from Barry Allen is: "He ain't no hero. That man took the law into his own hands, man. He got to be punished."

Towne also has a pretty good file on what *Newsweek* (May 27, 1985) headlines as "Tragedy In Philadelphia," the whole thing of the attack on the MOVE house which destroyed a neighborhood. He is especially pleased with a remark which was attributed (in several newspapers) to Mayor W. Wilson Goode: "It was a perfect plan except for the fire."

Probably the most recent clipping in Towne's miscellaneous collection is dated in Towne's own hand with the note—"Received from Henry Sutton 25 May 1985." The clipping, itself, is not dated, though the dateline is Paris. And there is no indication of the source of the clipping.

28 WOMEN
SAID TO DIE
IN CARGO BOX

Twenty-eight young women were found suffocated in a sealed container in which they were being smuggled from St. Martin island to St. Thomas in the U.S. Virgin Islands, a Paris newspaper reported yesterday.

According to the newspaper, about 40 other women, all believed to be prostitutes, survived the two-day journey in the metal box with no air holes.

A correspondent in Guadeloupe for the Paris daily Le Matin quoted an unnamed immigration official in the Dutch zone of St. Martin as saying,"This was one of numerous transports of prostitutes that didn't work out."

The official reportedly told Le Matin that dock workers found the container Thursday while unloading material of the Caribbean Amusement Co., which sells or rents bumper cars to carnivals in the Caribbean sea region.

A worker opened the container—for a reason not given in the dispatch—and saw the 28 bodies scattered about, mouths open "as if they had appealed for air before perishing," Le Matin said.

"The survivors could scarcely say a word," the newspaper said.

The whereabouts of the survivors were not reported.

The Dutch official was quoted as saying that the fatal journey began for the women, identified as residents of the Dominican Republic, in the port of Phillipsburg on St. Martin in the Dutch zone, where a house of prostitution is operated.

The immigration official said prostitutes are shipped around the islands about every 15 days in containers with air holes.

In a brief note on an attached piece of paper Towne has written: "Like a poem for our times. Almost every line, indeed every word is a jewel of wonder.

255

Building steadily to the final sentence. Which is beautifully matter-of-fact. Do you wonder how it is, living in this century, fellers? Well, you can learn more from this clipping than a whole year of *The New Yorker*. Call this the flip side of all the slick and glossy travel magazines. . . ."

As per Henry Sutton. It is uncertain exactly who this is, though it may possibly be the same Henry Sutton who was a Pop Novelist. That Henry Sutton was the pen name for David Slavitt—poet, novelist, translator.

Just be glad you aren't a Caribbean prostitute, Christie. Imagine getting shipped around in a container every 15 days! Those women could use some support from their Feminist sisters in America.

Meantime the clipping itself, and the fact that Towne chose to keep it, are additional evidence (if additional evidence is needed) of a deep-rooted psychic hostility towards women on his part.

It is difficult to imagine that he would have any hostile feelings toward you, Christie; though he might have some (hee-hee) hard feelings.

Those other cracks about women in Towne's poem don't apply. That was long, long before you came along.

His favorite woman of that period was (I kid you not) a Playmate of the Year named Donna Michelle. She was really something! (I can remember her, too. Probably a lot of guys do.) She wasn't as pretty as you are and not one tenth as successful, I would venture. But she was really stacked. And very acrobatic, too, as I recall. She came along before Feminism was invented. So I know absolutely nothing about her character or her intellect. *Playboy* didn't mention things like that in those days.

Just in passing. I think Feminism has improved things on the whole. I believe everyone should have a fair shake, including women and minorities. Including me. Including everybody but Towne. But some of these feminists have gone too far. They won't ease off. I have a literary friend who claims that they will not be satisfied or rest content until *Playboy* uses Alicia Ostriker as their centerfold. He's got to be joking.

Anyway, I didn't mean to go on and on like this. I was only trying to give a brief world picture at the time of writing (sort of like a message in a time capsule) so you can compare it with the way the world is when you finally get this in your hands.

That's an exciting thought, that you might be holding a book with these words in it *in . . . your . . . naked . . . hands.*

It is also a strange thought that, even as I write this, some places or others, people like Idi Amin and the Emperor Bokassa are still out there. John Z. DeLorean ("that rabbit pellet," as Towne would say) is out there, too, maybe scheming and dreaming. James L. Dickey and Bookie Binkley are, separately and equally, living their interesting lives.

Hello Ben Greer and Madison Bell and Allen Wier and Pete La Salle and Phil Kimball and the Bausch Boys.

Hi Richard and Cathy!

Greetings Carolyn Chute and Denise Giardina and Jane Gelfman.

256

Ho-ho-ho, Tahiti Mama! And Yo-ho-ho, Dark Czarina!

Keep on trucking, Patsy Chappell.

Keep on writing, Fred Chappell.

Hello to Hilary and Brendan and the Tillinghasts and Alan Cheuse and Nick Delbanco.

My love to . . . Listen, I have to stop this right now. Suddenly I see it could just go on and on and on. Like those lists in R.H.W. Dillard's wonderful novel, *First Man On The Sun*.

I have suddenly realized, Christie, here and now, that I am blessed with a huge number of friends, some only casual acquaintances, some as close as close can be. I couldn't possibly list them here, not if I had pages and pages to do so. Well, I am grateful for that. For the huge number of you, the overwhelming majority, who didn't get mentioned here, just let me say that I will greet you personally as soon as possible.

And if you want, I will write your name in the book. Right here. My friend _____ Okay? All you have to do is buy a copy of *Poison Pen* and I will put your name in it. Okay.

Meanwhile.

Greetings to all my new and old friends. Hope I can include you, too, among them, Mrs. Joel.

Middle finger and a thumb of the nose to all my enemies, known and unknown. You know who you are.

Enough!

My wife said to me, simply: "Public life is an illusion. Only private life is real and matters." I expect she is right. I expect that is the theme of this letter. I expect, also, that it is the subtext, the hidden theme and true subject of all of Towne's work. Thus it is the major theme of *Poison Pen* and, as well, of the larger work (unfinished and unpublished)—*Life With Kim Novak Is Hell*, from which *Poison Pen* is excerpted.

We have been talking about and trading in illusions. Laughter and tears (if any) have been the counterfeit currency of illusion. Illusions can cause real pain, but that's not my fault. Yours either.

Let us try to return to reality where we belong.

Now I will wave my magic (pardon) wand. And all of it—*Poison Pen* and *Kim Novak*, Towne and I, and, I'm afraid Billy Joel and you, Christie (except for your splendid poster and colorful calendars making a mockery of their two dimensions on my attic wall) will disappear.

For good.

Stay well, Christie.

Have a nice private life.

Take good care of your privates.

Lord bless you and keep you. lord lift up His countenance upon you. Etc. . . .

Love XXX
The Author

FINAL LIST OF TRULY PUBLIC PEOPLE

Here's a little alphabet of public figures who, as far as I know and can recollect, do not appear anywhere in this whole book except right here, but who sure enough deserve to—as do ever so many more.

This list is dedicated to the memory of Tab Hunter.

The 'eighties are here. It's a new era and I vow the world hasn't heard the last of Britt Ekland.—Britt Ekland, *True Britt.*

    J.T.

Arquette, Rosanna	Norris, Chuck
Boom, Boom, Sister	O'Grady, Desmond
Chambers, Marilyn	Perry, William
Donaldson, Sam	Quinlan, Karen Ann
Eastwood, Clint	Rajneesh, Bhagwan Shrebe
Farrakhan, Louis	Simon, John
Goldberg, Whoopi	Tomlin, Lily
Hall, Jerry	Udall, Mo
Iaccoca, Lee	Vogelsang, Arthur
Johnson, Don	Wouk, Herman
Koch, Mayor Ed	Xiaoping, Deng
Lauper, Cyndi	Yeager, Chuck
Marcos, Imelda	Zadora, Pia

THE END